Preface Books

A series of scholarly and critical studies of major writers intended for those needing modern and authoritative guidance through the characteristic difficulties of their work to reach an intelligent understanding and enjoyment of it.

General Editor: MAURICE HUSSEY

A Preface to Hardy

Merryn Williams

Longman London and New York

To John with love.

'But criticism is so easy, and art so hard: criticism
so flimsy, and the life-seer's voice so lasting.'
Thomas Hardy, writing about William Barnes

LONGMAN GROUP UK LIMITED
*Longman House
Burnt Mill, Harlow, Essex, CM20 2JE, England
and Associated Companies throughout the world.*

Published in the United States of
America by Longman Inc. New York

This edition © Longman Group Ltd 1976

This edition first published 1976
Seventh impression 1989

Library of Congress Cataloging in Publication Data

Williams, Merryn.
A preface to Hardy.

(Preface books)
Bibliography: p.
Includes index.
I. Hardy, Thomas, 1840–1928. I. Title.
PR4753.W53   823'.8   75 28382

*Produced by Longman Group (FE) Ltd
Printed in Hong Kong*

ISBN 0-582-35114-6

Contents

List of illustrations

vi

Foreword

A century on from their original reception the Wessex Novels of Thomas Hardy have entered into the national store of fictional masterpieces and are still eagerly read. Possibly Dickens alone of the great Victorian writers can equal or surpass Hardy's continuing success, a thought that would have pleased him most deeply. For many of us, though made aware of the unhappy social conditions of life in Hardy's Dorset, persist in finding colour, humanity and nostalgia present to a degree in the novels that almost excludes the darker emotions. There is still to this day a recognizable Hardy country and it stands fairly free from that more modern rural tragedy that goes by the name of development.

In this most readable, and unexpectedly positive study of Hardy's prose and verse, Merryn Williams offers a variety of scholarly approaches to her subject to demonstrate the depths of his power to release tragic emotion and universal humanity within the closely studied visual realism. In Part One she provides a firm historical perspective, reminding us that Hardy, for all his apparent isolation, could not escape the pervasive influence of the scientists and agnostics of Victorian England. We are invited to consider especially Charles Darwin, Thomas Huxley, John Stuart Mill and Matthew Arnold. The last-named writer's key poem, 'Dover Beach', quoted on p. 77, seems now to be part of a range stretching all the way to Beeny Cliff in Cornwall (see p. 150), that Cliff without a Name, the setting of one of the most imaginative of all post-Darwinian fantasies, that to be found in Hardy's *Pair of Blue Eyes*. For a further instance of Victorian thought in the present book look at the emblem of Doubt beside a grave on p. 74: while it symbolizes the spiritual condition of so many Victorian intellectuals it might have been painted to illustrate a typical Hardy scene among dead bodies and the things growing in a churchyard.

Incidentally, one wonders why it is that no art historian seems to have offered the genre paintings of the Pre-Raphaelite period or even the popular engravings for the Victorian drawing-room as unsuspected sources of Hardy's imagination. He was, after all, much more than a man devoted to a single art. In his diaries and notebooks we are continually aware of his discussions of paintings, architecture, music and even the problems of modern philosophy as discussed in the distinguished periodical, *Mind*. It seems to me quite possible that these magazine engravings with their almost operatic emotions could to some degree have influenced the drama of some of the stories which he wrote for just such illustration. The one reprinted on p. 114 is one example among the many that have never been reprinted.

Dr Williams continually seeks to dismiss the image of Hardy as a pessimist. There is, of course, no doubt that the tragic novels have their bitterness and bleakness, but we tend to ignore the more optimistic side of his character and writings. Where else can we find better and more delightful images of fields, woods and heaths or a more Franciscan love of the animal creation, devoid of sentimentality, in his period? Because it is the expressed aim of this book to draw attention to the positive aspect of his art I have chosen to quote a brief incident in *The Woodlanders*, said to have been his own favourite, and one of the Novels of Character and Environment. That last word arouses in us images of the conservationist and the environmentalist. Hardy anticipates us in this tree-planting episode of *The Woodlanders*:

> What he [Giles Winterborne] had forgotten was that there were a thousand young fir trees to be planted in a neighbouring spot which had been cleared by the wood-cutters, and that he had arranged to plant them with his own hands. He had a marvellous power of making trees grow. Although he would seem to shovel in the earth quite carelessly there was a sort of sympathy between himself and the fir, oak, or beech that he was operating on; so that the roots took hold of the soil in a few days. He put most of these roots towards the south-west; for he said, in forty years' time, when some great gale is blowing from that quarter, the trees will require the strongest holdfast on that side to stand against it and not fall.

MAURICE HUSSEY
General Editor

Introduction

Thomas Hardy's place on the shadowline between nineteenth- and twentieth-century literature has often puzzled his readers. He is neither quite Victorian nor quite modern, although his work combines elements of both. His poetry is too individual to be fitted into any tradition, and his great novels are a disconcerting mixture of the modern and the oldfashioned. The contradictions within his work are mirrored in his life. He was born in the early years of Queen Victoria, in a countryside with no railways or electricity and where most people could neither read nor write, and he lived to see the first great modern war and the first general strike. In some respects his novels read as if they had been written today. In others he seems to be writing about a way of life that has vanished for good.

This book lays its main emphasis on the tensions which make Hardy's work so unique. The first chapter gives an outline of his life, and tries to show how he never quite fitted into society as it was then, and his difficulties in making his work understood. The next two chapters are complementary. 'Hardy the Countryman' gives an account of his deep roots in Dorset, and of the social structure of rural England at that time. Hardy's major work is all written about that region, yet he could not have written it if he had not gone away as a young man to London and absorbed all he could from this new way of life. Chapter 3 looks at Hardy as an intellectual in Victorian England, reading the Romantic poets, and Darwin, Mill, and Huxley; and working out a philosophy (although he never called it that) which seemed revolutionary to the men of his time. The last three chapters are concerned with how that philosophy was expressed in his creative work, with special reference to one novel and ten poems (which are all very different from each other, because it was my purpose to show Hardy as a writer with a very wide range). Some of them could be called poems and novels of protest, springing as they do from a deep dissatisfaction with the world as it is. This might be called the main negative impetus behind Hardy's work. But when he protests against what is wrong with society, it is always in the name of something better, and his work appeals time and time again for more kindness and sympathy between living things. The strong belief in human values which he held to all his life makes his work not only angry, but compassionate, tender, and comic as well. His *positive* values as a writer were almost all derived from the people and the countryside of Dorset, though he seemed to have moved beyond both.

Any attempt to see Hardy in his social and intellectual context, instead of looking at the works by themselves, is bound to show him as an awkward, craggy and obstinately nonconformist writer. But I feel that there is no other honest way to show him. No writer can ever be completely cut off from the society he lives in, and Hardy throughout his life was more committed than most. This is why I have kept referring to political and philosophical concepts in discussing what are, after all, works of literature. Change, progress, conservatism, tradition: these are the raw materials of Hardy's work.

M.W.

MERRYN WILLIAMS devoted her Cambridge doctorate thesis to Hardy, publishing it as *Thomas Hardy and Rural England* (Macmillan 1972). From 1970 to 1971 she was a lecturer at the Open University, producing Humanities Course Units and the anthology, *Revolutions: 1765–1830*. She is married to a scientist and lives in Oxford.

Abbreviations

x

Part One
The Writer and his Setting

Chronological table

HARDY'S LIFE	HISTORICAL EVENTS
1840 Born at Higher Bockhampton, Dorset, 2 June.	
1846	Repeal of Corn Laws.
1847	Railway to Dorchester.
1848	Chartist petition. 'The Year of Revolutions.'
1849 At Isaac Last's school, Dorchester.	
1851	Great Exhibition.
1854	Cholera epidemic in Dorchester.
1856 Apprenticed to architect, John Hicks.	
1858 First poems; met Horace Moule.	
1859	Darwin's *Origin of Species*.
1860–1 Read Greek and helped with church restoration.	
1862 Moved to London to work as assistant architect.	
1865 Planned to train for Church at Cambridge University; gave up plan owing to religious doubts.	

1866		Swinburne's *Poems and Ballads*.
1867	Returned to Dorchester. Engaged to cousin, Tryphena Sparks. Began *The Poor Man and the Lady*.	
1870	Met Emma Gifford at St Juliot in Cornwall.	Education Act. Dickens died. Franco-Prussian war.
1871	*Desperate Remedies* published.	
1872	Designed schools for London Board. *Under the Greenwood Tree*.	Joseph Arch's Union. George Eliot's *Middlemarch*.
1873	*A Pair of Blue Eyes*.	
1874	*Far from the Madding Crowd* appeared in *Cornhill Magazine*. Married Emma Gifford.	
1875	*The Hand of Ethelberta*.	
1876–8	Lived in Sturminster Newton, Dorset; wrote *The Return of the Native*.	
1878–80	At Upper Tooting; *The Trumpet-Major*.	
1880–1	Wrote *A Laodicean* during a serious illness.	George Eliot died.
1881	Moved to Wimborne, Dorset.	
1882	Went to Darwin's funeral. *Two on a Tower*.	
1883	Moved back to Dorchester; wrote *The Dorsetshire Labourer*.	

3

1885	*The Mayor of Casterbridge.*	
1886		William Barnes died.
1887	*The Woodlanders.*	D.H. Lawrence born.
1891	*Tess of the d'Urbervilles.*	
1895	*Jude the Obscure.* The novels appeared revised as 'Wessex Novels'.	
1898	*Wessex Poems.*	
1899		Boer War began.
1901	*Poems of the Past and Present.*	Queen Victoria died.
1902		End of Boer War.
1903	First part of *The Dynasts.*	
1905	Degree from Aberdeen University.	
1906	Second part of *The Dynasts.*	Liberals won general election; Labour Party got 30 seats.
1908	Third part of *The Dynasts.*	
1909	*Time's Laughingstocks.* President of Society of Authors.	Swinburne died.
1910	Awarded Order of Merit.	
1912	Emma Hardy died on 27 November.	
1913	Degree from Cambridge University.	

4

1914	Married Florence Dugdale. *Satires of Circumstance.* On war committee of writers.	Great War began.
1916	Visited German prisoners of war in Dorchester.	
1917	*Moments of Vision.*	Russian Revolution.
1918		End of war.
1920	Honorary degree from Oxford University.	
1922	*Late Lyrics and Earlier.*	
1923	Prince of Wales visited Hardy.	
1925	Degree from Bristol University.	
1928	Died, 11 January. *Winter Words* published later the same year.	

1 Hardy's Life

Childhood and Youth

Thomas Hardy was born on 2nd June 1840, in a small thatched cottage in the little hamlet of Higher Bockhampton, three miles from Dorchester. It was a picturesque place. There were several quaint-looking houses, with 'trees, clipped hedges, orchards, white gatepost-balls' in the avenue of cherry trees which led up to the cottage, and behind it stretched the vast expanse of Egdon or Puddletown Heath. The cottage is still standing, and is used as a Hardy museum, but the other houses, the cherry trees, and much of the heath have all gone.

Fifty years earlier the heath had come right up to the door, and bats had flown in and out of the house when the first Thomas Hardy settled there with his wife. This was the novelist's grandfather. He was said to have used the house for smuggling, a tradition which may have inspired Hardy's long short story, 'The Distracted Preacher'. The second Thomas Hardy was a skilled violinist and a 'master mason' or building contractor who employed about a dozen men. His wife, Jemima Hand, had been a cook. She had been orphaned at an early age and her son recorded that she had had a hard time:

> By reason of her parent's bereavement and consequent poverty under the burden of a young family, Jemima saw during girlhood and young womanhood some very stressful experiences of which she could never speak in her maturer years without pain, though she appears to have mollified her troubles by reading every book she could lay hands on.

She was the person who gave the young Thomas Hardy his interest in books.

They had only been married for five months when the baby was born. The mother had a difficult labour, and the child was at first thought to be dead, but, fortunately for English literature, the nurse revived him just in time. They had three more children; Mary, born in 1841; Henry, in 1851; and Katharine, in 1856. None of them married, and there were no Hardys in the next generation.

Hardy often seems to have had a foreboding that there was something wrong with his family and that it was doomed to die out. At one time the Hardys had been well known in Dorset; one ancestor had founded Hardye's Grammar School in Dorchester and another had been the famous Admiral Hardy who was with Nelson when he died. They had owned a good deal of land, but lost all of it. Hardy noted in his diary, 'The decline and fall of the Hardys much in evidence hereabout. . . . So we go down, down, down (*Life*, 214–15). His father was not an ambitious man, and lost his chance of expanding his business by refusing to move from Higher Bockhampton. And, although the Hardys belonged to the upper class of the village, he was to discover later on that in the world outside they were regarded as peasants. This is one reason why his novels are so full of class-consciousness; it may also help to explain why he brooded over the decline of old families in *The Woodlanders* and *Tess of the d'Urbervilles*, and why he created a family which was marked down by fate, and unfit for marriage, in *Jude the Obscure*.

Little Thomas went on being a fragile child after his dramatic introduction to the world. His parents kept him at home till he was eight, as they did not expect him to live. He was precocious, 'being able to read almost before he could walk, and to tune the violin when of quite tender years' (*Life*, 15). He enjoyed wrapping up in a tablecloth and reading out the services from the prayer book, and everybody thought that as he was no good at anything else he would have to be a parson. The family went regularly to Stinsford church, which Hardy later immortalized under the name of Mellstock, and this church, where many of his ancestors were buried, was 'to him the most hallowed spot on earth':

> In this connection he said once — perhaps oftener — that although invidious critics had cast slurs upon him as Nonconformist, Agnostic, Atheist, Infidel, Immoralist, Heretic, Pessimist, or something else equally opprobrious in their eyes, they had never thought of calling him what they might have called him much more plausibly — churchy; not in an intellectual sense, but in so far as instincts and emotions rule. As a child, to be a parson had been his dream; moreover, he had had several clerical relatives who held livings; while his grandfather, father, uncle, brother, wife, cousin, and two sisters had been musicians in various churches over a period covering altogether more than a hundred years.
>
> (*Life*, 376)

Unconscious of religious controversy at this age, he soaked in the atmosphere of this small country church and gradually acquired the deep knowledge of the Bible which is so evident in his work. He read a good many other books which his mother gave him, and soon picked up arithmetic and geography when, at the age of eight, he was sent to the village school. After a year he seemed a good deal stronger, and his mother, who wanted the best possible education for him, decided that he should go to Isaac Last's Academy in Dorchester. He walked the three miles there and back through the country lanes every day.

It was a Nonconformist school but took pupils from all kinds of homes. Isaac Last was 'an exceptionally able man, and a good teacher of Latin', and it is impossible not to feel that the boy was unusually lucky in finding so good a school as this in a quiet country town. He was an outstanding pupil, won a prize for Latin, and also learned advanced mathematics and French. But he shunned the other schoolboys. He 'loved being alone', and he was already showing signs of the extreme sensitiveness which was to be a torment to him in later life. He has recorded that, like his own hero, Jude Fawley, he 'did not wish to grow up... to be a man, or to possess things, but to remain as he was, in the same spot, and to know no more people than he already knew (about half a dozen) (*Life*, 16). He also saw things, before he was sixteen, which he remembered for the rest of his life; a shepherd's boy who starved to death, and two public hangings in Dorchester. One of them was of a woman who had killed her lover, and it is very likely that this was in his mind when he wrote *Tess*.

He left school in 1856. His parents had been worrying for some time about what they were to do with him, for although there was still some idea that he might be a clergyman, this would have meant sending him to Oxford or Cambridge, and they were not sure that they could find the money. But a friend of the family, John Hicks, an architect who practised in South Street, Dorchester, offered to take the boy into his office as a pupil, and this was agreed. As it turned out he could hardly have done better. Hicks was 'a kindly-natured man, almost jovial, and allowed the two youths some leisure for other than architectural study' (*Life*, 28), being an old classical scholar himself. Hardy would get up at four or five in the morning and read Greek or Latin for a few hours before walking to work. In the office Hicks and the students used to argue about the classics, and also about religion. The other student was a Baptist, and the two boys used to have noisy theological discussions which disturbed the people on the next floor. So he was not by any means getting into a mental rut after he left school, and he had a remarkably helpful friend who saw that he went on reading.

This was Horace Moule, a young man eight years older than Hardy, who had just left Cambridge to become a freelance writer. His father was the Reverend Henry Moule, the Vicar of Fordington, who is the original of old Mr Clare in *Tess*. He was a devoted clergyman who had saved hundreds of lives when cholera epidemics had broken out in the Dorchester slums. Horace was a brilliant scholar, who had, however, failed to take his degree and suffered badly from depression. He was very kind to the young Hardy, introduced him to literary criticism and liberal theology, and advised him about his career. He felt compelled to tell the boy to go on studying architecture, as there was no other obvious way for him to earn a living. Nevertheless, at about the same time, Hardy began to write poetry.

He was eager to get out of Hicks's office. There is a story (not yet fully proved) that he applied to the authorities at Salisbury Cathedral to train as a clergyman, but was turned down on account of his rather ordinary background. This must have hurt him deeply, if it happened, but in any case the idea was shelved. Instead, in 1862, he 'started alone for London, to pursue the art and science of architecture on more advanced lines (*Life*, 35).

He was twenty-one then. He found a place with Arthur Bloomfield, in Adelphi Terrace, and stayed there for the next five years, until 1867. London must have overwhelmed him at first, but he soon got used to the great city,

> knowing every street and alley west of St Paul's like a born Londoner, which he was often supposed to be; an experience quite ignored by the reviewers of his later books, who, if he only touched on London in his pages, promptly reminded him not to write of a place he was unacquainted with, but to get back to his sheepfolds.
>
> (*Life*, 62).

These were the years which completed his education. During the day he worked conscientiously at architectural drawings, and in his spare time went round the museums and art galleries and read all he could. When he was twenty-five he thought again about going to Cambridge to study for the Church, but gave up the idea when he realized that he had no deep belief in it as a vocation. So in the end he never went to a university, and this has led many people to suppose that he was only half-educated:

> His environment cut him off from any tradition of culture that might have instilled into him that critical sense that was not implanted by nature. When he came to maturity, he made a conscientious effort to get over this disability. Hardy was a great self-educator, and his novels are marked by the fruits of his labours ... They have the touching pedantry of the self-educated countryman naïvely pleased with his hardly acquired learning. Indeed, it is the inevitable defect of a spontaneous genius like Hardy's that it is impervious to education. No amount of painstaking study got him within sight of achieving that intuitive good taste, that instinctive grasp of the laws of literature, which is the native heritage of one bred from childhood in the atmosphere of a high culture.
>
> (David Cecil, *Hardy the Novelist*, 145-6)

What this means, presumably, is that Hardy did not have the conventional public school and Oxbridge education which the English upper class assumes is the only education worth having. Neither did the Brontës, nor George Eliot, nor D. H. Lawrence, nor Dickens. Nor, if we look at the English poets, did Keats, nor Blake, nor Shakespeare. (Many people think that it would have been literally impossible for someone who went to the grammar school at Stratford-on-Avon to write Shakespeare's plays.) It is an appallingly snobbish attitude, and it has not died out yet. It helps to explain why so many

9

Victorian critics patronized Hardy, telling him to write about sheep and cows and to keep off philosophy. Even today, it is still fashionable for critics to describe Hardy as an imperfectly educated countryman, although he had read more widely and thought more deeply than many of them.

In fact, Hardy was more fortunate in his education than most people. He went to a very good school and had very good teachers outside it; without this background, it is not likely that he would have found the will-power to go on educating himself in his spare time. He was interested in a very wide range of subjects. He knew classical literature and mathematics at least as well as the average undergraduate, and, more important, by the end of his time in London he thoroughly knew the classics of our own literature: Shakespeare, the Bible, and the English poets who, until our own century, were never studied in Oxford and Cambridge.

By the time he reached London he was determined to be a poet, but he did not try to get introductions to famous writers, as a more pushing young man would have done. Although he was living very close to two of the poets he admired most, Swinburne and Browning, he never met them in those days. He once sat next to Dickens in a coffee-shop, and he listened to John Stuart Mill give a speech in the open air. But he did not presume to think that he himself would ever be a famous man. He wrote a good many poems during these years and sent them to the literary magazines, whose editors invariably sent them back. If we look at these poems, we recognize that his literary style was already formed by the time he was twenty-five. Like every young poet, he began by imitating the great writers of the past (in his case, Wordsworth and Shakespeare). But there are many more which could not have been written by anybody other than Hardy; 'The Ruined Maid' and 'Hap' display his characteristic philosophy and his characteristic tone.

If his literary career was not encouraging, he was excited by London in many other ways. He watched from the windows of his office while Charing Cross Bridge and the Embankment went up. He helped the Midland Railway to carry a cutting through Old St Pancras churchyard, removing many hundreds of graves. He visited the Great Exhibition of 1862 and the Science Museum, and discovered an interest in modern industry and science which he never lost. He also won two architectural prizes. But a good deal of his time in the capital must have been miserable. He was lonely there, although he saw his friend Moule sometimes, and he was deeply shocked by what he saw of the squalor, vice, and human misery in the richest city in the world. As his early religious convictions weakened and died, he began to feel 'a passion for reforming the world'. One of his early poems, 'Dream of the City Shopwoman', expresses the frustration that he felt at this time:

Thomas Hardy at 21.

O God, that creatures framed to feel
A yearning nature's strong appeal
Should writhe on this eternal wheel
In rayless grime;

And vainly note, with wan regret,
Each star of early promise set;
Till Death relieves, and they forget
Their one life's time!

$(CP, 576)$

By the summer of 1867 he was beginning to be ill, partly because of the stench from the river mud near his office, 'the Metropolitan main-drainage system not having been yet constructed', and partly because he shut himself up every evening to read. His employer told him to go down to the country for a rest, and Hardy felt that he might stay there for good. The business of getting on in the world repelled him, and he thought he had had enough, but in the end he left his books and papers in London and went back to Dorchester to work for Mr Hicks for the summer. His family were shocked to see how pale he looked, but a few weeks in the country made him much better.

Tryphena Sparks

It was only as recently as 1966, when a book called *Providence and Mr Hardy*, by Lois Deacon and Terry Coleman, was published, that the world knew anything about Hardy's love affair with his cousin Tryphena Sparks. The evidence about it is very incomplete and almost all comes from statements by Tryphena's daughter, who died as a very old woman in 1965. We shall probably never know now how deep this relationship went, how long it lasted, or why it was broken off. What does seem certain is that when Hardy went back to Dorchester he met and fell in love with Tryphena, who had been a child when he left for London and was now sixteen. They went for long walks on the heath together. At some time they seem to have become engaged.

Tryphena was the youngest daughter of Hardy's mother's sister, Maria Sparks. She was a student-teacher at the village school in Puddletown, where her parents lived, and was hoping to go to a teacher training college afterwards. The few surviving photographs of her show an attractive dark-haired girl, and Hardy may have left some hints of how she seemed to him in those days in his description of the heroine of *Jude the Obscure*:

She looked right into his face with liquid, untranslatable eyes, that combined, or seemed to him to combine, keenness with tenderness, and mystery with both. . . . She was not a large figure. . . she was light and slight, of the type dubbed elegant. . . . There was nothing statuesque in her; all was nervous motion. She was mobile, living, yet a painter might not have called her handsome or beautiful.

Another description of Sue Bridehead runs:

Then a wave of warmth came over him as he thought how near he now stood to the bright-eyed vivacious girl with the broad forehead and pile of dark hair above it; the girl with the kindling glance, daringly soft at times—something like that of the girls he had seen in engravings from paintings of the Spanish school.

We also know that Tryphena, like Sue Bridehead, must have been a brilliant girl. She impressed the education authorities so much that she was made a headmistress at twenty-one. But in 1868, for no obvious reason, she was removed from Puddletown school. It has been suggested that this was because she was pregnant, and that she left home shortly afterwards to have Hardy's child. Scholars are still arguing bitterly about this question, but at present there are very few known facts.

If Tryphena did have a baby at this time she must have kept it a closely guarded secret, for no birth certificate and no clear proof of existence have ever been found. On the other hand, Tryphena's daughter, more than ninety years later, identified the photograph of a little boy in her mother's album as Hardy's son. She said that his name was Randal, that he was delicate, and that he was brought up by an uncle and died young. As she was in her eighties at the time, some people have thought that her statements cannot be trusted. Others, who do believe them, have suggested that this child may have inspired the extraordinary figure of Little Father Time in *Jude the Obscure*.

We do not know why Hardy never married Tryphena; particularly if she was going to have his child, it would have seemed imperative that he should. It may have happened for natural and unexciting reasons; perhaps they grew apart after a few years, or perhaps he fell in love with Emma Gifford and broke with Tryphena for her sake. It is also very likely that their families objected to their marriage because they were first cousins. But Deacon and Coleman have suggested that their relationship was in fact much closer, and that Hardy *could* not marry Tryphena because she was his niece. This theory is based on two assumptions which have not been, and probably never can be proved. The first is that Tryphena was the illegitimate child of her supposed elder sister, Rebecca Sparks, and that she was passed off as the daughter of her actual grandmother to avoid scandal. This certainly sometimes happened in Dorset. By itself it would not have mattered, but the suggestion is that Rebecca was the daughter of Hardy's mother, born before her marriage, and again passed off as another woman's child. Hardy would not have been told that he and Tryphena were too closely related to marry until it was too late.

It is an extraordinary story, but not quite impossible. As the facts did not come to light until about a hundred years after it happened, it seems unlikely that we shall ever know whether the theories in *Providence and Mr Hardy* are true, false, or a mixture of both. Another suggestion is that Tryphena became involved with Horace Moule while she was still engaged to Hardy and that this led to the estrangement of the two friends and Moule's death.

The only facts we definitely know about Tryphena, during the years following 1867, are that she went to a training college in London and apparently kept in touch with Hardy there. She did well at the college and then became the headmistress of a girls' school in Plymouth, where she met a publican, Charles Gale. At some point her engagement to Hardy was broken off, probably by her. If she had a child it was looked after by somebody else. In 1877 she and Charles Gale were married, and Tryphena gave up her job. They had four children. Tryphena died in 1890, aged only thirty-eight. Her death had a deep effect on Hardy, which will be studied in its own place.

Emma Gifford and the early novels

When he came back to Dorchester, that summer of 1867, Hardy was still uncertain what he wanted to do with his life. He did not feel committed to architecture (this will be discussed in the next section) but poetry, which he liked much better, seemed to offer him no future at all. So, while continuing to do occasional work for Hicks, he began to write his first novel, *The Poor Man and the Lady*. All the evidence we have about this lost book agrees that it was very much the work of an angry young man. Hardy's experiences of life in Dorset and London had made him a radical, and there are several signs that he had suffered very bitterly because people had treated him as a member of an inferior class. In 1867 the British labour movement was still in its infancy, and there were very few people, even in London, who called themselves Socialists. Yet Hardy had written what he himself called a Socialist novel, and in that respect he was a long way ahead of his time. He even depicted what had never yet happened, large gatherings of working men in Trafalgar Square.

He sent the novel to Macmillan's in July 1868. In later years Macmillan's were to publish all Hardy's works, but, while they admired a good deal of *The Poor Man and the Lady*, they felt that it was too uneven to be printed. The publisher wrote to Hardy that 'your description of country life among working men is admirable', but he felt that the young author was much too prejudiced against the upper class:

The utter heedlessness of *all* the conversation you give in drawing-rooms and ball-rooms about the working-classes, has some ground of truth, I fear, and might justly be scourged, as you aim at doing, but your chastisement would fall harmless from its very excess... Nothing could justify such a wholesale blackening of a class but large and intimate knowledge of it.

(Life, 58)

Hardy tried the firm of Chapman and Hall next, and was summoned to London to meet their reader, who turned out to be the novelist George Meredith. The older man warned him that he would find himself in the centre of a storm if the novel was published, 'for if he printed so pronounced a thing he would be attacked on all sides by the conventional reviewers, and his future injured' *(Life*, 61). He suggested that Hardy should write a novel with a more complicated plot and that his first book should be put on one side.

The Poor Man and the Lady was never published in its original form, but ten years afterwards Hardy turned it into a long short story which he called 'An Indiscretion in the Life of an Heiress'. This cut out some, but not all, of the radical passages, and it gives a fairly good idea of the young Hardy's style. He was to write much better things later, but even his first crude attempts at prose fiction won the admiration of several distinguished literary men.

He went back to the country and began to write *Desperate Remedies*, living mostly in Weymouth where he worked for Mr Crickmay, the architect who had succeeded John Hicks. This turned out to be a murder and mystery story, strongly influenced by the novels of Wilkie Collins, and very unlike anything that Hardy was to write later on. He called it a 'melodramatic novel, quite below the level of *The Poor Man and the Lady*, which was the unfortunate consequence of Meredith's advice to "write a story with a plot" ' *(Life*, 64). There are some good bits of writing in it, but it was a bizarre way for Hardy to start his career as a novelist. He finished it and sent it to the publishers in March 1870.

In the same month he went down to Cornwall, at Mr Crickmay's request, to make an estimate for the repairs to St Juliot Church. The parish was a very lonely one, and the journey of a hundred miles by road and railway took him all day. Late in the evening he arrived at the rectory, where he was to stay, and where there lived an elderly clergyman, the Reverend Caddell Holder, his much younger wife, and her sister, Emma Lavinia Gifford, who was Hardy's own age, twenty-nine.

The two girls were the daughters of a Plymouth solicitor and their uncle was a Canon of Worcester Cathedral, later to be made an Archdeacon of London. Socially her family was much above Hardy's but they had had troubles recently — their father drank, and had gone bankrupt, and one of their brothers was insane. Emma must have been very lonely in this isolated place, for she loved excitement and an active social life. She received Hardy alone, as her brother-in-law was ill, and was interested in him at once:

> I was immediately arrested by his familiar appearance, as if I had seen him in a dream — his slightly different accent, his soft voice; also I noticed a blue paper sticking out of his pocket. . .I thought him much older than he was. He had a beard, and a rather shabby greatcoat, and had quite a business appearance. Afterwards he seemed younger, and by daylight especially so. . . . The blue paper proved to be the MS of a poem, and not a plan of the church, he informed me, to my surprise.
>
> (*Life*, 70)

Hardy stayed in St Juliot for four days and when he had finished work on the church Emma showed him the countryside, including the massive Beeny Cliff a few miles away. In later years Hardy always associated that romantic countryside with his own love for Emma:

> I found her out there
> On a slope few see,
> That falls westwardly
> To the salt-edged air,
> Where the ocean breaks
> On the purple strand,
> And the hurricane shakes
> The solid land.
>
> (*CP*, 322)

At what stage he actually fell in love with her is not known. When he went down to St Juliot he was almost certainly still engaged to Tryphena, and he did not marry Emma for another four years. But he was attracted by her vivacity, by what he called her *aliveness*, although there were deep differences between them — class differences, she took it for granted that she should ride everywhere while he walked; and religious differences too, for she was a devout Anglican. At this time it did not seem important. He went to Cornwall several more times, partly to see her and partly to finish restoring the church. They wrote to each other, and he talked to her about his hopes of becoming a writer.

Desperate Remedies was turned down by Macmillan's and accepted by Tinsley Brothers, on condition that Hardy paid seventy-five pounds. It was a bold step for a young man with very little money, but he paid it nevertheless, and got most of it back. The novel, which came out anonymously in March 1871, sold quite well. But Hardy was bitterly hurt by a review in the *Spectator* which said that the novel should never have been published, 'the reason for this violence being mainly the author's daring to suppose it possible that an unmarried lady owning an estate could have an illegitimate child' (*Life*, 84). Horace Moule, who reviewed the novel much more favourably, told him not to mind. Hardy was to discover that he needed the encouragement of his friends if he was to go on writing, for he was always very sensitive about hostile reviews.

Still, he wanted his next novel to be quite different, and for the next few months, while continuing to work on designs for Gothic churches, he wrote a much shorter book, *Under the Greenwood Tree*. Macmillan's were doubtful about publishing it, and Hardy very nearly threw the manuscript away. He was so depressed that he wrote to Emma to say that he was giving up literature altogether. She is not often given the credit which she deserves for her reaction to this. She begged him to go on writing whatever happened, although this was a very uncertain way of earning an income and they had to have more money before they could get married.

At first he took no notice and went on working doggedly at architecture. But he was impressed when Horace Moule advised him earnestly not to give up writing. He then bumped into Mr Tinsley, who asked him for another novel. Hardy refused to take any interest at first, but in the end he dug out his manuscript and gave it in without looking at it. *Under the Greenwood Tree* was published in 1872. It 'met with a very kindly and gentle reception' (*Life*, 89), although not many copies were sold. The story was shorter than Victorian readers liked, and although it was pleasant to read it was not very exciting. He could not give up architecture and become a professional writer on the strength of such a mild success.

Tinsley then made a proposal which was to alter Hardy's whole career, and to dominate his life for the next twenty-odd years. He asked him to write another, longer novel which would run for twelve months as a serial in his magazine and be published as a book after that. Shortly afterwards Leslie Stephen, the editor of the *Cornhill Magazine*, who had been greatly impressed by *Under the Greenwood Tree*, wrote to him with a similar request. Hardy, who was living in London again and drawing designs for the new Board Schools (education had in 1870 been made compulsory for all children) thought this over carefully, and then agreed. It seemed that this was a real chance to devote himself to literature and still earn a reasonable income.

We must look briefly at the conditions of the publishing trade in Victorian England in order to understand what this meant. Most established and successful novelists, including some of the greatest writers of the age, first published their work as a weekly or monthly serial in one of the circulating magazines. These magazines (examples are Dickens's *Household Words* and *All the Year Round* in which several of his own novels first saw the light) had an enormous public because more and more people were learning to read in the second half of the century, and magazines were considerably cheaper than books. After serialization these novels came out in hardback (usually in three volumes) and found their way to the public libraries, where they reached another vast group of readers. Quite often the final version was very different from the serial one; Hardy himself had to make several changes in his novels before they came out in book form, as we shall see, especially in the Appendix.

The advantage of this way of publishing books was that they reached a much wider public than the novels of Scott or Jane Austen had done. It also made it possible for an author to live entirely on his work and, if it was popular, to make a fortune. But there were drawbacks. A writer had to produce the sort of novel that his public and his editor wanted. He had to work to a deadline, and he had to see that each instalment was equally interesting and packed with action; if it was not, readers might stop buying the magazine. Even the length was not under the writer's control for he was under great pressure to produce a novel which would fill three volumes when it came out. (This led to a good deal of padding, and is one of the reasons why Victorian novels tend to be so enormously long.) Above all, he had to see that his work contained nothing that could conceivably offend anyone's prejudices. The magazines were designed for family reading, and almost everybody believed that the young girls into whose hands they might fall must be carefully shielded from dangerous knowledge; this led to the famous saying that an author must never write anything which 'might bring a blush to a young person's cheek'. This did not mean working-class girls in Dorset, like Tess Durbeyfield, who had always had the facts of life forced on them at an early age and in an extremely brutal way, but the daughters of middle-class families, 'young ladies', whose education was satirized by Dickens:

> Nothing disagreeable should ever be looked at. Apart from such a habit standing in the way of that graceful equanimity of surface which is so expressive of good breeding, it hardly seems compatible with refinement of mind. A truly refined mind will seem to be ignorant of the existence of anything that is not perfectly proper, placid, and pleasant.
>
> (*Little Dorrit*, II, 5)

Later on Hardy was to rebel against the tyranny of the 'young person', but in 1872 it never occurred to him that anybody could be offended by his writings, and even if he had known what difficulties he would have to face he would probably have done the same thing. He was anxious to get married, anxious to give up the architectural work which consumed so much of his time, and his main ambition at this stage seems to have been recognition as a good writer of serials.

He asked his employer for a holiday and went into the country, where he wrote most of *A Pair of Blue Eyes*. When it began to appear in print he gave notice that he would not be coming back, and his career as an architect came to a stop. The novel was well received; it was, indeed, the best thing that Hardy had yet written. It was a love story, set in Cornwall, and the fair-haired heroine, Elfride Swancourt, was in many ways very like Emma Gifford. Some critics have gone further, and suggested that the young architect, Stephen Smith, who wants to marry Elfride, is a portrait of Hardy himself. Hardy denied this strongly, but it is a fact that this novel, like *The Poor Man and the Lady* and many others which he was still to write, is preoccupied with class and its effect on human relationships. Stephen is turned out by Elfride's father when he is discovered to be the son of a labourer, and Hardy, although he never admitted it, was also having trouble with his fiancée's family around this time. When he and Emma went to Plymouth to see her father, Mr Gifford made it very clear that he did not want Hardy as a son-in-law. In later years he called him 'a low-born churl who has presumed to marry into my family'.

Hardy classified *A Pair of Blue Eyes* among a group of his works which he called Romances and Fantasies, 'as if to suggest its visionary nature' (*Life*, 73). It is not one of his greatest books. But it does have an interest and a poetry of its own, and Hardy was glad to think that it was much admired by Tennyson and by Coventry Patmore, two of the most popular poets of the day. When it came out in the standard three-volume edition Hardy's name appeared on the cover for the first time. Horace Moule again wrote an encouraging review. Next month Hardy went up to Cambridge to see him, and they climbed on to the roof of King's College chapel and looked out over the flat country towards Ely Cathedral. Hardy never forgot that morning, for it was to be the last time he saw his friend. In September 1873 Moule committed suicide in his rooms at Queens' College by cutting his throat. Over the last few years he had turned to drink, probably because he felt that his academic career was a failure and feared that he could not go on working. Hardy had cared for Moule deeply; perhaps he owed him his own success as a writer. It made him miserable that this good and talented man should have come to such an end. Possibly he thought that the University killed him; there are signs that he was thinking of Moule years later when he began to write *Jude the Obscure*. Other people have conjectured that Moule is Knight in *A Pair of Blue Eyes*. Hardy also wrote some poems which are undoubtedly about his friend; to the end of his life he never forgot him.

He was living at home then, writing *Far from the Madding Crowd* for the *Cornhill*. He always found that the quietness of Dorset, and the rhythm of life in the countryside, helped him to do good work. The new novel began to appear in the *Cornhill* in the first month of 1874. It was published anonymously, and one reviewer suggested, to Hardy's surprise, that the author might be George Eliot, who was recognized now as the leading novelist of the day. 'If *Far from the Madding Crowd* is not written by George Eliot,' this review continued, 'then there is a new light among novelists.' But not all the criticisms were so encouraging. Leslie Stephen was a most distinguished intellectual, but he could not and dared not overlook the prejudices of his readers if he wanted them to go on taking his magazine. He warned Hardy that the seduction of Fanny Robin must be treated in 'a gingerly fashion', and when 'three respectable ladies' wrote to him to complain about 'an improper passage' he was extremely upset. When Hardy pointed out that the same passage had been admired by *The Times* Stephen remarked, 'I spoke as an editor, not as a man. You have no more consciousness of these things than a child' (*Life*, 99). It was a bad omen. But the story had been so successful that Hardy felt he could at last afford to get married, and on 17 September 1874 he and Emma had a quiet wedding in London. None of their parents was there. After a short honeymoon, they went to live in Surbiton.

Architecture and literature

Hardy was struck off the list of the Architectural Association in 1872 for not having paid his subscription; in the same year, as we have seen, he gave up architecture as a career. He cannot have regretted it much. It had been chosen by his parents rather than entered freely by him, and except for short periods of work on an amateur basis he never took it up again.

Yet in some ways it must have seemed to be the natural career for him. For the last four generations all the Hardys had been mastermasons. 'For Hardy craftmanship was innate' (a modern architect has written), 'something inherited from his master-mason father and forebears who could think and work in no other way' (C.J.P. Beatty, Introduction to *The Architectural Notebook of Thomas Hardy*). He went on with architecture for long enough to be sure that he could have made a success of it, and his one surviving notebook shows that he took his work seriously. He was 'an all-round man', like his hero, Jude Fawley; sketches of Gothic pillars and winged angels alternate, in his notebook, with detailed notes about drains. He worked, not only on churches (though this is what he is remembered for) but also on labourers' cottages, railway buildings and schools. He used some of these experiences in his later writing; particularly the weak but interesting novel *A Laodicean*. The heroes of *The Poor Man and the Lady*, *Desperate Remedies* and *A Pair of Blue Eyes* are all young architects, and the hero of *Jude the Obscure* is a stonemason.

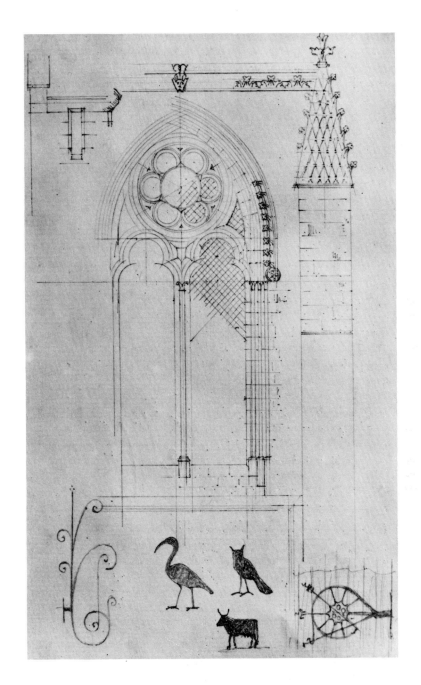

Gothic art and architecture in Hardy's surviving sketchbook.

During the years when Hardy was learning his trade English architecture was undergoing great changes. Glass and iron were used much more than they had been, in structures like the Crystal Palace and the roof of Paddington Station. With this increased modernity, architecture also began, in other ways, to look backwards. A.C. Pugin (1812–52) had made the English more aware of the beauty of medieval buildings, and during the early years of Queen Victoria a great campaign of church restoration began. Most churches and cathedrals were at this time in a bad state. They had been neglected for many hundreds of years, and if they had not been drastically repaired and brought up to date by the restorers they would probably be in ruins today. But the Victorians were very insensitive craftsmen. They tore down a great deal of beautiful medieval work, which was lost for ever, and put in greatly inferior work of their own. An entire church might be pulled down sometimes:

> The original church, hump-backed, wood-turreted, and quaintly hipped, had been taken down, and either cracked up into heaps of road-metal in the lane, or utilized as pig-sty walls, garden seats, guard-stones to fences, and rockeries in the flower-beds of the neighbourhood. In place of it a tall new building of modern Gothic design, unfamiliar to English eyes, had been erected on a new piece of ground by a certain obliterator of historic records who had run down from London and back in a day. (I, 1)

This is how Hardy describes the destruction of Marygreen village church in *Jude*. We have seen how he called himself 'churchy', in a strictly non-religious sense, and the village church in its role as the 'historic record' of the community it served seemed to him very valuable. 'The human interest in an edifice ranks before its architectural interest, however great the latter may be', he once said. This was in a speech to the Society for the Protection of Ancient Buildings, which had been founded by William Morris to resist the vandalism of church restorers. Hardy was an active member of this society in his later years, partly because he felt guilty that, as a young architect, he had been practically forced to destroy a good deal of fine Gothic work himself. In the same speech he had some interesting things to say about the role of an architect who is asked to restore a decaying church:

> The true architect, who is first of all an artist and not an antiquary, is naturally most influenced by the aesthetic sense, his desire being, like Nature's, to retain, recover, or recreate the idea which has become damaged, without much concern about the associations of the material that idea may have been displayed in. . . .
> Thus if the architect have also an antiquarian bias he is pulled in two directions—in one by his wish to hand on or modify the

drawings, as if the original dream and vision of the conceiving master-mason were for a brief hour flashed down through the centuries to an unappreciative age. (V)

Another passage, from *The Mayor of Casterbridge*, shows that he was accustomed to looking at towns with the architect's eye:

> To birds of the more soaring kind Casterbridge must have appeared on this fine evening as a mosaic-work of subdued reds, browns, greys, and crystals, held together by a rectangular frame of deep green. To the level eye of humanity it stood as an indistinct mass behind a dense stockade of limes and chestnuts, set in the midst of miles of rotund down and concave field. The mass became gradually dissected by the vision into towers, gables, chimneys, and casements, the highest glazings shining bleared and bloodshot with the coppery fire they caught from the belt of sunlit cloud in the west. (IV)

It was his architectural training which enabled him to say that Casterbridge met the countryside in 'a *mathematical* line', and that *Jude the Obscure* was 'almost *geometrically* constructed'. There are very many other examples in his work of how he had been affected by his training. But in 1874 he had virtually given up architecture, and was being recognized as a successful novelist for the first time.

The middle years

When *Far from the Madding Crowd* came out in book form with the author's name attached Hardy found to his surprise that he had written a popular novel at last. Whenever he and his wife went into London they saw people carrying copies, and on both sides of the Atlantic the novel was warmly reviewed. One of the most interesting of these reviews was written for the New York *Nation* by the young Henry James, who remarked:

> Mr Hardy describes nature with a great deal of felicity, and is evidently very much at home among rural phenomena. The most genuine thing in his book, to our sense, is a certain aroma of the meadows and lanes—a natural relish for harvesting and sheep-washings. He has laid his scene in an agricultural county, and his characters are children of the soil—unsophisticated country-folk. ...Everything human in the book strikes us as factitious and insubstantial; the only things we believe in are the sheep and the dogs. But, as we say, Mr Hardy has gone astray very cleverly, and his superficial novel is a really curious imitation of something better.

This was to be the tone of most reviewers towards Hardy for the next twenty years. Again and again they were to tell him patronizingly that his only talent was for writing about simple rustic scenes, and that *Far from the Madding Crowd* was his best novel. Perhaps this was why he deliberately made his next book, *The Hand of Ethelberta*, as different as he could. Published in *The Cornhill* in 1875, this was a comedy about a butler's daughter who gate-crashes high society and eventually marries a wicked old peer. It was badly received by the public, who wanted him to go on writing about country life, and Hardy noted unhappily: 'It was, in fact, thirty years too soon for a Comedy of Society of that kind—just as *The Poor Man and the Lady* had been too soon for a socialist story, and as other of his writings —in prose and verse—were too soon for their date' (*Life*, 108). As a general observation this had a lot of truth in it, but on this occasion the critics were right and Hardy was wrong. *The Hand of Ethelberta* is a weak novel; the scenes in high society are unconvincing, and the whole is distinctly inferior to anything that Hardy ever wrote about his own people. After finishing it, he wrote nothing for a while. He was moving restlessly about the country, looking for somewhere to settle, and he was not at all sure which direction to take next:

> One reflection about himself at this date sometimes made Hardy uneasy. He perceived that he was 'up against' the position of having to carry on his life not as an emotion, but as a scientific game; that he was committed by circumstances to novel-writing as a regular trade, as much as he had formerly been to architecture; and that hence he would, he deemed, have to look for material in manners —in ordinary social and fashionable life as other novelists did. Yet he took no interest in manners, but in the substance of life only. So far what he had written had not been novels at all, as usually understood—that is pictures of modern customs and observances —and might not long sustain the interest of the circulating library subscriber who cared mainly for those things. On the other hand, to go about to dinners and clubs and crushes as a business was not much to his mind. Yet that was necessary meat and drink to the popular author.
>
> (*Life*, 104)

This uncertainty about his own talents, his own real strength as a writer, went very deep at this time and never entirely died. It is now that we find him studying Addison, Macaulay, Newman, Gibbon, and leading articles in *The Times* in an effort to polish up his style. It led to many disastrous attempts at sophisticated prose which disfigure

Bridge at Sturminster Newton (Stourcastle) where the Hardys passed two happy years.

even his finest novels, and it was to shape the pattern of his life for many years to come. Even after he had settled in Dorchester he came up to London every year to go the rounds of polite society for as long as his first wife was alive. She enjoyed it more than he did, but all his life Hardy seems to have felt that he needed the approval of 'the world' and to have been unhappy if he did not get it. He also made notes for several novels about 'fashionable life', to be written if the public would read nothing else. Fortunately it never happened, and almost the only way in which these experiences touched his work was in a few short stories about titled ladies, which were published as *A Group of Noble Dames*.

After a short rest from novel-writing he got his nerve back. He and Emma rented a small cottage in Sturminster Newton, in the Vale of Blackmore, and he settled down to write *The Return of the Native*. The two years they spent, almost without a break, in the countryside were the happiest they were to know. Only one thing worried them; they had been married three years and there was still no sign of a child.

It was a good period for Hardy; the new novel was the best thing he had written yet. It was set on Puddletown Heath, which had played so great a part in his life, and his childhood memories of the mummers, the reddleman, and the old men's stories about Napoleon were interwoven with the theme of a hero born ahead of his time, one which was to absorb him more and more in the years to come. It was a splendid achievement. But his publishers made him alter the ending to conform to what the readers wanted, and although the ending which he actually wrote could probably not have been bettered it still depressed him that he was not allowed to write what he liked. He must have been even more depressed when the novel was published and most reviews said that it was worse than his earlier work. The English edition did not even sell out. It was many years before *The Return of the Native* was acknowledged to be a masterpiece, and meanwhile Hardy moved back to London and relapsed into writing inferior stuff.

It was at about this time that Hardy was first asked for a short story and during the rest of his career as a novelist he went on writing them at the rate of about two a year. They were popular at the time, but have not been much noticed since his death. Yet Hardy was a master of this particular art form, and some of his short stories are among the finest in the language. The best of them are collected in *Wessex Tales* and *Life's Little Ironies*; among those particularly well worth reading are 'The Three Strangers', 'A Tragedy of Two Ambitions', 'The Melancholy Hussar', 'The Son's Veto', 'The Grave by the Handpost', and 'The Fiddler of the Reels'.

Back in London he started to do research into the Napoleonic wars with the idea of writing a novel about them. It was hard work, but by the end of 1879 he had finished *The Trumpet-Major* and it was published the year. This novel, well known to generations of schoolchildren as a set book, is pleasant and entertaining but, compared to the novel which had gone before, very slight. While it was still running as a serial Hardy had promised to begin work on another novel, but before he had written more than one instalment he realized he was ill. The doctor found that he had an internal haemorrhage and told him to stay in bed for six months.

Lying with his feet propped higher than his head, and in a good deal of pain, he dictated the rest of *A Laodicean* to Emma. He did not feel particularly creative in the circumstances, but he was determined to do it, for the publishers would have been in an awkward position if he had let them down and there was very little money for his wife if he died. The result of all this was a long and poor novel. Some parts of it are memorable for his discussions of Gothic architecture, and the book also shows his interest in the discoveries of modern science, such as railway engineering and a device for faking photographs (unheard of at the time). But on the whole it was a novel which Hardy preferred to forget. It is usual to lay the whole blame for its failure on the fact that he was a sick man when he wrote it, but actually the first few chapters, written before he fell ill, are not much better than the rest of the book. It seems more likely that living in London and going about socially had a bad effect on his work: 'residence in or near a city tended to force mechanical and ordinary productions from his pen' (*Life*, 149). As soon as he was better he and Emma decided to move to the country for good.

They found a little house in the picturesque town of Wimborne Minster, and almost as soon as they had settled there, Hardy began to feel more cheerful:

> Our garden. . . has all sorts of old-fashioned flowers, in full bloom: Canterbury Bells, blue and white, and Sweet Williams of every variety, strawberries and cherries that are ripe, currants and gooseberries that are almost ripe, peaches that are green, and apples that are decidedly immature.
>
> (*Life*, 150)

A comet which he saw that year gave him the idea for a new story, about a young man in a quiet country village who wants to be an astronomer. In the Preface to *Two on a Tower* he said that the book ('this slightly-built romance', as he called it) had been inspired by the wish 'to set the emotional history of two infinitesimal lives against the stupendous background of the stellar universe, and to impart to readers the sentiment that of these contrasting magnitudes the smaller might be the greater to them as men'. He wrote it quickly, in about six months, and it was published in 1882. It was not one of his greatest novels, but he had tried to write a serious story about man's place in the universe, about achievement, and about self-sacrifice. He was therefore rather horrified when the book was attacked for being 'immoral', and also for being a satire on religion. It was not the first or the last time that readers were to see meanings in his novels of which he had never dreamed.

Soon afterwards, in April 1883, an article on Hardy's novels appeared in the *Westminster Review*. It was written by the critic and future apostle of sexual freedom, Havelock Ellis, and it showed a warm appreciation of Hardy's work:

> The English agricultural labourer is a figure which few novelists have succeeded in describing. Few, indeed, have had an opportunity of knowing him. George Eliot, who has represented so much of the lower strata of English rural life, has not reached him. At best he is only visible in the dim background.... It is difficult to find anywhere fit company for the quaint and worthy fellowship, so racy of the earth, who greet us from the pages of *Far from the Madding Crowd* and *The Return of the Native*.

This is a fair example of the attitude of enlightened critics to Hardy at this time. Most people tended to think of him as the author of *Far from the Madding Crowd*, although he had written five novels since that one, and to assume that the one thing he could do supremely well was to paint a picture of 'English rural life'. But it was not so usual for critics to see that Hardy was the *only* considerable novelist who had written about agricultural labourers, a class which was generally treated as rather funny and described, by educated people, under the nickname of 'Hodge'. In July of the same year Hardy published an article, 'The Dorsetshire Labourer', in *Longman's Magazine*, which ridiculed this crude conception:

> This supposedly real but highly conventional Hodge is a degraded being of uncouth manner and aspect, stolid understanding, and snail-like movement. His speech is such a chaotic corruption of regular language that few persons of progressive aims consider it worth while to enquire what views, if any, of life, of nature, or of society, are conveyed in these utterances.... But suppose that, by some accident, the visitor were obliged to go home with this man ... he would, for one thing, find that the language, instead of being a vile corruption of cultivated speech, was a tongue with grammatical inflection... the unwritten, dying Wessex English....
>
> Six months pass, and our gentleman leaves the cottage, bidding his friends goodbye with genuine regret. The great change in his perception is that Hodge, the dull, unvarying, joyless one, has ceased to exist for him. He has become disintegrated into a number of dissimilar fellow-creatures, men of many minds, infinite in difference; some happy, many serene, a few depressed; some clever, even

Grey's Bridge, Dorchester (Casterbridge)

to genius, some stupid, some wanton, some austere; some mutely Miltonic, some Cromwellian; into men who have private views of each other, as he has of his friends; who applaud or condemn each other; amuse or sadden themselves by the contemplation of each other's foibles or vices; and each of whom walks in his own way the road to dusty death. Dick the carter, Bob the shepherd, and Sam the ploughman, are, it is true, alike in the narrowness of their means and their general open-air life; but they cannot be rolled together again into such a Hodge as he has dreamed of, by any possible enchantment.

(PW 168–9)

This article, with its clear message that people who worked on the land must be respected as human beings, in some ways marked a turning-point in Hardy's career. From now on he was to go back to writing novels about Dorset and its people, and he was to do his most creative work as a novelist. He had also decided to settle in Dorchester for good. Over the previous ten years he and his wife had been moving restlessly from the town to the country and back again, never staying in one place for more than a couple of years. Probably

31

they lacked the stability which a family would have given them, and they must have realised by this time that they were never going to have children. But Hardy was definite that he wanted to live in Dorset, both for reasons of health and for reasons of work, and only go to London occasionally. So in the summer of 1883 they took lodgings in Dorchester, and Hardy began to design a house about a mile from the town. It was finished in another two years, and was called Max Gate. He was to write all the rest of his novels and poetry there.

Meanwhile he was working on *The Mayor of Casterbridge*, one of the finest of his novels. Almost certainly it turned out well because he refused to be rushed, and also because he was writing about the town which he had known all his life. A good deal of the real Dorchester went into Hardy's portrait of Casterbridge, and the hero, Michael Henchard, is one of the most vital characters that he ever conceived. But he had some trouble getting it published, and not all the copies were sold. Reviewers complained that it was too gloomy, and, predictably, that it was not as good as *Far from the Madding Crowd*. Fortunately Hardy was becoming more and more indifferent to what the public thought. Moving back to Dorchester seems to have given him confidence, and from then on his novels were to become steadily more unorthodox and more individual.

He finished *The Mayor* a couple of months before he moved into Max Gate, and his next novel, *The Woodlanders*, was written entirely in the study there. It was his own favourite work, although not many people agreed with him at the time. Some called it disagreeable, or even immoral. But it was enough of a success, both with the public and in his own judgement, to make Hardy happy to go on writing novels.

He was now contemplating a more ambitious work than any he had yet written. In September 1888 he went to look at some of the houses and lands which his family had owned, long before, and wrote,

> The Vale of Blackmoor is almost entirely green, every hedge being studded with trees. On the left you see to an immense distance, including Shaftesbury. The decline and fall of the Hardys much in evidence hereabout ... 'All Woolcombe and Froom Quintin belonged to them at one time'.

(*Life*, 214)

Out of this grew the idea for a story, set in the Vale of Blackmoor, which would deal with the decline and fall of ancient families. This mingled with memories of a woman whom he had seen hanged, as a boy, for a crime of passion, and with his own knowledge about the exploitation of country girls. He began to write *Tess of the d'Urbervilles*, although it was not known by that name at first; in the manuscript the heroine was called Rose Mary Troublefield. Troublefield is a corruption of Turberville, the real name of an aristocratic Norman family which had died out by that time, and which is commemorated in the Dorset church of Bere Regis.

He offered the first few chapters to a magazine editor without, apparently, seeing anything controversial about what he had written. It was sent back to him, 'virtually on the score of its improper explicitness' (*Life*, 222). He could not yet afford to do without serial publication, so he spent the year 1890 cutting up the manuscript, leaving out some parts and drastically altering others, to make it fit for the great British public. He said that he did this in a spirit of cynical amusement, but in an essay which he wrote that year, 'Candour in English Fiction', it can be seen that he bitterly resented what he was having to do to his novel. 'The great bulk of English fiction of the present day is characterized by its lack of sincerity', he stated truthfully enough, and the reason for this was that writers were forced to rely for their livelihood on the circulating magazines from which any frank treatment of sex or religion was carefully excluded:

It may be urged that abundance of great and profound novels might be written which should require no compromising, contain not an episode deemed questionable by prudes. This I venture to doubt. In a ramification of the profounder passions the treatment of which makes the great style, something unsuitable is sure to arise; and then comes the struggle with the literary conscience. The opening scenes of the would-be great story may, in a rash moment, have been printed in some popular magazine before the remainder is written; as it advances month by month the situations develop, and the writer asks himself, what will his characters do next? What would probably happen to them, given such beginnings? On his life and conscience, though he had not foreseen the thing, only one event could possibly happen, and that therefore he should narrate, as he calls himself a faithful artist. But, though pointing a fine moral, it is just one of those issues which are not to be mentioned in respectable magazines and select libraries. The dilemma then confronts him, he must either whip and scourge those characters into doing something contrary to their natures, to produce the spurious effect of their being in harmony with social forms and ordinances, or, by leaving them alone to act as they will, he must bring down the thunders of respectability upon his head, not to say ruin his editor, his publisher, and himself.

What he often does, indeed can scarcely help doing in such a strait, is, belie his literary conscience, do despite to his best imaginative instincts by arranging a *dénouement* which he knows to be indescribably unreal and meretricious, but dear to the Grundyist and subscriber. If the true artist ever weeps it probably is then, when he first discovers the fearful price that he has to pay for writing in the English language—no less a price than the complete extinction, in the mind of every mature and penetrating reader, of sympathetic belief in his personages.

(*PW*, 129–30)

He ended with a plea for a literature in which writers would be able to deal honestly with the profounder passions which he had described:

Nothing in such literature should for a moment exhibit lax views of that purity of life on which the well-being of society depends; but the position of man and woman in nature, and the position of belief in the minds of man and woman—things which everybody is thinking but nobody is saying—might be taken up and treated frankly.

After the expurgated version had appeared in serial form the complete novel was published at the end of 1891. The storm which followed took Hardy by surprise. He had not thought that so many readers would be shocked by what he was trying to do in *Tess*, or that he would be so widely accused of holding immoral views. But, as is always the case with so-called 'immoral' novels, the sales were enormous, and many discerning critics greeted *Tess* as a great work of art. Hardy became at once one of the most widely read English authors both at home and abroad.

An interesting glimpse of Hardy at this time is provided by a journalist, Raymond Blathwayt, who interviewed him after the book had come out. He wrote:

Mr Hardy is in himself a gentle and a singularly pleasing personality. Of middle height, with a very thoughtful face and rather melancholy eyes, he is nevertheless an interesting and an amusing companion. ... His wife ... is so particularly bright ... so evidently a citizen of the wide world, that the, at first, unmistakable reminiscence that there is in her of Anglican ecclesiasticism is curiously puzzling and inexplicable to the stranger.

Hardy showed him around Max Gate and talked about his latest novel. On the character of Tess he said:

'She had done exactly what I think one of her nature under similar circumstances would have done in real life. It is led up to right through the story. One looks for the climax. One is not to be cheated out of it by the exigencies of inartistic conventionality. And so there come the tears of faithful tragedy in place of the ghastly and affected smile of the conventionally optimistic writer.'

He said that the public's growing willingness to accept tragic endings was a hopeful sign for the future. Blathwayt went on to say:

'And the ultimate result of your book, Mr Hardy, will be, I hope, that a greater freedom will exist for the decent, grave consideration of certain deep problems of human life.'

'Well,' replied Mr Hardy with a smile, 'that would be a very ambitious hope on my part. Remember I am only a learner in the art of novel writing. Still I do feel very strongly that the position of man and woman in nature, things which everyone is thinking and nobody saying, may be taken up and treated frankly. Until lately novelists have been obliged to arrange situations and *dénouements* which they knew to be indescribably unreal, but dear to the heart of the amiable library subscriber. See how this ties the hands of a writer who is forced to make his characters act unnaturally, in order that he may produce the spurious effect of their being in harmony with social forms and ordinances.'

(Lerner and Holmstrom, 90–7)

It is very clear from everything Hardy said and wrote at this time that he was moving in the direction of greater realism, and this tendency can be seen, still more clearly, in his next novel, *Jude the Obscure*. For some years now he had been thinking of writing a story about a young man who failed to go to Oxford and committed suicide, and it is difficult not to feel that this was inspired by the fate of Horace Moule. Later he dropped the idea of suicide for his hero, and something which happened in 1890 made him alter his plans once more. While he was in a train on the way to London he found himself thinking about Tryphena, and composed the first few lines of a poem to her which he called, 'Thoughts of Phena', and which was later published in *Wessex Poems*. In it he called her 'my lost prize'. It was, he said, ' a curious instance of sympathetic telepathy' (*Life*, 224), for Tryphena was dying at the time, and the poem was not finished until after Hardy had heard about her death. They had had no contact with each other for nearly twenty years. He went to see her grave at Plymouth and left a wreath there. In the Preface to *Jude the Obscure* he said that parts of the novel had been suggested by 'the death of a woman' in the year Tryphena died.

Opinion has always been divided about Hardy's last novel, which is the story of two cousins who fall in love but each marry the wrong person, as well as the story of a young working man who is excluded from Oxford. Some people, notably Swinburne, thought and still think that it is one of the greatest things Hardy ever wrote. Others found it depressing and a failure, and this included the majority of those who reviewed it at the time. Typical headlines for these reviews were 'Jude the Obscene', 'Hardy the Degenerate', and 'The

35

Anti-Marriage League'. The novel was banned from public libraries and thrown on the fire by a bishop. One lady wrote:

Nothing so coarsely indecent as the whole history of Jude in his relations with his wife Arabella has ever been put in English print —that is to say, from the hands of a Master. There may be books more disgusting, more impious as regards human nature, more foul in detail, in those dark corners where the amateurs of filth find garbage to their taste; but not, we repeat, from any Master's hand.

(Quoted, Lerner and Holmstrom, 127)

An American wrote that the novel showed:

the studied satyriasis of approaching senility, suggesting the morbidly curious imaginings of a masochist or some other form of sexual pervert. The eagerness with which every unclean situation is seized upon and carefully exploited recalls the spectacle of some foul animal that snatches greedily at great lumps of putrid offal which it mumbles with a hideous delight in the stenches that drive away all cleanlier creatures. ... It is simply one of the most objectionable books that we have ever read in any language whatsoever. ... Mr Hardy is merely speculating in smut.

(Quoted, *ibid*, 133)

This kind of review, and the anonymous letters he received, upset Hardy profoundly. It made him almost ill to find himself at the centre of the greatest literary scandal for years. He did not feel he had written an immoral book; his only aim was to write honestly, but at the time he did not try to defend himself, and retreated into his shell. The 1912 Preface to *Jude*, and poems like 'Wessex Heights' and 'In Tenebris' give some indication of how deep his suffering went. And perhaps the most painful thing of all was that his wife was against him too. She not only did not understand the novel; she had gone so far as to try to get it stopped.

We do not know exactly when Hardy and Emma began to be miserable in their marriage, but it seems certain that things grew much worse about the time he wrote *Jude the Obscure*. Not unnaturally she felt that a book which criticized marriage would be interpreted as an insult to her; moreover she was shocked by Hardy's cynicism about the Church, for as she got older she had become more devout. Her attitude towards that novel becomes unforgiveable when it is discovered that she secretly sided with attempts to suppress it altogether. Part of the difference between them may be reflected in the novel itself. Hardy writes of Jude: 'One thing troubled him more than any other; that Sue and himself had mentally travelled in opposite directions... events which had enlarged his own views of life, laws, customs, and dogmas, had not operated in the same manner on Sue's' (VI, iii).

36

Later in the novel this becomes a general observation; 'Strange difference of sex, that time and circumstance, which enlarge the views of most men, narrow the views of women almost invariably' (VI, x). Hardy felt this had happened to Emma. She would apologize to visitors for his unorthodox opinions, explaining that he did not really mean what he said. And this was only one example of how she snubbed him in public; on another occasion she had said, 'Try to remember, Thomas Hardy, that you married a lady!' This was the root of the problem. She did feel that her family was much more distinguished than her husband's; it is said that she refused to visit his parents; she liked entertaining and visiting London much more than he ever did. There was too a streak of madness in her family, and about this time Emma was growing more and more eccentric. Hardy's poem, 'The Interloper', shows that at times he feared she might really go mad. He continued to live with her; in a way he even continued to love her, but increasingly they lived like strangers.

Another source of unhappiness during these years was Hardy's deep feeling for a married woman, Mrs Florence Henniker, an authoress and society hostess whom he had met in 1893. But there was never any intrigue between them and after a while it became an ordinary friendship. Perhaps her greatest importance in Hardy's life lies in the fact that she introduced him to another woman, Florence Dugdale, who eventually became his wife.

Meanwhile, he tried to rebuild his life as far as he could. He prepared his novels for a new general edition, which came out in 1895. But he was determined not to write any more fiction, partly, or perhaps entirely, because of the reception of *Jude*. He no longer had any need to write for money, for *Jude*, like *Tess*, had been a great success just because it was so scandalous and he had earned enough to retire. He found his thoughts turning back to poetry, which was what he had always wanted to write and indeed had been writing in private for the last thirty years. His first collection, *Wessex Poems*, came out in 1898. It was rather a shock to the public, who had never thought of him as anything but a novelist, but it was quite well received. He went on writing poetry exclusively for the rest of his life. What has only gradually been realized is that he was a great poet, an artist of wonderful depth and versatility, in spite of the fact that most of his poems were written as an elderly man. He himself said that he would like to be remembered as a poet who had also written some novels, and as time went on his prose works began to seem less and less important to him.

In the early years of the century he began work on *The Dynasts*, an epic drama in blank verse which he had been planning for years. It was born out of the deep interest in Napoleon which he shared with many other writers of his own and the previous generation, and it aimed to give a picture of what happened to Europe at the time of

Emma Lavinia Gifford
(afterwards Mrs Thomas Hardy)
1870

Emma Hardy

Tryphena Sparks

Florence Emily Hardy

Mrs Florence Henniker

the Napoleonic wars. The actual history of these wars and the politics which led up to them was observed by the blind cause of things, which Hardy called 'It', or the Immanent Will, by the remote unsympathetic Spirit of the Years, and by the Spirit of the Pities, which represents Hardy's own point of view. The whole work is deeply imbued with a sense of the horrors of war. It took him some six years to write, and was published in three parts.

The Dynasts is not easy to read today, partly because of its length and partly because it illustrates several of Hardy's bad habits as a poet, particularly his weakness for a cramped syntax and archaic words. But it was a heroic attempt to write a modern epic, and as such it was welcomed by the public. Indeed, Hardy must have been surprised at how respectable he was becoming. While almost all his novels had been abused or sneered at, his work as a poet was universally praised. He was getting to be a grand old man of letters. Aberdeen University gave him a doctorate in 1905, and in 1910, after the completion of *The Dynasts*, he was awarded the Order of Merit.

'Poems of 1912–13' and after

Hardy was still on very cold and distant terms with his wife when she died suddenly in November 1912. It was a terrible shock to him. Looking back over the years, he found that he could only remember the long-ago time when they had been young and in love, and much of what had happened since seemed to him to be more his fault than hers. He found a manuscript among her papers, headed 'What I Think of my Husband', which deepened his feelings of guilt. After the first shock, he found that he was writing poem after poem about her, and these became a cycle, called 'Poems of 1912–13', which are among the greatest love lyrics in English. But, after they had been written, he found that he could not work. Celebrity hunters broke into the house demanding to see him, and his life became completely disorganized. One of the poems he wrote in 1913 shows us something of his loneliness and hopelessness at this time:

> Something tapped on the pane of my room
> When there was never a trace
> Of wind or rain, and I saw in the gloom
> My weary Beloved's face.

> 'O I am tired of waiting,' she said,
> 'Night, morn, noon, afternoon;
> So cold it is in my lonely bed,
> And I thought you would join me soon!'

I rose and neared the window-glass,
But vanished thence had she:
Only a pallid moth, alas,
Tapped at the pane for me.

(Something Tapped *CP*, 436)

He felt that he could not go on without companionship of some sort. He got a wire-haired terrier, named Wessex, whom he spoiled like a child. But what saved him at this juncture was the friendship of a much younger woman, Florence Dugdale, whom he and his wife had known for many years. She was a teacher's daughter, wrote children's stories, and had done some research for Hardy in the British Museum. After Emma died she had come to Max Gate at his request and made all the arrangements for the funeral. During the year which followed he became more and more attached to her, and they were quietly married in February 1914. She brought back meaning and order to his life and looked after him lovingly throughout the fourteen years they were to spend together. It is doubtful whether he could have gone on working but for her.

The Great War which broke out six months later was a profound shock to Hardy. He had been fascinated by the European wars of a century earlier, but never thought the same thing could happen again. It destroyed his belief that the world was gradually getting better. He hated everything he saw of the war, but like most English people he accepted the official version that the country was fighting for its life and offered to help in any way he could. He joined the Writers' War Committee and wrote several mildly patriotic poems which had a wide circulation. But he never hated Germans or joined in the hysterical propaganda which was so common during those years. He visited the wounded prisoners of war in Dorchester and tried to persuade them that the war was not against Germany as such, which they found hard to believe. The war brought him a personal sadness as well. A distant cousin, Frank George, to whom he had hoped to leave Max Gate, was killed in 1915, and Hardy commemorated him in the poem, 'Before Marching and After'.

When at last the war ended he wrote, 'And there was a Great Calm', which asked if there had been any reason for the holocaust:

Calm fell. From Heaven distilled a clemency;
There was peace on earth, and silence in the sky;
Some could, some could not, shake off misery:
The Sinister Spirit sneered: 'It had to be!'
And again the Spirit of Pity whispered, 'Why?'

(*CP*, 557)

Afterwards his life settled down into a quiet routine. He was nearly eighty now, and too old to go far from home, but many admirers came down to Max Gate to see him. Young poets sent him their work. One of these was the antiwar writer Siegfried Sassoon, who found Hardy much more sympathetic than most of the older generation, and who organized a tribute to him on his birthday from a large number of young writers. Hardy was very touched by this. 'It was almost his first awakening to the consciousness that an opinion had silently grown up as it were in the night, that he was no mean power in the contemporary world of poetry' (*Life*, 390).

In 1920 the University of Oxford, doubtless earlier offended by *Jude*, decided to give Hardy an honorary doctorate seven years after Cambridge had done the same thing. Hardy seemed to enjoy the occasion. An undergraduate, Charles Morgan, later a novelist and dramatist, showed him round the city and reflected:

> It seemed very strange to be driving solemnly up the High and down the Broad with the author of *Jude*. It seemed strange because, after all, it was so natural. ... When we are under-graduates we expect writers to be literary men in all things; we cannot easily dissociate them from their works; and it seemed to me very odd that Thomas Hardy should bother about the Martyrs' Memorial.
>
> (*Life*, 401)

It must have been hard to realize that the distinguished visitor had been at one time something very like what we would now call an angry young man. But Morgan sensed that a good deal of the passion of that young man was still there, beneath the surface:

> He was not simple; he had the formal subtlety peculiar to his own generation; there was something deliberately 'ordinary' in his demeanour which was a concealment of extraordinary fires— a method of self-protection common enough in my grandfather's generation, though rare now.
>
> There are many who might have thought him unimpressive because he was content to be serious and determined to be un-spectacular. But his was the kind of character to which I lay open. He was an artist, proud of his art, who yet made no parade of it; he was a traditionalist and, therefore, suspicious of fashion; he had that sort of melancholy, the absence of which in any man has always seemed to me to be a proclamation of blindness.
>
> There was in him something timid as well as something fierce, as if the world had hurt him and he expected it to hurt him again. But what fascinated me above all was the contrast between the plainness, the quiet rigidity of his behaviour, and the passionate boldness of his mind, for this I had always believed to be the tradi-tion of English genius, too often and too extravagantly denied.
>
> (*Life*, 403)

Thomas Hardy, O.M. doy en of English letters.

There is another revealing glimpse of Hardy as a very old man, written by an Oxford don, Godfrey Elton, who met him when Hardy again visited the university as an honorary fellow of Queen's College in 1923:

> A smallish, fragile, bright-eyed man, elderly certainly but as certainly not old. . . . An elderly gentleman, one would have said, who had always lived in the country and knew much of the ways of wild creatures and crops. . . .
>
> I should not have guessed that I was with a man who wrote; rather an elderly country gentleman with a bird-like alertness and a rare and charming youthfulness—interested in everything he saw, and cultured, but surely not much occupied with books: indeed almost all of us, his new colleagues, would have struck an impartial observer as far more *bookish* than the author of the Wessex novels.
>
> (*Life*, 421)

He went on living quietly in the country with Florence and Wessex, writing poetry almost to the end. He used to walk regularly to Stinsford churchyard and put flowers on the family graves. He was still interested in everything that went on round him, in poetry, religion and politics, never showing the faintest trace of senility. In November 1927 Florence noted: 'Speaking about ambition T. said today that he had done all that he meant to do, but he did not know whether it had been worth doing. His only ambition, so far as he could remember, was to have some poem or poems in a good anthology like the Golden Treasury' (*Life*, 444).

He had prepared another book of poems, *Winter Words*, for publication on his eighty-eighth birthday, but he was never to see it in print. Shortly after this note was written he found that he could not work any more and in the New Year he died. He had expressed a wish to be buried in Stinsford churchyard but in the end only his heart was laid there and he was given an elaborate funeral in Westminster Abbey. He lies next to Dickens in the Poets' Corner. It was an irony which he would have appreciated, for only a few years earlier he had written a sarcastic poem about the Abbey's refusal to erect a memorial in the same place to Byron, on the grounds that he had been a most immoral writer.

2 Hardy the Countryman

To understand Hardy's life and work we have to know something about Dorset in the nineteenth century, the region which lay at the heart of what he called Wessex, and where most of his novels are set. When Hardy was growing up it was very different from the rest of England. It had its own culture, its own traditions, even its own language, in a sense.

It was a very remote and old-fashioned county. When Hardy wrote about it in his novels, he was often asked, 'even by educated people', where exactly it lay. Traditions lingered on for a long time in this neighbourhood. Hardy's grandmother remembered hearing the news of the French Revolution, and many men still living had joined the militia to fight Napoleon, when it looked as if Dorset would be invaded from the sea. These memories were very real to him; he knew a great deal more about his ancestors, who had lived, died and been buried in Dorset, than most of us do about ours. Some of his earliest memories were of 'men in the stocks, corn-law agitations, mail-coaches, road-waggons, tinder-boxes, and candle-snuffing' (*Life* 21); he had also seen two public hangings by the time he was sixteen. He had also seen or heard of such customs as the skimmity-ride, the maypole, the mummers who gave the play of St George and the Dragon at Christmas, the old-fashioned hiring fairs for farm labourers, and the sale by husbands of wives. But things were changing. When he was seven the railway came to Dorchester, and Hardy noted with regret that this killed off the countryside's traditional ballads — 'the orally transmitted ditties of centuries being slain at a stroke by the London comic songs that were introduced' (*Life*, 21). This is a complaint which we often hear in our own century, from Scotland to Eastern Europe, wherever the culture of a country or province is superseded by a new 'pop culture' which has no real roots there. The ballads were not the only thing Hardy regretted. His family had a long connection with the cultural life of the parish which had come to an end when he was only one year old. For forty years before that, his grandfather, and then his father and his uncle, had been the nucleus of a little group of musicians who accompanied the services at Stinsford church. In those days it was normal for such groups, rather than an organ, to provide the church music, and there

Victorian genre picture of village music group resembling Mellstock Quire.

was a small gallery for the players which has long since been pulled down. They were excellent performers: 'the Hardy instrumentalists, though no more than four, maintained an easy superiority over the large groups in parishes near'. Hardy drew a detailed and loving picture of this little group in an early novel, *Under the Greenwood Tree*, although he

> invented the personages, incidents, manners, etc., never having seen or heard the choir as such, they ending their office when he was about a year old. He was accustomed to say that on this account he had rather burlesqued them, the story not so adequately reflecting as he could have wished in later years the poetry and romance that coloured their time-honoured observances.
>
> (*Life*, 12)

Hardy felt a deep respect for these people, and a deep regret that choirs like this should have been abolished all over the West Country when he was a boy. He noted that the musicians were 'mainly poor men and hungry', but very good at and devoted to their work, which included playing at weddings and parties as well as in church. Not surprisingly, when the village choirs were killed the attendance at the village church (which also had the disadvantage of being associated with the landlords) began to decline.

Later Hardy came to think that one of the most important events of his childhood had been the Great Exhibition which was held in London in 1851:

> For South Wessex, the year formed in many ways an extraordinary chronological frontier or transit-line, at which there occurred what one might call a precipice in Time. As in a geological 'fault' we had presented to us a sudden bringing of ancient and modern into absolute contact, such as probably in no other single year since the Conquest was ever witnessed in this part of the country.
>
> (*The Fiddler of the Reels*)

Special 'exhibition trains' were laid on, and literally thousands of people, who had never left their village or got on a train before, were whirled up to London to see the wonders of modern science and industry. Hardy did not go, but already as a boy he had begun to feel the contrast between old and new. Dorchester was an old-fashioned place, just as he was to describe it later in *The Mayor of Casterbridge*, but, compared with Higher Bockhampton, it seemed very modern:

> Owing to the accident of his being an architect's pupil in a county town of assizes and aldermen, which had advanced to railways and telegraphs and daily London papers; yet not living there, but

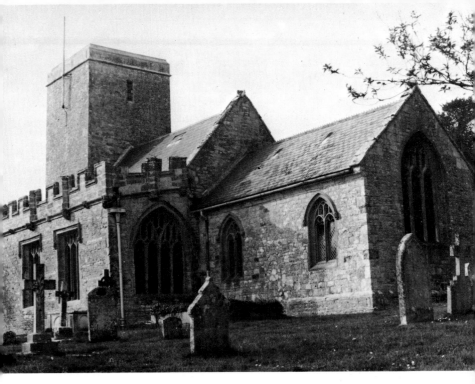

Stinsford Church, where the Hardys are buried, original of Mellstock.

walking in every day from a world of shepherds and ploughmen in a
hamlet three miles off, where modern improvements were still
regarded as wonders, he saw rustic and borough doings in a juxta-
position peculiarly close. To these externals may be added the
peculiarities of his inner life, which might almost have been called
academic — a triple existence unusual for a young man — what
he used to call, in looking back, a life twisted of three strands—the
professional life, the scholar's life, and the rustic life, combined in
the twenty-four hours of one day.

(*Life*, 31–2)

This 'triple existence' was in fact to continue all the rest of his life,
for as well as being a scholar and a professional man Hardy was
always to remain deeply committed to the Dorsetshire countryside,
its people and its culture. Instinctively, he felt that he belonged here,
although at a very early stage he began to be conscious of something
beyond.

47

William Barnes and 'provincialism'

When Hardy was working at John Hicks's office in South Street, he would often look in next door, where the Reverend William Barnes kept a school. Hardy used to ask his advice about knotty points in Greek and Latin grammar (he was an expert on all kinds of linguistic problems) and later they became friends in spite of forty years' difference in age. Barnes was one of Hardy's greatest teachers at this formative time in his life.

This extraordinary man, probably the best-known person in Dorchester, was born a farmer's son in the Vale of Blackmore in 1801. He took an external degree at Oxford and eventually became a clergyman, during which time he taught himself an amazing number of languages. 'He was almost always ready', Hardy wrote, 'with definite and often exclusive information on whatever slightly known form of human speech might occur to the mind of his questioner, from Persian to Welsh, from the contemporary vernaculars of India to the tongues of the ancient British tribes' (*PW*, 102). But his particular love was the Dorsetshire dialect, and he is remembered today as our only significant dialect poet since Burns. Not that he is remembered widely, because many readers are naturally reluctant to tackle poems which they assume will be very difficult. Hardy was conscious of this obstacle when he wrote, in the Preface to a new edition of his friend's work:

> I chance to be (I believe) one of the few living persons having a practical acquaintance with letters who knew familiarly the Dorset dialect when it was spoken as Barnes writes it, or, perhaps, who know it as it is spoken now. Since his death, education in the West of England, as elsewhere, has gone on with its silent and inevitable effacements, reducing the speech of this country to uniformity, and obliterating every year many a fine old local word. The process is always the same: the word is ridiculed by the newly taught; it gets into disgrace; it is heard in holes and corners only; it dies.
>
> (*PW*, 76)

This was all the more sad, from Hardy's point of view, because he felt that Barnes, at his best, had been a very great poet. He was essentially a writer of simple lyrics; he did not often go deeply into social conditions, but his descriptions of nature were often uniquely lovely — Hardy cited his phrase 'the blue-hilled worold' to describe the landscape of Blackmore Vale. He was also deeply impressed with Barnes's poetry about the people of Dorset, particularly one called 'The Wife-a-Lost'. This sad little poem is not difficult to translate into ordinary English, particularly if one substitutes 's' where Barnes writes 'z', and leaves most of the 'w's out:

Since I noo mwore do zee your feäce,
Up-steäirs or down below,
I'll zit me in the lonesome pleäce,
Where flat-bough'd beech do grow.
Below the beeches' bough, my love,
Where you did never come,
An' I don't look to meet ye now,
As I do look at hwome.

Since you noo mwore be at my side,
In walks in zummer het,
I'll goo alwone where mist do ride
Drough trees a-drippèn wet :
Below the rain-wet bough, my love,
Where you did never come,
An' I don't grieve to miss ye now,
As I do grieve at hwome.

Since now bezide my dinner bwoard
Your vaïce do never sound,
I'll eat the bit I can avword,
A-vield upon the ground ;
Below the darksome bough, my love,
Where you did never dine,
An' I don't grieve to miss ye now
As I at hwome do pine.

What Hardy admired about poems like these was that they used the
regional dialect *seriously*. Most writers only put it into the mouths of
their 'comic rustics', a vulgarization of the real country people
which never failed to make him angry. As he said in 1908, in the
Preface to Barnes's poems :

For some reason or none, many persons suppose that when anything is penned in the tongue of the countryside, the primary
intent is burlesque or ridicule, and this especially if the speech be
one in which the sibilant has the rough sound, and is expressed by
Z. Indeed, scores of thriving story-tellers and dramatists seem to
believe that by transmuting the flattest conversation into a dialect
that never existed, and making the talkers say 'be' where they
would really say 'is', a Falstaffian richness is at once imparted to its
qualities.

(*PW*, 78)

Hardy's own use of dialect was considerably more subtle and varied
than the older poet's. As a young man he tried writing a few poems in
broad Dorset, but they were not a success. In his novels, the less
well educated characters do normally speak in the language of the

province, but Hardy was careful not to reproduce their speech phonetically, as Barnes had done:

> The rule of scrupulously preserving the local idiom, together with the words which have no synonym among those in general use, while printing in the ordinary way most of those local expressions which are but a modified articulation of words in use elsewhere, is the rule I usually follow.
>
> (*PW*, 92)

He was more reluctant than Barnes to use words which would not have been easily understood by his readers. Occasionally he showed how the older people, like Grammer Oliver in *The Woodlanders*, used expressions like 'ch woll' or 'Ich woll' for 'I will'.* Even an educated girl like Tess Durbeyfield speaks in a fairly broad dialect sometimes: 'Had it anything to do with father's making such a mommet of himself in thik carriage this afternoon? Why did 'er? I felt inclined to sink into the ground with shame!' (*Tess*, III). But, normally, Hardy found that he could give his readers a good idea of the rhythm and quality of west country speech without actually using dialect words:

> 'My brother-in-law told me, and I have no reason to doubt it,' said Creedle, 'that she'll sit down to her dinner with a gown hardly higher than her elbows. "O, you wicked woman!" he said to himself when he first see her, "you go to the Table o' Sundays, and kneel, as if your knee-joints were greased with very saint's anointment, and tell off your hear-us-good-Lords as pat as a business-man counting money; and yet you can eat your victuals a-stript to such a wanton figure as that!" Whether she's a reformed character by this time I can't say; but I don't care who the man is, that's how she went on when my brother-in-law lived there.'
>
> (*Woodlanders*, IV)

And at other times in the Wessex novels he showed how the dialect could be transformed into great literature, as in the backward labourer Whittle's description of the last days of Michael Henchard:

> 'He was kind-like to mother when she wer here below, sending her the best ship-coal, and hardly any ashes from it at all; and taties, and such-like that were very needful to her. I seed en go down street on the night of your worshipful's wedding to the lady at yer side, and I thought he looked low and faltering. And I followed en over Grey's Bridge, and he turned and zeed me, and said, "You go back!" But I followed, and he turned again, and said, "Do you hear, sir? Go back!" But I zeed that he was low, and I followed on still. Then 'a said, "Whittle, what do ye follow me for when I've

*The Dorset dialect was in some ways very like German, and Hardy commented on this in a poem, 'The Pity of It', which he wrote in 1915. It seemed to him to make the war all the more tragic.

told ye to go back all these times?" And I said, "Because, sir, I see things be bad with 'ee, and ye wer kind-like to mother if ye were rough to me, and I would fain be kind-like to you". Then he walked on, and I followed; and he never complained at me no more. We walked on like that all night; and in the blue o' the morning, when 'twas hardly day, I looked ahead o' me, and I zeed that he wambled, and could hardly drag along. By that time we had got past here, but I had seen that this house was empty as I went by, and I got him to come back; and I took down the boards from the windows, and helped him inside.'

(*Mayor of Casterbridge*, XLV)

In the hands of a great master like Hardy, or indeed a less great one like Barnes, dialect could become a wonderful means of showing how Dorset people felt and thought. But, as Hardy was well aware, it was dying out. The coming of universal education helped to kill it; Tess Durbeyfield speaks 'two languages, the dialect at home, more or less; ordinary English abroad and to persons of quality'. It was also a fact that many of these people thought it was vulgar to speak anything except 'ordinary English'; Hardy shows Henchard becoming furious with his daughter because of her 'occasional pretty and picturesque use of dialect words — those terrible marks of the beast to the truly genteel':

> The sharp reprimand was not lost upon her; and in time it came to pass that for 'fay' she said 'succeed'; that she no longer spoke of 'dumbledores' but of 'humble bees'; no longer said of young men and women that they 'walked together', but that they were 'engaged'; that she grew to talk of 'greggles' as 'wild hyacinths'; that when she had not slept she did not quaintly tell the servants next morning that she had been 'hag-rid', but that she had 'suffered from indigestion'.

(*Mayor of Casterbridge*, XX)

Hardy's own feelings about the substitution of correct, but colourless English phrases for the 'pretty and picturesque' dialect words come over very clearly. Although he could only use them sparingly in his novels, he wrote:

> It must, of course, always be a matter for regret that, in order to be understood, writers should be obliged thus slightingly to treat varieties of English which are intrinsically as genuine, grammatical, and worthy of the royal title [the King's English] as is the all-prevailing competitor which bears it; whose only fault was that they happened not to be central, and therefore were worsted in the struggle for existence, when a uniform tongue became a necessity among the advanced classes of the population.

(*PW*, 92–3)

51

What he was protesting against was the assumption that the dialect of one particular region (London and the south-east) was somehow superior to the dialects of all the other regions, and that people must all speak with identical accents and use identical forms of speech if they wished to be 'truly genteel'. Indeed his whole work can be seen as a vindication of the dignity, the essential value of the culture and the people of his own region. After reading Matthew Arnold, he wrote:

> Arnold is wrong about provincialism, if he means anything more than a provincialism of style and manner in exposition. A certain provincialism of feeling is invaluable. It is of the essence of individuality, and is largely made up of that crude enthusiasm without which no great thoughts are thought, no great deeds done.
>
> (*Life*, 146–7)

It was at that time, and still is, customary to run Hardy down because he was a 'provincial' writer. But so were the Brontës and George Eliot and D.H. Lawrence; indeed *Middlemarch*, which is often called the greatest of English novels, is subtitled 'A Study of Provincial Life'. Hardy's attempts to write about the smart London scene which he discovered in later life were almost invariably flat and boring. His best novels were written not only *about* but actually *in* Dorset; he found that he could not work well when he was living anywhere else. And although we may sometimes find a difficult word or phrase in the Wessex novels, Hardy almost certainly solved the problem of making a dialect readable in the only possible way. Emily Brontë and George Eliot did what Barnes had done and copied dialect straight on to the page, and as a result these parts of their novels are difficult to read. Hardy was more flexible, and he made the Dorset-shire dialect immortal, but it is a matter of regret that we have no recording of his voice (as far as is known) or even of authentic readings of the period dialect to which we may turn for verifications of our studies.

Social conditions in Dorset

Six years before Hardy was born, a group of labourers in the little village of Tolpuddle, a few miles away across Puddletown Heath, banded together to form a trade union branch. They were George Loveless and his brother James, Thomas and John Standfield, James Hammet and James Brine. Five of them were Methodists, a fact which automatically made them suspicious characters to parsons and squires. Strictly speaking, trade unions were not illegal, but Lord Melbourne's government meant to stamp them out by any means it could. The men were found guilty of taking an illegal oath (they had sworn to keep faith with each other) and transported to Australia. They became known to history as the six Tolpuddle Martyrs. There was a good deal of agitation after the sentence, but it took four years to get all the men back from Australia, and by this time many of them were so disgusted with conditions in England that they emigrated to Canada and never came back (The only one who stayed behind, James Hammett, died in the workhouse and is buried in Tolpuddle churchyard). Hardy must have known this story well. He grew up where it happened, and it was not to be forgotten in his lifetime or after that.

It is pleasant to know that there are six cottages in Tolpuddle today, each named after one of the Martyrs, for the use of agricultural labourers when they retire. But at the time the incident did a great deal of harm, and not only to the six men themselves. It killed agricultural trade unionism for the best part of forty years, and during this time the labourers went on suffering, as they had done for as long as anybody could remember. Dorset was one of the very poorest counties in England, and in the absence of railways or big towns it was practically impossible to get away from the land. Years later, in 1902, Hardy wrote to the novelist Rider Haggard:

> As to your first question, my opinion on the past of the agricultural labourers in this county: I think, indeed know, that down to 1850 or 1855 their condition was in general one of great hardship.... As a child I knew a sheep-keeping boy who to my horror shortly afterwards died of want — the contents of his stomach at the autopsy being raw turnip only.
>
> (*Life*, 312)

A popular song, 'The Fine Old English Labourer', tells us a little about how these people used to live, and why some of them died:

> He used to take whatever wage the farmer chose to pay,
> And work as hard as any horse for eighteenpence a day;
> Or if he grumbled at the nine, and dared to ask for ten,
> The angry farmer cursed and swore, and sacked him there and
>   then.

> He used to tramp off to his work while town folk were a-bed,
> With nothing in his belly but a slice or two of bread;
> He dined upon potatoes, and he never dreamed of meat,
> Except a lump of bacon fat sometimes by way of treat.

> He used to find it hard enough to give his children food,
> But sent them to the village school as often as he could;
> But though he knew that school was good, they must have bread
>   and clothes,
> So he had to send them to the fields to scare away the crows.

When Hardy was a boy, women and children still worked on the land, diseases like cholera still lingered, and the old and sick usually ended up in Dorchester workhouse. This is the place described in *Far from the Madding Crowd*, where Fanny Robin dies with her baby. It was 'a picturesque building':

> The view from the front, over the Casterbridge chimneys, was one of the most magnificent in the country. A neighbouring earl once said that he would give up a year's rental to have at his own door the view enjoyed by the inmates from theirs – and very probably the inmates would have given up the view for his year's rental.
>
> (*Far from the Madding Crowd*, XL)

Many of Hardy's greatest novels reflect the social realities of Dorset in the nineteenth century. In *Far from the Madding Crowd* and *The Mayor of Casterbridge* he shows us the old fashioned hiring fairs, held every year, where labourers stood up to be picked over by farmers. In *Jude* he shows child labour; in The *Woodlanders* and *Tess* the system whereby, after living in the same house for three generations, a family could be turned out of doors. (This only applied to the better-off villagers; most labourers could be turned out anyway, whenever the farmer wished). But in his later novels, which have a more modern setting than the early ones, we can see how the system was changing. *Tess* and *Jude* show exactly how horrible work on the land could be, but the characters are free to leave the land if they wish. There is a great difference between them and an earlier generation of people who remained in their villages for the whole of their lives.

During the 1840s two things happened which were profoundly to alter life in Dorset. One was the extension of the railway to Dorchester; the other was the abolition of the Corn Laws. The coming of railways made labourers much more mobile; able to look for work where they liked if they could not find it at home. The repeal of the Corn Laws by Sir Robert Peel's government (Peel is the 'Corn Law convert' whom Hardy mentions in Book 2 of *Jude*) meant that the country could import cheap grain from abroad when the home crop failed. This was necessary because people in England and Ireland were starving, but the farmers claimed that it would ruin them, and in a sense they were right. Although the full effects were not felt for another quarter of a century, it meant that the British corn trade lost most of its old importance. There were two 'great depressions', in the periods 1875–84 and 1891–99, when the harvest failed and the country had to buy vast quantities of Russian and American corn. The farmers lost heavily, and those who had not already done so began to change over from arable to pasture farming. It was very profitable for them to do so. They only needed about half as many labourers, and there was a growing demand for more animal food. People were beginning to eat bacon and eggs for breakfast instead of bread and potatoes, and the living standards of those labourers who stayed on the land went up.

Agriculture in traditional manner.

By this time there had been several other changes. Education was making the labourers dissatisfied with their conditions; the growth of industry was offering them better-paid jobs; and a new Agricultural Labourers' Union was founded in 1872. Its leader, Joseph Arch, was worried at first about its chances:

> I remembered the Labourers' Union in Dorsetshire, started in the thirties—what had become of that? Poor Hammett had had to pay a heavy price for standing up with his fellow-labourers against the oppression.... For daring to be Unionists they had been sent to the hulks in Australia.... What if the Union we meant to start in this corner of Warwickshire tonight should fall to bits like a badly made box?
>
> (*Life of Joseph Arch, IV*)

But it was no longer possible to treat agricultural labourers as the Martyrs had been treated, and although the Union broke up after only twelve years it did what it was intended to do. In many places (including parts of Dorset) it pushed up wages, and where this could not be done it helped the labourers to move to the towns or abroad. Once started, this process was irresistible. Thousands of labourers left the villages for ever, and those who did not give up work on the land altogether tended to move about from place to place, changing jobs every year. This happened often in Dorset, and Hardy shows something of its effect on ordinary people in *Tess of the d'Urbervilles*.

What were Hardy's feelings about these great changes in the countryside? He respected Arch, whom he once heard addressing a crowd of labourers, and he felt that the labourers had been 'greatly wronged' in the days when the farmers had it all their own way. He was delighted that their standards of living had gone up so much during his lifetime:

> But changes at which we must all rejoice have brought other changes which are not so attractive. The labourers have become more and more migratory—the younger families in especial, who enjoy nothing so much as fresh scenery and new acquaintance. The consequences are curious and unexpected. For one thing, village tradition—a vast mass of unwritten folklore, local chronicle, local topography, and nomenclature—is absolutely sinking, has nearly sunk, into eternal oblivion. I cannot recall a single instance of a labourer who still lives on the farm where he was born, and I can only recall a few who have been five years on their present farms. Thus you see, there being no continuity of environment in their lives, there is no continuity of information, the names, stories, and relics of one place being speedily forgotten under the incoming

Agricultural machinery: steam-threshing machine of 1868.

facts of the next. For example, if you ask one of the workfolk (they always used to be called 'workfolk' hereabout – 'labourers' is an imported word) the names of surrounding hills; streams; the character and circumstances of people buried in particular graves; at what spots parish personages lie interred; questions on local fairies, ghosts, herbs, etc., they can give no answer; yet I can recollect the time when the places of burial even of the poor and tombless were all remembered, and the history of the parish and squire's family for 150 years back known. Such and such ballads appertained to such and such a locality, ghost tales were attached to particular sites, and nooks wherein wild herbs grew for the cure of divers maladies were pointed out readily.

(*Life*, 312–13)

Still, he realized that these quaint and charming traditions probably had to go if the labourers were ever to be freed from their shackles. It is only the old story that progress and picturesqueness do not harmonise. They are losing their individuality, but they are widening the range of their ideas, and gaining in freedom. It is too much to expect them to remain stagnant and old-fashioned for the pleasure of romantic spectators.

(*PW*, 181)

What he did regret bitterly, and felt to be quite unnecessary, was the destruction of the class to which he and his parents had belonged. Almost every village had at one time had its own elite, consisting of skilled craftsmen, shopkeepers, and a few other people who were not directly employed on the land. They had provided most of the local leadership of Arch's Union, and they were the people who kept the village traditions (such as church choirs) alive. But towards the end of the century they were gradually squeezed out by the farmers and landowners who disliked their independence (Hardy describes the kind of thing which happened in chapter LI of *Tess*). They usually held cottages on a long lease, and when these leases ended, they generally had to leave their homes, like the Durbeyfields, or Giles. In the end there was nobody left in the villages except farmers and labourers, and village life became much poorer as a result.

Hardy summed up, rather sadly, that the modern labourer had 'a less intimate and kindly relationship with the land' than had been the case in earlier times. In many novels he shows people who do have this kind of relationship with the land: Gabriel Oak, Marty. Giles Winterborne, Tess. But his later novels reveal these people in a tragic light; Marty, Giles and Tess are all destroyed or defeated, and the hero of his last novel, *Jude the Obscure*, knows nothing about the dead traditions of his village and dislikes the very thought of working on the land.

Conclusion

When he was in London, as a young man and later after he had
become a successful novelist and was invited to fashionable parties,
Hardy always felt a sense of constraint. As soon as he could afford it he
had a house built at Max Gate, near Dorchester, and settled down
there, and in his later years he became more and more reluctant to go
far from home. He knew Dorset intimately—the countryside, the
churches and the local traditions; he spent long hours bicycling along
country lanes and through obscure villages, and he found that he did
his best work when he was at home. In this sense he undoubtedly was
what is called a provincial novelist, and this comes over very strongly
in passages like his description of 'the beautiful vale of Blakemore or
Blackmoor':

> This fertile and sheltered tract of country, in which the fields are
> never brown and the springs never dry, is bounded on the south by
> the bold chalk ridge that embraces the prominences of Hambledon
> Hill, Bulbarrow, Nettlecombe-Tout, Dogbury, High Stoy, and
> Bubb Down. The traveller from the coast...is surprised and de-
> lighted to behold, extended like a map beneath him, a country
> differing absolutely from that which he has passed through....
> Here, in the valley, the world seems to be constructed upon a
> smaller and more delicate scale; the fields are mere paddocks, so
> reduced that from this height their hedgerows appear a network of
> dark green threads over-spreading the paler green of the grass. The
> atmosphere beneath is languorous, and is so tinged with azure that
> what artists call the middle distance partakes also of that hue,
> while the horizon beyond is of the deepest ultramarine. Arable
> lands are few and limited; with but slight exceptions the prospect is
> a broad rich mass of grass and trees.
>
> (*Tess*, II)

Again, if we look at his autobiography we find the same feeling for
nature in the Dorset region:

> So Hardy went on writing *Far from the Madding Crowd*—some-
> times indoors, sometimes out, when he would occasionally find
> himself without a scrap of paper at the very moment that he felt
> volumes. In such circumstances he would use large dead leaves,
> white chips left by the wood-cutters, or pieces of stone or slate that
> came to hand. He used to say that when he carried a pocket-book
> his mind was barren as the Sahara.
>
> This autumn Hardy assisted at his father's cider-making – a
> proceeding he had always enjoyed from childhood – the apples
> being from huge old trees that have now long perished. It was the

last time he ever took part in a work whose sweet smells and oozings in the crisp autumn air can never be forgotten by those who have had a hand in it.

(Life, 96)

Or again, in a passage from his diary for 1884, just before he started writing The Mayor of Casterbridge:

> When trees and underwood are cut down, and the ground bared, three crops of flowers follow. First a sheet of yellow; they are primroses. Then a sheet of blue; they are wild hyacinths, or as we call them, graegles. Then a sheet of red; they are ragged robins, or as they are called here, robin-hoods. What have these plants been doing through the scores of years before the trees were felled, and how did they come there?

(Life, 164)

Such concern for man and that environment in which he lives, the physical, spiritual and moral ecology which Hardy continuously examines is one of the reasons that lie behind his continuing popularity after a further century of change.

3 Hardy the Victorian

Hardy the Victorian

We call Hardy a Victorian because he spent the first sixty years of his life in the nineteenth century and it was that century which formed many of his beliefs and ideas. But he was not a *typical* Victorian; to many of us he now seems to exemplify the more modern, adventurous, questioning spirit which came into literature about the turn of the century and led on directly to the work of D.H. Lawrence. Many of the most cherished Victorian beliefs (in Providence, for example) were just those which Hardy found that he could not accept. Another way in which he seems untypical is in his preoccupation with the life of the countryside, which we looked at in the last chapter. He was interested in the railways which came to the countryside, and the ideas brought by the railways, but he did not, like many contemporary novelists, write about industrialisation or life in big towns. The consciousness of most educated Victorians, writers or not, was decidedly *urban*; Hardy was very different from them in this way.

But in other ways he could not help being influenced by the contemporary intellectual climate. This chapter will look briefly at his relationship with various thinkers and currents of thought in his time. The first section tries to show how Hardy fitted into the Victorian literary tradition, and suggests that other novelists did not influence him, except in a negative way. Other poets did, and this section will look at the admiration for Romanticism which he shared with his age, and at the influence of the great Victorian rebel, Swinburne.

The second section is about Hardy's agnosticism, and here he did belong to a very definite tradition. Few ages have been more conscious of religion than the Victorian, and Hardy himself (like most other agnostics) had been brought up in a strongly Christian home. One result of this was a strong and naïve belief in what was called Providence, which led to a popular demand that art should be 'uplifting', and illustrate the principles of poetic justice. This accounts for the unnaturally happy endings which are foisted on to so many Victorian novels, and which Hardy, in the end, very much disliked. His pessimism, as the Victorians called it, and his interest in Darwin's discoveries had a powerful effect on his work.

Perhaps the most distinguished agnostic thinker of the century was John Stuart Mill, who also influenced Hardy in other ways. His teaching on freedom was particularly important, and can be traced in Hardy's last novel, *Jude the Obscure*.

Hardy emerges from any study of his ideas as a man of the Left, extremely suspicious of all conventional ideas about politics and religion. But he was a lonely figure all his life and joined no political movement. He took no part in the great debate about the nature of Victorian society and its destiny associated with the names of Carlyle, Ruskin, Morris, Pugin, Kingsley and Disraeli. This had something to do with his comparative isolation from the big towns where most Victorians lived, and also with his own diffidence. He often said that any opinions which he might seem to express in his novels and poems were offered as impressions rather than convictions. Nevertheless, he did have views about society, and particularly strongly about war, and it seemed worth putting a short note at the end of this chapter to describe them.

Hardy, the Romantics and Swinburne

If Hardy's style has often been criticized, it is partly because he himself was often very unsure of what was the 'best' technique. At times, remembering the sophisticated public which was only too ready to sneer at him, he became very self-conscious and tried to smarten up his writing—usually by sprinkling it with fragments of poetry and long Latin words. We hear of his reading Defoe, Fielding, Addison, Scott and *The Times* editorials in an effort to improve his own style. Of course this did him no good. When Hardy was writing at his best the style came naturally, and there was no need for him to look over his shoulder at anyone else.

It is hard to say whether he was much influenced by other novelists. He admired Fielding, who had lived in the same part of England, and thought that he was not appreciated enough 'as a local novelist'. Dickens was still alive when he first went to London, and the young man often went to hear him reading from his own novels, but in general they wrote about very different subjects and in still more different ways. At this time, Thackeray was generally thought to be the best living novelist, and in 1863 Hardy wrote home to his sister:

> He is considered to be the greatest novelist of the day—looking at novel-writing of the highest kind as a perfect and truthful representation of actual life—which is no doubt the proper view to take. Hence, because his novels stand so high as works of Art or Truth, they often have anything but an elevating tendency, and on that account are particularly unfitted for young people—from their very truthfulness. People say that it is beyond Mr Thackeray to paint a perfect man or woman—a great fault if novels are intended to instruct, but just the opposite if they are to be considered merely as Pictures.

(*Life*, 40)

It is clear from this that Hardy at twenty-three was already aware of the tension between writing with one eye on the public which largely consisted of 'young people' and writing what he felt to be true. But Thackeray died in the year this was written, and by this time a new novelist was appearing on the horizon—George Eliot. Hardy had, as we have seen, the strange experience of being mistaken for her when *Far from the Madding Crowd* was first published in the *Cornhill Magazine*. Like him, she wrote mainly about the countryside, and her ideas on many subjects were not very different from his. He thought that she was a 'great thinker—one of the greatest living', but 'not a born storyteller by any means', and that her novels were not representative of real country life.

The other great novelist of the late nineteenth century was Henry James, but although he and Hardy met several times they were really incompatible. James wrote that *Tess of the d'Urbervilles* was 'vile', while Hardy accused him of 'saying nothing in infinite sentences'. Later he wrote: 'The great novels of the future will certainly not concern themselves with the minutiae of manners. . . . James's subjects are those one could be interested in at moments when there is nothing larger to think of' (*Life*, 211). It emerged in time that readers of fiction polarized similarly so that James's admirers have been prominent in denigrating Hardy and his work.

But during his growing period in London he was reading hardly any novels, and a great deal of poetry. We know that in later life he said that he had always wanted to be a poet, and had only written the novels for money, and, while we need not take this too seriously, it is true that he was influenced by poets much more than by novelists. He had a thorough knowledge of Milton and Shakespeare, yet his real roots were in the English Romantic tradition, the tradition which, in one way or another, helped to form almost all English poets until it was killed by the First World War. It began about the time of the French Revolution, when a group of young poets, of whom Wordsworth was the spokesman, became tired of the artificial and conventional nature of eighteenth-century verse. With the rise of this group strong emotions came back into poetry; new ideas and original verse forms were tried out freely, and a new conception of the poet came into circulation. Instead of stringing platitudes together (like Pope and Johnson) he must 'look in his heart and write'. Naturally, the Romantics were very different from one another. The whole essence of the Romantic outlook was that each writer should develop his individuality to the full. One other point may be noted: that Romanticism was above all a *democratic* movement. It stressed that literature belonged not just to the civilized few but to the whole people; and the Romantic poets, at least while they were young, were very sympathetic to the French Revolution and to progressive ideas.

Wordsworth had insisted in his Preface to *Lyrical Ballads* that poetry must be written in 'the real language of men'. Hardy must have felt very much the same, as he incorporated a good deal of ordinary language, including dialect, in his poems and novels. Perhaps he had more in common with Wordsworth than with any other Romantic writer. He is not a rich and colourful poet like Keats; his language is more often careful, restrained, deliberately sober and plain. And, again like Wordsworth, he is deeply interested in man's relationship to his natural environment—in his case Dorset, in Wordsworth's the Cumberland hills. Like Wordsworth, he writes about men and women who live in constant communion with nature, shepherds, for example, or tramps, or rural workers, and he feels that nature provides these people with a permanent source of strength.

As a boy Hardy wrote at least one quite good imitation of Wordsworth (a poem about his father's cottage which is studied in chapter 6) At twenty-eight, when he had come back from London and was writing *The Poor Man and the Lady*, he noted in his diary:

Cures for despair:
To read Wordsworth's 'Resolution and Independence'
 „   „   Stuart Mill's 'Individuality' (in *Liberty*)

(Life, 58)

We must look more closely at Wordsworth's 'Resolution and Independence' to see what he meant. This poem, also known as 'The Old Leech-Gatherer', begins with Wordsworth walking out on to the moors on a beautiful spring day. At first he is happy and cheerful, but then, without warning, he becomes very depressed:

> I heard the skylark warbling in the sky;
> And I bethought me of the playful hare:
> Even such a happy child of earth am I;
> Even as these blissful creatures do I fare;
> Far from the world I walk, and from all care;
> But there may come another day to me—
> Solitude, pain of heart, distress and poverty.

While he is still in this mood he comes across an old man, who makes his living by gathering leeches from the pools on the moor. He is one of those odd characters, like the reddleman in *The Return of the Native*, whose mode of life is so strange and old-fashioned that they seem to belong to another world. But the old man is not held up to us as a curiosity. He is courteous and dignified, and seems perfectly cheerful although the leeches which provide his income are gradually disappearing:

> Once I could meet with them on every side;
> But they have dwindled long by slow decay;
> Yet still I persevere, and find them where I may.

After leaving him the poet finds that he is haunted by the thought of the old man. It makes his own troubles appear very petty:

> I could have laughed myself to scorn, to find
> In that decrepit man so firm a mind.
> 'God,', said I, 'be my help and stay secure;
> I'll think of the leech-gatherer on the lonely moor.'

There is something here of the courage of ordinary people which Hardy shows us in books like *The Woodlanders* and *Tess*. It may also have helped to suggest his well-known description of Egdon Heath: 'a place perfectly accordant with man's nature—neither ghastly, hateful, nor ugly: neither commonplace, unmeaning, nor tame; but, like man, slighted and enduring' (*Return of the Native*, 1).

In the same novel Hardy spoke of 'the view of life as a thing to be put up with, replacing that zest for existence which was so intense in early civilization' (III, i), and here he seems to be thinking along the same lines as Wordsworth in this poem. The instinctive, joyful response to the world which we find in children is not enough, because pain and death are realities which cannot be overlooked. But what is heroic in man is his ability to put up with 'solitude, pain of heart, distress and poverty' and still carry on. This is an essential part of Hardy's philosophy, which the Victorians called pessimism, and which he himself thought was the only realistic and possible creed. That was why Wordsworth's poetry seemed to him so good as a 'cure for despair'.

Surprisingly it seems that Hardy's favourite Romantic poets were Keats and, above all, Shelley. He called him 'our most marvellous lyrist', and was always deeply moved when he 'impinged on the penumbra of the poet he loved'. While in Italy he wrote a poem, speculating about what had happened to 'the dust of the lark that Shelley heard'. Indeed Shelley's 'To a Skylark', and Keats's 'Ode to a Nightingale', were to inspire one of his own most famous poems, 'The Darkling Thrush'. He felt a strong sympathy for both of them as people: Shelley because he had been persecuted for unorthodox ideas, and Keats because he had been abused by the critics (like Hardy himself) and died in obscurity. One of his late poems, 'At Lulworth Cove a Century Back', comments on the way in which the genius of Keats was ignored until after his death.

Of course this does not mean that Hardy wrote the same kind of poetry as Keats or Shelley. This would hardly have been possible, nearly a hundred years later, and in any case his temperament was very different from theirs. But he did find himself in sympathy with many of Shelley's ideas—Shelley who had been sent down from Oxford for writing *The Necessity of Atheism* and whose poem 'Queen Mab' had caused a scandal because of its left-wing and antireligious ideas. Hardy's own attitude to religion was very much the same as

Shelley's. He believed in what he called 'the *spirit* of the Sermon on the Mount', but, except as a very young man, he didn't believe in a personal God. Another way in which he was very close to Shelley was in his shrinking from other people's pain. He was much the same kind of man as his hero, Jude Fawley:

> Though Farmer Troutham had just hurt him, he was a boy who could not himself bear to hurt anything. He had never brought home a nest of young birds without lying awake in misery half the night after, and often reinstating them and the nest in their original place the next morning. He could scarcely bear to see trees cut down or lopped, from a fancy that it hurt them; and late pruning, when the sap was up and the tree bled profusely, had been a positive grief to him in his infancy. This weakness of character, as it may be called, suggested that he was the sort of man who was born to ache a good deal before the fall of the curtain upon his unnecessary life should signify that all was well with him again. He carefully picked his way on tiptoe among the earthworms, without killing a single one.
>
> (*Jude*, I, ii)

Hardy continued throughout his life to be haunted by the suffering of the innocent, even when they were only earthworms. When he was over eighty he expressed the hope that 'whether the human and kindred animal races survive till the exhaustion or destruction of the globe...pain to all upon it, tongued or dumb, shall be kept down to a minimum by loving-kindness' (*PW*, 53). This has a great deal in common with the beliefs of Shelley, who was a vegetarian, a pacifist, and a believer that tyranny could be defeated by moral force. 'I wish no living thing to suffer pain', he makes the hero say, rejecting the idea of revenge, in 'Prometheus Unbound'. Both of them hated war, unnecessary suffering and any kind of cruelty. The Spirit of the Pities in *The Dynasts*, who looks on in horror as Europe plunges into war, is a very Shelleyan conception.

Another important influence on Hardy's work was Shelley's concept of love. Both writers had unorthodox ideas about marriage, and some of them are discussed at length in the fourth book of *Jude the Obscure* when Sue's husband, after an agonising private struggle, decides that she would be happier with her lover. He explains his decision to a friend, who is naturally surprised:

> 'I found from their manner that an extraordinary affinity, or sympathy, entered into their attachment, which somehow took away all flavour of grossness. Their supreme desire is to be together —to share each other's emotions, and fancies, and dreams.'
> 'Platonic!'
> 'Well, no. Shelleyan would be nearer to it. They remind me of —what are their names—Laon and Cythna.' (IV, iv)

Laon and Cythna are the two lovers in Shelley's long narrative poem 'The Revolt of Islam'. There is something ethereal about their love, too:

She moved upon this earth a shape of brightness,
A power, that from its objects scarcely drew
One impulse of her being—in her lightness
Most like some radiant cloud of morning dew
Which wanders thro' the waste air's pathless blue,
To nourish some far desert; she did seem
Beside me, gathering beauty as she grew,
Like the bright shade of some immortal dream
Which walks, when tempest sleeps, the wave of life's dark
    stream.

The theme of a relationship from which 'all flavour of grossness' has been removed is taken up again when Sue makes Jude 'say those pretty lines ... from Shelley's "Epipsychidion" as if they meant me.' The lines are:

There was a Being whom my spirit oft
Met in its visioned wanderings far aloft...
A seraph of heaven, too gentle to be human,
Veiling beneath that radiant form of woman.

Both Shelley and Hardy believed that love is an affinity of the mind and spirit, which is a great deal more important than sex. In Shelley the loved object is seen as something radiant, divine, scarcely human, and this is how Jude sees the woman he loves, Sue. It comes as a slight shock, after all this, to realise that 'Epipsychidion' is a poem about the impossibility of faithfulness, which suggests that 'to divide is not to take away' from the person one loves:

I never was attached to that great sect,
Whose doctrine is, that each one should select
Out of the crowd a mistress or a friend,
And all the rest, though fair and wise, commend
To cold oblivion, though it is in the code
Of modern morals, and the beaten road
Which those poor slaves with weary footsteps tread,
Who travel to their home among the dead
By the broad highway of the world, and so,
With one chained friend, perhaps a jealous foe,
The dreariest and the longest journey go.

Shelley's ideas on sexual relationships were unconventional. After he had left his wife for Mary Godwin he suggested that she should come and live with them as a friend, and in the same way Sue optimistically hopes that she can go on being friends with her husband after she has left him. It would be a mistake, though, to think that Hardy necessarily agreed with Shelley's theories. He did reject the Victorian concept of marriage, and in *Jude the Obscure* he examined several arguments about divorce and free love. But his final conclusion was that 'Shelleyan' characters like Angel Clare and Sue Bridehead did more harm than good. Shelley's theory of love left out too many things—the 'fret and fever, derision and disaster', the human need for deep emotional commitments and the earthly, as opposed to the heavenly, aspects of love.

Jude the Obscure often refers to Shelley, whom Hardy describes as 'the last of the optimists'. Shelley did, indeed, have an idealistic faith in goodness:

> It is a modest thought, and yet
> Pleasant if one considers it,
> To own that death itself must be
> Like all the rest, a mockery.
>
> That garden sweet, that lady fair,
> And all sweet shapes and odours there,
> In truth have never passed away:
> 'Tis we, 'tis ours, are changed; not they.
>
> For love, and beauty, and delight,
> There is no death nor change; their might
> Exceeds our organs, which endure
> No light, being themselves obscure.
>
> ('The Sensitive Plant')

It was much more difficult for Hardy to believe this at the end of the century, when, as we shall see, he acquired a reputation for being a 'pessimist'. It looks on balance as if, despite his reverence for Shelley, he finally came to see some of his ideas as naïve.

The Victorian reading public admired Keats and Shelley without really knowing much about them. Controversial facts about these two men, particularly the radicalism in their writings, were hushed up, and they gained the reputation of being sweet, sentimental poets who died young because they were too good for the world. The Victorians' favourite writer was Tennyson, the Poet Laureate, a master of smooth and conventional verse, while the much more interesting and original Robert Browning was largely unread (and the most interesting of them all, Gerard Manley Hopkins, remained virtually unknown until 1918). The genius of the age made fiction the central literary form: Romanticism, history, politics, sociology and even the vision of townscape and landscape painting are all involved in it. On the other hand, English poetry had grown dull and stagnant when Algernon Charles Swinburne published his first book in 1866.

Swinburne is today only half-remembered, and we can see now that he was far from a great poet, but his work had an electric effect at the time on young men who were looking for inspiration. Hardy described this effect, many years later, in his elegy for Swinburne, 'A Singer Asleep':

> It was as though as a garland of red roses
> Had fallen about the hood of some smug nun
> When irresponsibly dropped as from the sun,
> In fulth of numbers freaked with musical closes,
> Upon Victoria's formal middle time
> His leaves of rhythm and rhyme.

He went on to describe his own reactions when Swinburne's poems first came out:

> O that far morning of a summer day
> When, down a terraced street whose pavements lay
> Glassing the sunshine into my bent eyes,
> I walked and read with a quick glad surprise
> New words, in classic guise—
>
> The passionate pages of his earlier years,
> Fraught with hot sighs, sad laughters, kisses, tears;
> Fresh-fluted notes, yet from a minstrel who
> Blew them not naïvely, but as one who knew
> Full well why thus he blew   (*CP*, 304-5)

This gives us a good idea of the reasons for Swinburne's great appeal for Hardy's generation. He was not in the least a naïve writer; on the contrary he was one of the most 'musical' (Hardy's word) of all English poets. His verse is easy, fluent, and intoxicating. We can get some impression of its quality from the lines from the 'Hymn to Proserpine' which are quoted by Hardy in *Jude the Obscure*:

> Thou hast conquered, O pale Galilean; the world has grown
>   grey from thy breath;
> We have drunken of things Lethean, and fed on the fullness of
>   death;
> Laurel is green for a season, and love is sweet for a day;
> But love grows bitter with treason, and laurel outlives not May.
> Sleep, shall we sleep after all? for the world is not sweet in the
>   end;
> For the old faiths loosen and fall, the new years ruin and rend.
> Fate is a sea without shore, and the soul is a rock that abides;
> But her ears are vexed with the roar and her face with the foam
>   of the tides.

But Swinburne had more to offer to his readers than a beautiful style. Hardy, and his other admirers, felt that his great merit was to have brought passion back into English poetry—'hot sighs, sad laughters, kisses, tears'—at a time when it had become stodgy, respectable, and very embarrassed by sex. Swinburne never made any secret of his convictions. Like Shelley, he was a passionate republican and atheist; the poem just quoted makes it clear that he thought Christianity was life-denying. Instead he worshipped the idea of liberty, natural beauty, and passionate physical love. In a notorious poem, 'Dolores', he contrasted 'the lilies and languors of virtue' with 'the raptures and roses of vice', leaving no doubt as to which he preferred. His sex life was as unorthodox as his religious and political views.

It need hardly be said that the Victorians were deeply shocked by *Poems and Ballads* and although Swinburne became a hero to many of the younger generation his poetry was viciously abused in the press. Hardy recalled this time, in a letter to a friend, after Swinburne died:

> No doubt the press will say some good words about him now he is dead and does not care whether it says them or no. Well, I remember what it said in 1866, when he did care, though you do not remember it, and how it made the blood of some of us young men boil.
>
> Was there ever such a country—looking back at the life, work, and death of Swinburne—is there any other country in Europe whose attitude towards a deceased poet of his rank would have been so ignoring and almost contemptuous?...To use his own words again, 'it makes one sick in a corner'—or as we say down here in Wessex, 'it is enough to make every little dog run to mixen'.
>
> (*Life*, 344)

This came after Hardy himself had been savaged for writing *Jude* (a novel which Swinburne praised enthusiastically). 'We laughed and condoled with each other', he noted, 'on having been the two most abused of living writers; he for *Poems and Ballads*, and I for *Jude the Obscure*' (*Life*, 325).

Why did Hardy admire Swinburne so greatly? He himself was a very different kind of poet—less showy and more genuine, we may feel now—and his own work is quite free from the 'decadent' quality which made Swinburne's so exciting to the youth of his day. Part of his admiration had to do with the literary tradition in which he had been raised. The Victorians liked poetry to be 'musical' and to deal with beautiful and romantic subjects; Tennyson was a great master of this kind of poetry and so was Swinburne, in his own way. But perhaps even more of Hardy's enthusiasm was for Swinburne as a

bold and independent thinker. Like him, Swinburne was what we would now call a humanist, one who believed that man, not God, was the most important being in the universe. He asserted this, deliberately provocatively, in his 'Hymn of Man', which announced that God was dead:

> By the name that in hell-fire was written, and burned at the
>   point of thy sword,
> Thou art smitten, thou God, thou art smitten; thy death is upon
>   thee, O Lord.
> And the love-song of earth as thou diest resounds through the
>   wind of her wings—
> Glory to Man in the highest! for Man is the master of things.

With his atheism went the belief that there was no such thing as Providence, and that man is necessarily alone and must work out his own destiny:

> Save his own soul's light overhead,
> None leads him, and none ever led,
> Across birth's hidden harbour-bar,
> Past youth where shoreward shallows are,
> Through age that drives on towards the red
> Vast void of sunset hailed from far,
> To the equal waters of the dead;
> Save his own soul he hath no star,
> And sinks, except his own soul guide,
> Helmless in middle turn of tide.
>
> (Prelude to *Songs Before Sunrise*)

These were some of Hardy's favourite lines (he often quoted 'Save his own soul he hath no star', which is the motto for Book II of *Jude the Obscure*). As we shall see in the next section, he believed very strongly that the universe was, by its nature, indifferent to man and his feelings and hopes. Both writers tended to see man as a lonely and heroic figure, 'slighted and enduring'. They were both 'pessimists' in the sense of believing that man must solve his own problems, without any help from a superhuman force.

During his later years Swinburne wrote hardly anything of importance. The promise of his early work (he had started publishing poetry many years before Hardy) was never fulfilled. Today, although his collected works fill several volumes, he is remembered only on the strength of a few lyrics, but even in his decline he still had useful things to say about the nature and purpose of literature, for example when he discussed the doctrine (very fashionable at the turn of the century) of 'art for art's sake':

71

The well-known formula of art for art's sake...has like other doctrines a true side to it and an untrue. Taken as an affirmation, it is a precious and everlasting truth. No work of art has any worth or life in it that is not done on the absolute terms of art...On the other hand, we refuse to admit that art of the highest kind may not ally itself with moral or religious passion, with the ethics or the politics of a nation or an age...In a word, the doctrine of art for art's sake is true in the positive sense, false in the negative; sound as an affirmation, unsound as a prohibition.

(Quoted in Harold Nicolson, *Swinburne*, 183)

If he read this, Hardy must have agreed with every word. Towards the end of his career as a novelist he complained bitterly about the people who denied him the right to speak his mind about moral or political issues, and one of his reasons for turning to poetry was that this made it easier for him to express his ideas. It was natural that both he and Swinburne should find themselves unpopular in an age which hated and feared originality and tried to reduce its artists to mere entertainers. For this reason Hardy had a fellow-feeling for Swinburne more than for any other living writer, and he records rather touchingly in the *Life* that after he had written 'A Singer Asleep' he 'gathered a spray of ivy and laid it on the grave of that brother-poet of whom he never spoke save in words of admiration and affection' (*Life*, 349).

Hardy, the Agnostics and 'Pessimism'

In 1859 two books came out which were to have a profound effect on the young Hardy; John Stuart Mill's *On Liberty*, and *The Origin of Species* by Charles Darwin. Twenty-three years later, when he went to Darwin's funeral in Westminster Abbey, Hardy said that he had been 'among the earliest acclaimers' of his work. At that time, he was in the minority. Conventional people tended to make fun of *The Origin of Species*, an unpretentious book which turned out, in the end, to be as revolutionary as the theories of Copernicus and Galileo that the earth moved round the sun.

Darwin had observed during his researches in South America that certain animals showed slight but quite definite differences from the animals on islands only a few miles away. This struck him as so interesting that it suggested a whole new theory about the origins of life. Had they been created with these slight differences when God made the world, as was taught in the Book of Genesis? Or was it not more likely that they all belonged to the same species, and had evolved their own differences to suit their special conditions of life?

Darwin came to the conclusion that vast numbers of species had existed at one time, but several had died out; those which survived being the ones which were best adapted to their environment. This became known as the doctrine of the *survival of the fittest*.

Darwin's discoveries could be applied to human beings as well as to animals. He did not, as many people thought, say that man was descended from the monkeys, but he did think that men and monkeys were collateral descendants of one ancestor. It was a theory that shook Victorian Christianity to its foundations. For if life evolved under its own laws, if it was not true that Adam and Eve and the animals had been created just as they were in the Garden of Eden, then there was no need for God.

As a matter of fact scientists had suspected for some time that parts of the Bible were inaccurate. Geologists like Charles Lyell (1795–1875) had become convinced, from their study of fossils, that the earth was much older than the six-thousand-odd years which the theologians claimed. But this was not the sort of thing that could be said aloud in Victorian England, where a highly bigoted form of Christianity was taught in the churches and schools. Darwin literally could not face publishing his discoveries for years because he knew how unpopular this would make him. When his book finally did come out, and the storm broke, he took no further part in the controversy. Most of the propaganda work for his theories was done by T.H. Huxley.

A distinguished biologist in his own right, Huxley is mainly remembered as the champion of Darwin and as the man who invented the word 'agnostic'. An agnostic means 'one who does not know', and Huxley maintained that human beings *cannot* know whether or not God exists:

> It is wrong for a man to say that he is certain of the objective truth of any proposition unless he can produce evidence which logically justifies that certainty. This is what Agnosticism asserts; and, in my opinion, it is all that is essential to Agnosticism. That which Agnostics deny and repudiate, as immoral, is the contrary doctrine, that there are propositions which men ought to believe, without logically satisfactory evidence, and that reprobation ought to attach to the profession of disbelief in such inadequately supported propositions.

> (*Agnosticism and Christianity*)

This is presumably the kind of argument which Hardy was thinking of when he showed Tess discussing religion with Alec d'Urberville, using arguments which he does not repeat but which 'might possibly have been paralleled in … Huxley's *Essays*' (*Tess*, XLVI). She has picked them up from her husband, Angel Clare, who

is typical of the educated young men, from strongly Christian backgrounds, who were beginning to turn to agnosticism in the latter half of the century. Hardy met Huxley in London a few times and thought very highly of him, 'speaking of him as a man who united a fearless mind with the warmest of hearts and the most modest of manners (*Life*, 122).

While he was still very young Hardy became absorbed in the problem which worried almost all the educated Victorians, of whether the Christian faith which he had been brought up to believe in was true. For many people, it was agony to believe that it might be a myth. Tennyson's great poem 'In Memoriam' (1850), written about his beloved friend Arthur Hallam who died suddenly when he was only twenty-two, put into words what many thousands of others were thinking and feeling. How could God be all-powerful and all-loving, in face of the overwhelming fact of human suffering? Pain and death were more real to the Victorians than perhaps they are to us, at a time when tuberculosis was a killer disease and about half of all children never grew up. And when one turned from the human to the animal world, it seemed even more frightening. Tennyson wrote about the dilemma of one:

> Who trusted God was love indeed
> And love creation's final law—
> Tho' Nature, red in tooth and claw
> With ravine, shrieked against his creed.

This was written earlier than *The Origin of Species*, but Darwin's book did still more to weaken the idea that love was the final law of the universe. Tennyson himself resolved his doubts in the end, but other distinguished poets, like Matthew Arnold and A.H. Clough, could not; nor could many other intellectuals. Even some churchmen began to feel that Christianity would have to be brought up to date. In 1860 a group of them published a controversial book, *Essays and Reviews* (rather like *Honest to God* in our own time) which made a deep impression on the young Hardy when Horace Moule gave it to him to read. But it seems that at quite an early age he began to move away from the liberal Christianity which Moule believed in and towards an acceptance of Darwinism, and all its implications. One of his finest poems, 'In a Wood', begun in 1887, shows how he saw even trees as 'red in tooth and claw':

Icon of Victorian agnosticism. 'Resurgam' (I shall rise again) falls in the shadow.

Pale beech and pine so blue,
Set in one clay,
Bough to bough cannot you
Live out your day?
When the rains skim and skip,
Why mar sweet comradeship,
Blighting with poison-drip
Neighbourly spray?

Heart-halt and spirit-lame,
City-opprest,
Unto this wood I came
As to a nest;
Dreaming that sylvan peace
Offered the harrowed ease—
Nature a soft release
From men's unrest.

But, having entered in,
Great growths and small
Show them to men akin—
Combatants all!
Sycamore shoulders oak,
Bines the slim sapling yoke,
Ivy-spun halters choke
Elms stout and tall.

Touches from ash, O wych,
Sting you like scorn!
You, too, brave hollies, twitch
Sidelong from thorn.
Even the rank poplars bear
Lothly a rival's air,
Cankering in black despair
If overborne.

Since, then, no grace I find
Taught me of trees,
Turn I back to my kind,
Worthy as these.
There at least smiles abound,
There discourse trills around,
There, now and then, are found
Life-loyalties.

(*CP*, 56)

This is a fine satirical retort to the complacent Victorian assumption that nature represented peace and innocence—'every prospect pleases, and only man is vile'. On the contrary, Hardy is arguing, *all* life is pervaded by the struggle for existence, and it can only be made bearable by solidarity between human beings. He wrote this poem at about the same time as *The Woodlanders* and if we turn to the novel we find many similar images. There is a well-known passage, often quoted to show Hardy's morbid frame of mind, which describes what actually happens in woods, 'The leaf was deformed, the curve was crippled, the taper was interrupted; the lichen ate the vigour of the stalk, and the ivy slowly strangled to death the promising sapling' (VII). The trees in chapter XLII are 'wrestling for existence, their branches disfigured with wounds resulting from their mutual rubbings and blows'. The animal world shows the same pattern— 'owls that had been catching mice in the outhouses, rabbits that had been eating the winter-greens in the gardens, and stoats that had been sucking the blood of the rabbits' (IV). Even human beings, at their worst, are no less ruthless; we see in this novel how men and women struggle for the possession of houses, lands and people, and how some of them fail to survive. A philosophy called 'social Darwinism', which was quite fashionable at this time although it was never sanctioned by Darwin, taught that human society illustrated the scientific principle of 'the survival of the fittest'; in other words the weak and incompetent were unsuccessful in life while the strong and clever naturally got to the top. Hardy had something to say about this in *The Mayor of Casterbridge*, and in *Jude the Obscure* he rejected it completely. He argued here that the greatest of mankind are usually failures in the worldly sense, and that a successful man is usually 'as cold-blooded as a fish and as selfish as a pig'—in other words, something less than human.

This meant that there was no room for optimistic assertions like Browning's 'God's in his heaven: all's right with the world', which was a commonplace for many for Hardy's contemporaries. 'God's *not* in his heaven: all's *wrong* with the world', Angel Clare says in anguish in *Tess*. Hardy himself noted wryly that most philosophers 'cannot get away from a prepossession that the world must somehow have been made to be a comfortable place for man' (*Life*, 179). But increasingly, Hardy's generation was coming to feel that the world was frightening, planless, and dangerous. Matthew Arnold wrote in his poem 'Dover Beach':

> the world which seems
> To lie before us like a land of dreams,
> So various, so beautiful, so new,
> Hath really neither joy, nor life, nor light,
> Nor peace, nor certitude, nor help from pain;
> And we are here as on a darkling plain,
> Swept with confused alarms of struggle and flight,
> Where ignorant armies clash by night.

This famous and beautiful image seems very appropriate to the world which Hardy created in his poems and novels (so appropriate, in fact, that one of the best books on Hardy, by Harvey C. Webster, is actually called *On a Darkling Plain*). Man must create his own values, for, living in a universe of cruelty and chaos, he will find no guidance from anything outside himself.

A great many of the most thoughtful and intelligent Victorians turned to agnosticism, among them John Stuart Mill, Herbert Spencer and George Eliot. Like Hardy, this great novelist had been brought up to be a devout Christian, and even her agnosticism had a religious tinge. She expressed her feelings in a nutshell:

> She, stirred somewhat beyond her wont, and taking as her text the three words which have been used so often as the inspiring trumpet-calls of man—the words *God*, *Immortality*, *Duty*—pronounced, with terrible earnestness, how inconceivable was the *first*, how unbelievable the *second*, and yet how peremptory and absolute the *third*.
>
> (Quoted in G.S. Haight, *George Eliot*, 464)

The agnostics were well aware of the difficulties involved in keeping hold of the idea of duty while abandoning the idea of God. Then as now, many people believed that if religion lost its hold men would become completely immoral. Hardy dramatizes this issue in the argument between Alec and Tess:

> 'Why, you can have the religion of loving-kindness and purity at least, if you can't have—what do you call it—dogma.'
>
> 'O no! I'm a different sort of fellow from that! If there's nobody to say, "Do this, and it will be a good thing for you after you are dead; do that, and it will be a bad thing for you," I can't warm up. Hang it, I am not going to feel responsible for my deeds and passions if there's nobody to be responsible to; and if I were you, my dear, I wouldn't either!'
>
> She tried to argue, and tell him that he had mixed in his dull brain two matters, theology and morals, which in the primitive days of mankind had been quite distinct. But ... she could not get on.
>
> (*Tess*, XLVII)

Long before he wrote this, Hardy had accepted the basic agnostic principle that 'theology' and 'morals' were two different things. Few people could have been more concerned with 'morals' than he was, but by the time he was twenty-five he had lost most of his youthful beliefs. As we have seen, he had some idea of studying to be a clergyman, but he decided in the end 'that he could hardly take the step with honour while holding the views which on examination he found himself to hold' (*Life*, 50). At about the same time he was reading

Cardinal Newman, the leader of the Oxford Movement (which is described in *Jude*) and perhaps the most brilliant orthodox thinker of the nineteenth century. But he was not convinced:

> July 2 (1865). Worked at J.H. Newman's *Apologia*, which we have all been talking about lately. A great desire to be convinced by him. . . . Only—and here comes the fatal catastrophe—there is no first link to his excellent chain of reasoning, and down you come headlong. (*Life*, 48)

Later he said that Newman had 'a feminine nature, which first decides and then finds reasons for having decided' (*ibid*, 305). He himself would not indulge in wishful thinking. However much he might want to believe in Christianity (and poems like 'The Impercipient' and 'The Oxen' suggest that he did want to sometimes) he refused to let himself be persuaded against his judgement. He went on being an agnostic all his life.

So Newman was a weaker influence on the young man than Darwin, Mill and Swinburne. Another strong influence, although this came later, was that of Leslie Stephen, whom Hardy described as 'the man whose philosophy was to influence his own for many years, indeed, more than that of any other contemporary' (*Life*, 100). He wrote several essays on religion and morals, of which the most famous is 'An Agnostic's Apology':

> Overpowered, as every honest and serious thinker is at times overpowered, by the sight of pain, folly, and helplessness, by the jarring discords which run through the vast harmony of the universe, we are yet enabled to hear at times a whisper that all is well, to trust to it as coming from the most authentic source, and to know that only the temporary bars of sense prevent us from recognizing with certainty that the harmony beneath the discords is a reality and not a dream. This knowledge is embodied in the central dogma of theology. God is the name of the harmony; and God is knowable. Who would not be happy in accepting this belief, if he could accept it honestly? Who would not be glad if he could say with confidence: 'The evil is transitory, the good eternal: our doubts are due to limitations destined to be abolished, and the world is really an embodiment of love and wisdom, however dark it may appear to our faculties'. And yet, if the so-called knowledge be illusory, are we not bound by the most sacred obligations to recognize the facts? Our brief path is dark enough on any hypothesis. We cannot afford to turn aside after every *ignis fatuus* without asking whether it leads to sounder footing or to hopeless quagmires. Dreams may be pleasanter for the moment than realities; but happiness must be won by adapting our lives to the realities.

Hardy was in the central agnostic tradition when he denied that there was any such thing as Providence—a force which saw to it that everything in the world worked towards good. This was one of the Victorians' favourite beliefs. Wordsworth wrote about 'Nature's holy plan'; Browning 'never dreamed, though right were worsted, wrong would triumph'. To Hardy these bland assertions seemed intolerably smug. In his later novels, which became steadily more unconventional, he drove home the message again and again that there is no supernatural force which looks after the innocent:

It grew darker, the fire-light shining over the room. The two biggest of the younger children had gone out with their mother; the four smallest, their ages ranging from three-and-a-half years to eleven, all in black frocks, were gathered round the hearth babbling their own little subjects. Tess at length joined them, without lighting a candle.

'This is the last night that we shall sleep here, dears, in the house where we were born,' she said quickly. 'We ought to think of it, oughtn't we?'

They all became silent; with the impressibility of their age they were ready to burst into tears at the picture of finality she had conjured up, though all the day hitherto they had been rejoicing in the idea of a new place. Tess changed the subject.

'Sing to me, dears,' she said.

'What shall we sing?'

'Anything you know; I don't mind.'

There was a momentary pause; it was broken, first, by one little tentative note; then a second voice strengthened it, and a third and a fourth chimed in unison, with words they had learnt at the Sunday-school—

> Here we suffer grief and pain,
> Here we meet to part again;
> In Heaven we part no more;

The four sang on with the phlegmatic passivity of persons who had long ago settled the question, and there being no mistake about it, felt that further thought was not required. With features strained hard to enunciate the syllables they continued to regard the centre of the flickering fire, the notes of the youngest straying over into the pauses of the rest.

Tess turned from them, and went to the window again. Darkness had now fallen without, but she put her face to the pane as though to peer into the gloom. It was really to hide her tears. If she could only believe what the children were singing; if she were only sure, how different all would now be; how confidently she would leave them to Providence and their future kingdom! But, in default of that, it behoved her to do something; to be their Providence; for to Tess, as to some few millions of others, there was ghastly satire in the poet's lines.

(Tess, LI).

If Tess is to play Providence, and save the children from the workhouse, she will have to live with a man she hates. We may think now that it is greatly to Hardy's credit that he doesn't shrink from showing us how and why this girl is destroyed. But in his own time most people criticized his novels for their 'morbidity' and 'pessimism', and many readers today still have the impression that Hardy is a gloomy and depressing writer. It is worth looking at what he himself had to say:

> As to pessimism. My motto is, first correctly diagnose the complaint —in this case human ills—and ascertain the cause: then set about finding a remedy if one exists. The motto or practice of the optimists is: Blind the eyes to the real malady, and use empirical panaceas to suppress the symptoms.
>
> (Life, 383)

It saddened him that critics 'approached his work with an ignorant prejudice against his "pessimism" which they allowed to stand in the way of fair reading and fair judgement' (ibid, 402). He preferred to describe himself as a 'meliorist', that is, one who believes that the world can be made better, if people try. But he insisted, in a poem, 'In Tenebris', from which he often quoted, that 'if way to the Better there be, it exacts a full look at the Worst'. It was no good pretending that pain did not exist or did not matter:

> Pain has been, and pain is: no new sort of morals in Nature can remove pain from the past and make it pleasure for those who are its infallible estimators—the bearers thereof. And no injustice, however slight, can be atoned for by her future generosity, however ample, so long as we consider Nature to be, or to stand for, unlimited power.
>
> (Life, 315)

Because he rejected the idea of a God of love some people accused him of believing in the opposite, a malignant old gentleman who enjoyed tormenting the human race. Hardy always said that he believed in no such thing:

> In connection with this subject it may be here recalled, in answer to writers who now and later were fond of charging Hardy with postulating a malignant and fiendish God, that he never held any views of the sort, merely surmising an indifferent and unconscious force at the back of things 'that neither good nor evil knows'. His view is shown, in fact, to approximate to Spinoza's—and later

Einstein's—that neither Chance nor Purpose governs the universe, but Necessity.

(ibid, 337)

After the Great War, which destroyed a good many of his hopes for the future, he became more and more inclined to think that 'the never-ending push of the Universe was an unpurposive and irresponsible groping in the direction of the least resistance. Some of his ideas about what this force might be can be found in the poem "New Year's Eve". (*CP.* 260)

Mill and the idea of liberty

It is possible that John Stuart Mill had a deeper influence on Hardy than did any other Victorian thinker. Hardy saw him only once, in 1865, when he was making an open-air speech as the Liberal candidate for Westminster—a speech pitched well over the heads of the crowd. He called him 'one of the profoundest thinkers of the last century' when he described this occasion over forty years later, and he was particularly impressed by Mill's essay *On Liberty*, 'which we students of that date knew almost by heart'. It was two or three years afterwards that he noted that the chapter on Individuality in this essay, along with Wordsworth's 'Old Leech-Gatherer', was his best 'cure for despair'.

Mill had an extraordinary life. His father, James, together with Jeremy Bentham (1748–1832), was responsible for working out the philosophy of Utilitarianism, based on the idea that 'it is the greatest happiness of the greatest number that is the measure of right and wrong'. They believed that human beings were motivated only by the desires of obtaining pleasure and avoiding pain. Together they founded the *Westminster Review*, a radical philosophical magazine, for which George Eliot was later to be a leading writer. The younger Mill was brought up strictly according to his father's ideas.

In his *Autobiography* (1873) Mill has recorded how his education began at the age of three. 'I never was a boy; never played at cricket.' He was taught Latin, Greek, mathematics and logic, but not English poetry. The Utilitarians tended to feel that nothing was valuable if it was not useful (an attitude which Dickens savagely sent up in *Hard Times*). As a young man Mill had some sort of nervous breakdown, and strangely enough what cured him was reading the poetry of Wordsworth. He began to feel that Utilitarianism left out too much of human experience and would have to be reappraised. In his essay *Utilitarianism* (1861) he argued that, while it was true that all human beings sought happiness, there were many different kinds of happiness, including the delight in doing good for its own sake. It was not true, as Bentham had said, that people were motivated only by self-interest. Human beings might be conscientiously compelled to sacrifice themselves for the general happiness of the human race.

Mill was perhaps the most enlightened and far-seeing thinker of his generation. He campaigned for women's rights, and for the rights of colonial peoples. He was interested in and sympathetic to the new Socialist ideas. But probably the most important thing he wrote was *On Liberty*. It is one of the two greatest arguments for freedom of speech in the English language (the other is Milton's *Areopagitica*), and its thesis is that if freedom is denied to the individual, the whole of society will suffer as a result.

We know that Hardy had it 'almost by heart', particularly the third chapter on Individuality. He quotes from this chapter in *Jude the Obscure*, when Sue is trying to persuade her husband to let her leave him:

> Sue continued: 'She, or he, "who lets the world, or his own portion of it, choose his plan of life for him, has no need of any other faculty than the ape-like one of imitation". J.S. Mill's words, those are. I have been reading it up. Why can't you act upon them? I wish to, always.'
>
> 'What do I care about J.S. Mill!' moaned he. 'I only want to lead a quiet life!'

(Jude, IV, iii)

It is not a bad answer. But, starting from this point, Hardy shows how Phillotson eventually comes to realize that the kindest thing is to dissolve his marriage. There is a dreadful incompatibility between him and Sue which is intellectual as well as sexual: 'Her intellect sparkles like diamonds, while mine smoulders like brown paper.' Although he loves his wife and knows that society would support him in making her stay with him, he feels conscientiously forced to let her go. Hardy prefaces this part of the novel with a quotation from Milton: 'Whoso prefers either Matrimony or other Ordinance before the Good of Man and the plain Exigence of Charity, let him profess Papist, or Protestant, or what he will, he is no better than a Pharisee.'

It is clear that Hardy agreed with Mill and Milton that human happiness was more important than institutions. If a marriage makes either the husband or wife unhappy, then the marriage should go. It is true that Phillotson has to sacrifice himself to what Mill would have called the 'general good', but ultimately it would not make him happy, either, to go on exploiting another person. 'His mild serenity at the sense that he was doing his duty by a woman who was at his mercy almost overpowered his grief at relinquishing her.'

In fact, the whole of *Jude the Obscure* shows how deep the influence of *On Liberty* went. Mill's argument was that all human beings ought to have the fullest possible freedom of speech and action, so long as this did no harm to anyone else. A good many people would have argued at the time that it *did* do harm; that those who attacked religion, for example, or conventional morals would corrupt other people and might undermine the whole of civilization. The Victorians were very harsh with anyone who stepped out of line on these matters, and in some ways, Mill claimed, English society was actually tyrannical:

> Society . . . practises a social tyranny more formidable than many kinds of political oppression, since, though not usually upheld by such extreme penalties, it leaves fewer means of escape, penetrating much more deeply into the details of life, and enslaving the soul itself. Protection, therefore, against the tyranny of the magistrate is not enough: there needs protection also against the tendency of society to impose, by other means than civil penalties, its own ideas and practices as rules of conduct on those who dissent from them; to fetter the development, and, if possible, prevent the formation, of any individuality not in harmony with its ways, and compel all characters to fashion themselves upon the model of its own . . . In our times, from the highest class of society down to the lowest, everyone lives as under the eye of a hostile and dreaded censorship.

Jude the Obscure (which Hardy at first called *The Recalcitrants*) is all about this 'tyranny of the prevailing opinion and feeling'. The characters are all unconventional people who behave in unorthodox ways. Phillotson, as we have seen, agrees to his wife leaving him, and as a result gets persecuted and loses his job. Jude is a working-class boy with the wild dream of going to Oxford; Sue is an emancipated girl who laughs at religion and makes her own decisions on matters of sex. They are persecuted, too, when the neighbours find out that they are living together without being married. In the end, all three of them are defeated. Sue breaks down completely and forces herself to go back to Phillotson ('We must conform,' she tells herself), Phillotson pretends to conform although his views have not really changed, and Jude dies. 'Our ideas were fifty years too soon to be any good to us,' he says near the end, and Hardy definitely seems to have felt that, in the present state of things, people who dissented from the received opinions were bound to suffer. In the story of Clym Yeobright, in *The Return of the Native*, he showed the same thing.

What frightened Mill about the tyranny of society was that this was bound to produce distorted human beings.

> Its ideal of character is to be without any marked character; to maim by compression, like a Chinese lady's foot, every part of human nature which stands out prominently, and tends to make the person markedly dissimilar in outline to commonplace humanity.

This 'narrow theory of life' led to a 'pinched and hidebound type of human character':

> Many persons, no doubt, sincerely think that human beings thus cramped and dwarfed, are as their Maker designed them to be; just as many have thought that trees are a much finer thing when clipped into pollards, or cut out into figures of animals, than as nature made them.

In fact this kind of repression was harmful to everybody, and particularly to the small but precious group of exceptional people, 'the salt of the earth', who were responsible for all the improvements in the human condition:

> Genius can only breathe freely in an *atmosphere* of freedom. Persons of genius are ... *more* individual than any other people—less capable, consequently, of fitting themselves, without hurtful compression, into any of the small number of moulds which society provides in order to save its members the trouble of forming their own character.

Perhaps unconsciously, Hardy took over several of these images when he came to write *Jude the Obscure*. Modern marriage was described in the Preface as 'the forced adaptation of human instincts to rusty and irksome moulds that do not fit them'. The same image, of a *mould*, comes up again when Sue says:

> 'I have been thinking...that the social moulds civilization fits us into have no more relation to our actual shapes than the conventional shapes of the constellations have to the real star-patterns. I am called Mrs Richard Phillotson, living a calm wedded life with my counterpart of that name. But I am not really Mrs Richard Phillotson, but a woman tossed about, all alone.'

> *(Jude, IV i)*

And later:

> 'I have only been married a month or two,' she went on, still remaining bent upon the table, and sobbing into her hands. 'And it is said that what a woman shrinks from—in the early days of her marriage—she shakes down to with comfortable indifference in half-a-dozen years. But that is much like saying that the amputation of a limb is no affliction, since a person gets comfortably accustomed to the use of a wooden leg or arm in the course of time.'

> (IV, ii)

It's the same idea that we find in *On Liberty*, that if people are forced to live in ways which they do not want then their whole personalities will become distorted. Just as Sue has to suppress the real, vital part of herself when she is married to Phillotson, so Jude, too, has to give up the dream of becoming a student which means almost everything to him:

> 'It is a difficult question...for any young man...whether to follow uncritically the track he finds himself in, without considering his aptness for it, or to consider what his aptness or bent may be, and re-shape his course accordingly. I tried to do the latter, and I failed...If I had ended by becoming like one of these gentlemen in red and black that we saw dropping in here by now, everybody would have said: "See how wise that young man was, to follow the bent of his nature!" But having ended no better than I began they say: "See what a fool that fellow was in following a freak of his fancy!"'
>
> (VI, i)

Mill had written:

> The man, and still more the woman, who can be accused either of doing 'what nobody does', or of not doing 'what everybody does', is the subject of as much depreciatory remark as if he or she had committed some grave moral delinquency.

Because they try to live in the way that suits them best, Jude and Sue are avoided by other people for being 'peculiar'. Their attitude to marriage is particularly unconventional, for they both find it psychologically impossible to go through a legal ceremony. Jude says:

> 'The intention of the contract is good, and right for many, no doubt; but in our case it may defeat its own ends because we are the queer sort of people we are—folk in whom domestic ties of a forced kind snuff out cordiality and spontaneousness.'
>
> Sue still held that there was not much queer or exceptional in them: that all were so. 'Everybody is getting to feel as we do. We are a little before-hand, that is all.'
>
> (V, iv)

This echoes two ideas that we find in Mill. In the first place, he insisted that people had an absolute right to live as seemed best to them: 'If a person possesses any tolerable amount of common-sense or experience, his own mode of laying out his existence is the best, not because it is the best in itself, but because it is his own mode.' Thus, Jude thinks that marriage is suitable for most people but not for him and Sue because of their unusual temperaments: 'Customs are made for customary circumstances, and customary characters: and his circumstances or his character may be uncustomary.' However, Sue believes that she and Jude are ahead of their time, and that in fifty or a hundred years everyone will feel as they do. Sue at the beginning of the novel, and Jude at the end, are both shown as people with enlightened ideas. Marriage is described as a system of 'devilish domestic gins and springes to noose and hold back those who want to *progress*'. Jude, speaking of the failure of his ambitions, says: 'It takes two or three generations to do what I tried to do in one.' They are among the exceptional few whom Mill called 'the salt of the earth; without them, human life would become a stagnant pool'. Mill was very conscious of belonging to a tiny minority of progressive thinkers whose position was always under attack from the prejudiced majority. Hardy, although he was a good deal younger, seems to have felt exactly the same. This is why he showed the characters in *Jude*, or Clym Yeobright in *The Return of the Native*, as lonely and misunderstood by other people. And after *Jude* had been denounced as the most immoral book of its generation, he apparently felt more strongly than ever that society was persecuting him for his beliefs.

The influence of Mill's great essay is particularly obvious in *Jude*, but it went further. It helped to determine Hardy's whole attitude to the problem of Victorian 'censorship', which we looked at in Chapter 1, for this seemed to him a particularly blatant denial of his own freedom to think and write.

Hardy's politics

When Hardy's first novel, *The Poor Man and the Lady*, was turned down on account of its politics he professed to be surprised that 'he had written so aggressive and even dangerous a work almost without knowing it'. It certainly does seem to have been aggressive, to judge from his own account:

> The story was, in fact, a sweeping dramatic satire of the squirearchy and nobility, London society, the vulgarity of the middle class, modern Christianity, church restoration, and political and domestic morals in general, the author's views, in fact, being obviously those of a young man with a passion for reforming the world— those of many a young man before and after him; the tendency of the writing being socialistic, not to say revolutionary.
>
> (*Life*, 61)

It is only surprising that he was surprised when the publishers sent the book back. Yet throughout his life Hardy always was rather surprised, and rather hurt, when his books were attacked for being angry, immoral, or subversive. He always said that he was not trying to argue anything in his novels, but only to put down his impressions of life. And alongside his radicalism went a deep need to be approved of and accepted by other people. 'There was in him something timid as well as something fierce', as Charles Morgan noted in 1920, and it was this combination of gentleness with 'passionate boldness' as a thinker that made Hardy unique.

He used to maintain that he was 'quite outside politics', but other people took it for granted that he would be on the progressive side. He was sometimes asked to sign the nomination papers for Liberal candidates, which he declined to do. During the crisis of 1911, when the Liberal Government had its great showdown with the House of Lords, Lloyd George threatened to create hundreds of Liberal peers to swamp it; among the names on his list was that of Thomas Hardy. This threat (which finally broke the power of the Lords) never had to be put into practice, so we cannot know whether Hardy would have taken a peerage or not. Probably not; he had earlier written in a private letter:

> I have always thought that any writer who has expressed unpalatable or possibly subversive views on society, religious dogma, current morals, and any other features of the existing order of things, and who wishes to be free and to express more if they occur to him, must feel hampered by accepting honours from any government —which are different from academic honours offered for past attainments merely.
>
> (*Life*, 327)

He did, however, accept the Order of Merit in 1910, perhaps because his novel-writing days were over and he felt that he would no longer be compromising himself. But he thought that he had 'failed in the accustomed formalities' when he met the King. Indeed he always felt rather ill at ease when he was mixing in London high society, and he gave it up altogether after his first wife died. This was another of the many paradoxes in his life. He had 'married a lady', and after he became an established novelist he spent a few months every year in London, where he mixed on equal terms with statesmen and peers. Yet his diaries show that he was deeply out of sympathy with these people, however much he may have been flattered at being accepted into the 'best' society. 'These women!' he noted about some society beauties. 'If put into rough wrappers in a turnip-field, where would their beauty be?' (*Life*, 224). Other scribbled notes suggest that he was not as indifferent to politics as he liked people to think:

> The offhand decision of some commonplace mind high in office at a critical moment influences the course of events for a hundred years. Consider the evening at Lord Carnarvon's, and the intensely average conversation on politics held there by average men who two or three weeks later were members of the Cabinet. A row of shopkeepers in Oxford Street taken just as they came would conduct the affairs of the nation as ably as these.
>
> (*Life*, 172)

On another occasion he noted that

> the talk was entirely political—of when the next election would
> be—of the probable Prime Minister—of ins and outs—of Lord
> This and the Duke of That—everything except the people for
> whose existence alone these politicians exist. Their welfare is never
> once thought of.
>
> (*Life*, 238)

This feeling went very deep in Hardy, and kept him from having
much respect for either of what were then the two big parties (although he is said to have supported the Labour Party as an old man).
Though he never formulated any clear political principles he was
always, like Dickens, on the side of the people against the government.* His major novels are all about the ordinary people of Dorset,
the men and women who do a real job of work in the world, as
opposed to the Mrs Charmonds and Alec Stoke-d'Urbervilles. We
have laid a great deal of emphasis on the ways in which Hardy was
different from other people—an unconventional thinker very conscious of being in a minority in his own time. But in fact he was
always stressing the *representative* quality of his heroes and heroines.
Tess, in her sufferings, is like 'some few millions of others'; Jude is
faced with a question 'which thousands are weighing at the present
moment in these uprising times', and Sue Bridehead is a representative of the new kind of woman 'who was coming into notice in her
thousands every year—the woman of the feminist movement'. Hardy
identified himself with these struggling masses of people, and, in his
own way, tried to speak for them. One of his comments on his critics
in the Preface to *Tess* was that they 'could not endure to have said
what everybody nowadays thinks and feels'.

One subject on which he never hid his feelings was his hatred of
war, and this for many years before 1914. The growing nationalism
and xenophobia of these years deeply worried him, as we can see
from a note which he wrote for a German professor in 1909:

> We call our age an age of Freedom. Yet Freedom, under her
> incubus of armaments, territorial ambitions smugly disguised as
> patriotism, superstitions, conventions of every sort, is of such
> stunted proportions in this her so-called time, that the human race
> is likely to be extinct before Freedom arrives at maturity.
>
> (*Life*, 347)

During the Great War he was abused by the Jingoists for saying in
a poem that the German and English peoples had the same interests
at heart. Yet he did support the war, seeing it as a crusade against
Great Power aggression, though never in a bigoted way. He hoped

*Dickens once said: 'My faith in the people governing is, on the whole, infinitesimal;
my faith in the People governed, on the whole, illimitable.'

to see an international League of Peace set up to prevent future wars, in which context he wrote:

> Nothing effectual will be accomplished in the cause of *Peace* till the sentiment of *Patriotism* be freed from the narrow meaning attaching to it in the past (still upheld by Junkers and Jingoists) and be extended to the whole globe.

> *(Life, 375)*

The kind of patriotism which meant affection for one's own country or region, and a feeling for human solidarity, came instinctively to Hardy. The kind which meant invading or bullying other nations he as instinctively loathed. He was not a pacifist, but when the aged Russian writer Tolstoy published a sermon denouncing war and was attacked for it he responded at once in a letter to *The Times*:

> The sermon may show many of the extravagances of detail to which the world has grown accustomed in Count Tolstoy's later writings. It may exhibit, here and there, incoherence as a moral system.... But surely all these objectors should be hushed by his great argument, and every defect in his particular reasonings hidden by the blaze of glory that shines from his masterly general indictment of war as a modern principle, with all its senseless and illogical crimes.

> *(Life, 322)*

Hardy did not, as Tolstoy did, work out a clear political philosophy for himself. But he did question almost all the common assumptions of his century, and he found himself in a very lonely and exposed position as a result. One of the great forces which shaped his art was his compelling need to seek out the truth, however uncomfortable or painful; the other was his passionate hatred of suffering. 'What are my books,' he said, 'but one long plea against "man's inhumanity to man"—to woman—and to the lower animals? Whatever may be the inherent good or evil of life, it is certain that men make it much worse than it need be.' (Quoted in F.B. Pinion, *A Hardy Companion*, 178). The cruelty of man and society; the immeasurable value of each human being and the tragic waste of human potentiality; these are the great themes of Hardy's writings, and in this sense it is true to say that he is a novelist of protest.

Hardy's influence on twentieth century literature

With Hardy's work still a potent force in modern writing it is too early to assess his influence. One on whom he certainly exerted a deep influence was D.H. Lawrence who during the First World War wrote a long essay, 'A Study of Thomas Hardy' which tells us less about its ostensible subject than it does about Lawrence himself. Like his predecessor he had come from a quite ordinary family and begun his career by writing about a class and a region (in his case, Nottinghamshire and its miners) which had scarcely been mentioned in literature before. He was interested too in exploring man's relation to the natural world, writing at length about the significance of Egdon Heath, and to modern society. He also recognized Hardy as one of the first English novelists to treat the relationship between the sexes with the seriousness it deserved. Lawrence's public was only a few degrees more emancipated than that which had abused Hardy; his work too was widely misunderstood and his novels went as far as being both censored and entirely banned. He must therefore have had personal reasons for sympathising with what Hardy wrote in 'Candour in English Fiction'. It is fascinating, further, to see how he virtually rewrote the plot of *Jude* in Lawrentian terms and how it ended up as something completely different. As Ian Gregor has written in *The Great Web*: 'where *Jude* ends, *The Rainbow* begins.'

Hardy may be felt as an influence too behind a great but little-known writer (who had strong affinities with Lawrence) Lewis Grassic Gibbon. In his trilogy, *A Scots Quair*, Gibbon was concerned with the life of a remote and old-fashioned community, untypical in even its language and with the relationship of its life to the land and its eventual destruction under the impact of vast social changes. The muted radicalism we find in Hardy becomes more pronounced and aggressive in Gibbon. He, however, had no successor. There have been English novelists of social protest (Walter Greenwood springs to mind) but they are hardly great writers. Nor are the rural novelists such as Mary Webb of Shropshire or A.G. Street of Wiltshire. On the other hand, the mainstream English novel since Lawrence has usually left out the social dimension and the novel today is a very different literary form from anything Hardy knew or himself created.

Even so, the influence of Hardy is still present in several ways. For example, in one of the most remarkable of modern English novels, *The French Lieutenant's Woman* by John Fowles which is set in Victorian times in Lyme Regis. The influence has been felt in U.S.A. and in Japan, the first entirely alien country to appreciate Hardy's work. In Australia, finally, there is the distinguished output of Patrick White. Because of his concern with the country in such a book as *The Tree of Man* one is barely aware that the village life is other than an English one. It is of a universal nature but has affinities with the Wessex novels that it may be read as part of the progeny of Hardy.

There is no final account of the influence of Hardy's poetry upon our own century either. During his lifetime there were more striking images and ideas to be found in the new writings of T.S. Eliot, Ezra Pound and W.B. Yeats but it is today admitted that Hardy must share a position of virtual equality with these by virtue of his preference for a conversationally low key and a carefully controlled stanzaic pattern as against blank verse and free verse which he particularly rejected. In Hardy, as we have seen, there is a recreation of the English Romantic tradition which has never failed to find adherents. Siegfried Sassoon has been mentioned already, but at much the same time the poets Edward Thomas, Robert Graves and the American, Robert Frost, were evidently and admittedly in his debt. Even writers as different in sensibility as Ezra Pound and Dylan Thomas proclaimed their adherence though it is far from easy to pinpoint Hardy's effect upon their own output. And, in our own day, W.H. Auden, who considered Hardy as the greatest master, C. Day Lewis, and Philip Larkin, are but three who have felt him as a vital force and one more lasting than the Anglo-American traditions that had been written so unnaturally large into the still incomplete histories of our poetry of the present century. Meantime readers may refer for more material to Donald Davie's suggestive *Thomas Hardy and British Poetry*.

Finally, because of the increased output of Hardy's works from the press and the demand for still more precise editions of what he wrote (a move that in 1974 and 1975 is at last being satisfied) he may be forming the consciousness of writers who are still in the process of self-discovery. There has at the same time been something of a renaissance in Hardy studies and scholarship, for although the public has long known that he was a great writer it has taken longer for critics to find this out and explain precisely why. Although the world in which Hardy grew up has gone for ever it is impossible to picture him as a Victorian. He has indeed transcended these limits and comes over to most people as a curiously modern and readily accessible writer of the highest order and of today.

Part Two
Critical Survey

4 The Hardy Hero and his Predicament

When Hardy began work on *The Poor Man and the Lady*, at the age of twenty-seven, he tells us that:

> He considered that he knew fairly well both West-country life in its less explored recesses and the life of an isolated student cast upon the billows of London with no protection but his brains—the young man of whom it may be said more truly than perhaps of any, that 'save his own soul he hath no star'. The two contrasting experiences seemed to afford him abundant materials out of which to evolve a striking socialistic novel—not that he mentally defined it as such, for the word had probably never, or scarcely ever, been heard of at that date.

(Life, 56)

As we have already noted the hero was a young architect from an obscure home in Wessex who wants to marry an heiress. Her parents turn him down and he gets mixed up in extreme left-wing politics; in the end he and the Lady decide to elope, but she dies. Other characters included an architect's mistress who works in a shop making religious symbols, and the whole novel was intended as a satire on 'the vulgarity of the middle class' and 'modern Christianity'. It was turned down by two publishers, as recorded in the first chapter, and he destroyed the novel. But the radicalism which came out so violently in this first novel persists, in a smouldering way, in most of the novels he wrote later on. Nearly all of them are in some sense about *class*, about the difficulties of rising from one class into another, about jobs and education and money, and about the inevitable pain and conflicts which happen when people from two different classes fall in love.

There were other themes that persisted too. Everybody knows that he wrote about 'West-country life in its less explored recesses'; what is not so obvious is that he very often took for his hero a young man who has been cast adrift, not necessarily in London, but in a moral and intellectual wilderness in which there are no fixed rules to guide him, only the promptings of his own soul. This is a central theme in *The Return of the Native, Tess of the d'Urbervilles* and *Jude the Obscure*. It forms what we can call the essentially *modern* part of his novels, while his descriptions of life in the remote parts of Dorset must have

Hobbema's 'The Avenue', Hardy's favourite Dutch landscape in which the blend of man and scenery, as in the novels, forms a perfect fusion.

seemed almost as old-fashioned to his earliest readers as they do to us now.

After *The Poor Man and the Lady* Hardy wrote a pot-boiler, *Desperate Remedies*; his next novel was *Under the Greenwood Tree*, or *The Mellstock Quire*. This is a very much better and more characteristic novel, for in it Hardy returned to the people and scenes he knew best. 'Mellstock' is Stinsford, the hamlet where he grew up, and the choir is based on the perished group of musicians which had included several members of his own family. Although, as Hardy said, the book is not to be taken too seriously, he did feel that the destruction of old-fashioned church choirs was a tragic symbol in its small way. This made him gently, but very definitely, critical of the pretty young organist, Fancy Day, who takes over from the choir, and of the Reverend Mr Maybold, who is a decent man but doesn't know how to communicate with ordinary people. When Fancy is forced to choose between him and young Dick Dewy, a member of the original choir, she is really having to choose between two ways of life. Dick is a little bit 'beneath' her, whereas Maybold is the sort of educated gentleman whom her father has always wanted her to marry. This is the kind of conflict which comes up over and over again in Hardy's novels, and although Fancy makes the right choice in the end there is a suspicion that she doesn't really care for Dick as much as he does for her.

Although they are only sketched in lightly, the 'hero' and 'heroine' are both recognizable Hardy types. Their names are symbolic; Dick represents dewy-eyed innocence; Fancy is ruled by her whims. She is a flirtatious girl, like so many Hardy heroines, while Dick is the unpretentious warm-hearted hero who is to become more important in the later and greater works.

In many ways the love story is not the real heart of the novel. Hardy wanted the title to be *The Mellstock Quire*, and his deepest sympathies are with the choir which is in the process of being destroyed. It is these people who represent what is really valuable in the life of the community, in a way that Fancy can never do, and there is a constant quiet suggestion that they are keeping alive, not only the best of the village traditions, but also a sympathetic awareness of nature which cannot be understood by those who have grown up in towns. The young Hardy never wrote anything finer than the first pages of this book, which show the choir assembling in the dark lanes on Christmas Eve:

> To dwellers in a wood almost every species of tree has its voice as well as its feature. At the passing of the breeze the fir-trees sob and moan no less distinctly than they rock; the holly whistles as it battles with itself; the ash hisses amid its quiverings; the beech rustles while its flat boughs rise and fall. And winter, which modifies

the note of such trees as shed their leaves, does not destroy its individuality.

(1)

We first meet Dick, the hero, walking through 'the darkness of a plantation that whispered thus distinctively to his intelligence'. It is only the first of many scenes in Hardy's novels where he shows people working or walking in the countryside in a total or partial darkness, with only their knowledge of the landscape to guide them. He is interested in more than the simple skill of distinguishing trees from one another (in a countryside without electricity) by sound rather than sight. This is only one example, he seems to be saying, of how people can develop a deeply intuitive relationship with their surroundings which can give meaning and purpose to their lives.

Gabriel Oak

Man is part of nature, in the Wessex novels, and also part of history. This is worked out much more fully in Hardy's next important novel, his first really good one, *Far from the Madding Crowd*. His description of the shepherd Gabriel Oak, watching his flock on the lonely down at midnight, is interesting enough to be worth quoting at length:

> The sky was clear—remarkably clear—and the twinkling of all the stars seemed to be but throbs of one body, timed by a common pulse. The North Star was directly in the wind's eye, and since evening the Bear had swung round it outwardly to the east, till he was now at a right angle with the meridian. A difference of colour in the stars—oftener read of than seen in England—was perceptible here. The sovereign brilliancy of Sirius pierced the eye with a steely glitter, the star called Capella was yellow, Aldebaran and Betelgueux shone with a fiery red.
>
> To persons standing alone on a hill during a clear midnight such as this, the roll of the world eastward is almost a palpable movement. The sensation may be caused by the panoramic glide of the stars past earthly objects, which is perceptible in a few minutes of stillness, or by the better outlook upon space that a hill affords, or by the wind, or by the solitude; but whatever be its origin the impression of riding along is vivid and abiding. The poetry of motion is a phrase much in use, and to enjoy the epic form of that gratification it is necessary to stand on a hill at a small hour of the night, and, having first expanded with a sense of difference from the mass of civilised mankind, who are dreamwrapt and disregardful of all such proceedings at this time, long and quietly watch your stately progress through the stars. After such a nocturnal reconnoitre it is hard to get back to earth, and to believe that the

consciousness of such majestic speeding is derived from a tiny human frame.

This is similar in some ways to a famous passage from *The Rainbow*, where Lawrence, who as a young man had been strongly influenced by Hardy's work, writes:

> But during the long February nights with the ewes in labour, looking out from the shelter into the flashing stars, he knew he did not belong to himself. He must admit that he was only fragmentary, something incomplete and subject. There were the stars in the dark heaven travelling, the whole host passing by on some eternal voyage. So he sat small and submissive to the greater ordering.

Both writers are expressing the sense of awe which is felt by a solitary man on looking at the stars (an experience, by the way, which fewer and fewer of us are likely to have in this century; neither Hardy nor Lawrence grew up in a town). Many of us feel at these times, and Lawrence appears to be saying, that man is something small and insignificant; Hardy doesn't say this. On the contrary, he feels that the whole universe takes its meaning from man's presence —'the consciousness of such majestic speeding is derived from a tiny human frame'.

But if Hardy is more humanist, more definitively centred on man than Lawrence, he too feels that man 'does not belong to himself'. He has a vital relationship with the natural world, which he ignores at his peril, and he also depends on other human beings to keep him alive. Gabriel, the hero of this novel, has a profound understanding of nature which helps to make him the most admirable character in the book. In the chapter we have just been studying, we see him nursing the newborn lambs, and telling the time of night from the stars. Later, when the sheep under his care are struck down by a mysterious disease, he is the only one who knows how to cure them, and when a whole harvest is threatened by rain he saves it by working in the darkness 'entirely by feeling with his hands'. But he is not merely a skilful farmer; he is also *morally* stronger and better than most people. Near the beginning of the story he says to Bathsheba, the rather flighty girl whom he is in love with: 'I shall do one thing in this life—one thing certain—that is, love you, and long for you, and *keep wanting you* till I die'. Bathsheba turns him down at first and marries the flashy Sergeant Troy, who is the opposite of Gabriel, an uncontrollable flirt. This type reappears several times in Hardy's novels (he satirizes it in a notorious late work, *The Well-Beloved*), and although he was not completely without sympathy he obviously felt that this type of man was very dangerous. Troy nearly ruins Bathsheba's life, and incidentally her farm as well, before the story works itself out and she is left thankfully free to settle down with Gabriel.

For the Hardy hero like Gabriel Oak there is no real 'predicament', because whatever disasters may hit him he will carry on, stoically and without self-pity, doing the work that lies to hand. Perhaps this type of man, based on the shepherds and small farmers of Dorset among whom Hardy had grown up, was the kind of 'hero' he most admired. But the Gabriel figure becomes less common in his later novels, because by this time Hardy was beginning to be obsessed by problems of a very different kind.

Diggory Venn and Clym Yeobright

We can see this happening in his next great novel, *The Return of the Native*. The people who live on barren Egdon Heath have the same feeling as Gabriel for the great underlying reality of nature, which is always there although human lives, and human civilizations, come and go. 'The sea changed, the fields changed, the rivers, the villages and the people changed', says Hardy in the first chapter, 'but Egdon remained'. In *Far from the Madding Crowd* Nature was a positive and on the whole a friendly force; in this novel, on the other hand, it is something you have to put up with. People who refuse to adapt to the heath will be broken. Hardy shows us two characters, Eustacia, who yearns for a life of luxury in Paris, and the gambler and compulsive flirt Wildeve, both of whom are forced to live on the heath, but hate it. In the end they both die, drowned in the flooded weir on a night of wind and storm. On the other hand, people who accept the heath and understand its moods can live on it without too much trouble. This is true of the sweet and unsophisticated Thomasin, who brings her baby out on to the heath quite happily, and the reddleman Diggory Venn. This weird character, although he appears to have come from a realm outside nature, is actually very much like Gabriel Oak. He is essentially kind and unselfish, devoted to the woman he loves even when there seems no hope of getting her, and, like Thomasin, thoroughly well adapted to life on the heath. At certain times, particularly in the remarkable scene where he plays dice with Wildeve by the light of glow-worms, we feel that he has powers which aren't quite human. Nature seems to work on his side, because he understands and knows how to relate to it, and, like Gabriel, he has his reward at the end of the novel, when most of the other characters are broken or die.

And yet the real hero of this novel is *not* Diggory, but—some would say—a much less admirable figure, Clym Yeobright. When we first meet him, nearly a third of the way through the novel, we are immediately made aware that Clym is different from other people— 'singular' is the word Hardy uses 'Had Heaven preserved Yeobright from a wearing habit of meditation, people would have said, "A handsome man!" Had his brain unfolded under sharper contours they would have said, "A thoughtful man" But an inner strenuousness was preying upon an outer symmetry, and they rated his look as singular' (II, 6).

Clym's physical health and good looks are fated to be shortlived because he worries too hard about himself, and about the whole human race. He has come back to the heath where he was born, throwing up a good career as a diamond merchant, because he wants to do something useful with his life. 'Can any man deserving the name waste his time in that effeminate way, when he sees half the world going to ruin for want of somebody to buckle to and teach them how to breast the misery they are born to?' His idea is to become a teacher to the heath workers' children, and he is content to live on Egdon because its roughness and wildness suit him: 'To my mind it is most exhilarating, and strengthening, and soothing. I would rather live on these hills than anywhere else in the world.'

Yet Clym has moved a long way away from the dwellers on the heath, who don't understand why he has come back to live there when he could be having a gay time in Paris. His plans to start a school never work out, and although he is quite happy to cut furze on the heath when he can do nothing better, he cannot really go back to being a land worker when his whole life has made him, inescapably, an intellectual. He has no clearcut social position and he is bound to be isolated from other people because, Hardy suggests, he is too far ahead of them. He has a 'typical countenance of the future', which means that, in the present, he is bound to look 'singular'. 'The rural world was not ripe for him. A man should be only partially before his time; to be completely to the vanward in aspirations is fatal to fame.'

But worse is to happen to Clym. Through a series of events over which he has very little control, he comes to feel responsible for the deaths of his mother and of his wife. By the end of the novel he is left a semi-invalid with a profound sense of guilt 'It is I who ought to have drowned myself. Those who ought to have lived lie dead, and here am I alive!' There is nobody left who cares much about Clym as a person, but he does, in the end, rebuild his life by staying on the heath, as he planned, and becoming an unorthodox preacher:

Yeobright had, in fact, found his vocation in the career of an itinerant open-air preacher and lecturer on morally unimpeachable subjects... He left alone creeds and systems of philosophy, finding enough and more than enough to occupy his tongue in the opinions and actions common to all good men. Some believed him, and some believed not; some said that his words were commonplace, others complained of his want of theological doctrine; while others again remarked that it was well enough for a man to take to preaching who could not see to do anything else. But everywhere he was kindly received, for the story of his life had become generally known. (VI, iv)

'I got to like the character of Clym before I had done with him', Hardy wrote, when he re-read the novel many years afterwards. 'I think he is the nicest of all my heroes and *not a bit* like me' (*Later Years* 151). Indeed there can hardly be any doubt, in this last paragraph, of his affectionate feelings towards his hero. Clym deserves kindness, because he has suffered so drastically, and his moral philosophy closely resembles Hardy's in being a simple system of ethics, not tied to philosophy in any way. (This ought to answer those critics, from D.H. Lawrence downwards, who think that Hardy deliberately drew Clym as a bit of a wet.) Whether it is equally obvious that Clym is 'not a bit like me', I am not sure. In many ways Hardy does seem to have been very like Clym in his unconventional ideas, his dubiousness about many received opinions, and his feeling that when life is cut off from its natural roots it is bound to be unhappy. What is certain is that in his later work Hardy definitely became more and more interested in this kind of hero, the lonely misfit; the intellectual whom most people think of as an eccentric; the man with a haunting and indestructible feeling of guilt.

Over the next eight or ten years, one of Hardy's less productive periods, the themes of loneliness and self-sacrifice become increasingly important in his work. John Loveday, the hero of *The Trumpet-Major*, renounces the woman he loves to his brother and goes off to the Napoleonic wars to be killed. Viviette in *Two on a Tower* gives up her lover for the good of his career and in the end she dies too. In *A Laodicean* (perhaps the weakest novel he ever wrote) Hardy again shows a girl sacrificing herself for the good of her lover and eventually going into a convent. And *The Mayor of Casterbridge,* which is discussed more fully in the next chapter, shows the hero progressively breaking all his human and social ties until he is driven out of the community, to die almost alone on Egdon Heath.

Giles Winterborne

The Woodlanders, written ten years after *The Return of the Native*, has some things in common with it, but the tone is sadder, more resigned, much less confident about the power of new ideas to change the world. There is nobody in the woodland community at all like Clym Yeobright. Mr Fitzpiers, the 'very clever and learned young doctor' whose light Grace watches in fascination as it changes to blue, then violet, and then red, represents 'like a tropical plant in a hedgerow, a nucleus of advanced ideas and practices which had nothing in common with the life around'. But Fitzpiers has no idealistic dreams about reforming the world; he is dabbling in strange studies for his own amusement and he is also a cold-hearted philanderer who boasts that he has been infatuated with five women at once. Both he and Mrs Charmond, the rich landowner with whom he has an affair, dislike living in the woods and don't know their way round them (just as Wildeve and Eustacia feel lost on Egdon Heath). But Mrs Charmond actually owns the despised woods and can pull down houses and trees at her pleasure, and without really wanting to harm the woodland workers she exercises a casual tyranny over their lives. This has ramifications into other than property relationships; as Creedle says to Giles Winterborne, the real hero of the novel:

> 'Ye've lost a hundred load of timber well seasoned; ye've lost five hundred pound in good money; ye've lost the stone-windered house that's big enough to hold a dozen families; ye've lost your share of half-a-dozen good wagons and their horses;—all lost!— through your letting slip she that was once yer own!'

(XXV)

What this means is that Giles has lost Grace, who later becomes the wife of Fitzpiers, because Mrs Charmond has turned him out of his house, and also because he is not thought good enough for a girl whose father has had her expensively educated. 'Learning is better than houses and lands', says Creedle, but in this novel the three go together, and cultivated upperclass people, the Charmonds and Fitzpierses of this world, have no difficulty in taking everything they want from the ordinary people who work in the woods, like Giles, and the girl Marty South.

'On taking up *The Woodlanders* and reading it after many years I think I like it, *as a story*, the best of all', Hardy said, and one is tempted to agree with him when one comes back to this beautiful and comparatively neglected novel—perhaps the most neglected of all his great works. Some of the things which we remember longest are the lyrical and lovely descriptions of the fertile country around the Hintocks, as in this passage:

> It was the cider country more especially, which met the woodland district some way off. There the air was blue as sapphire—such a blue as outside that apple-region was never seen. Under the blue the orchards were in a blaze of pink bloom, some of the richly flowered trees running almost up to where they drove along. At a gate, which opened down an incline, a man leant on his arms regarding this fair promise so intently that he did not observe their passing.
>
> 'That was Giles', said Melbury, when they had gone by.
> 'Was it? Poor Giles,' said she.
> 'All that apple-blooth means heavy autumn work for him and

Fordington near Dorchester, the Reverend Henry Moule's church.

his hands. If no blight happens before the setting the cider yield
will be such as we have not had for years.'

(XIX)

Giles and his fellow-workers are not merely figures in a landscape;
they actually *create* that landscape. He and Marty have an instinctive
love and knowledge of nature which seems miraculous to people who
don't work in the woods.

From the light lashing of the twigs upon their faces when brushing
through them in the dark either could pronounce upon the species
of the tree whence they stretched; from the quality of the wind's
murmur through a bough either could in like manner name its sort
afar off.

Of Giles we are told that 'he had a marvellous power of making
trees grow...There was a sort of sympathy between himself and the
fir, oak or beech that he was operating on; so that the roots took hold
of the soil in a few days.' But these skills, the basis of life itself, are much
less highly thought of than the possession of money, or of an aristo-

cratic name like Fitzpiers. In a famous passage, Marty says that the young trees sigh 'because they are very sorry to begin life in earnest—just as we be'. She is right, because life is intensely hard, even tragic, for people like Giles and herself. Unlike Gabriel Oak and Diggory Venn, whom he strongly resembles in some ways, Giles can find no fulfilment in the world of this novel. He sacrifices himself for Grace, and dies, to be forgotten by her in exactly eight months. She goes off to the Midlands with her husband, where, we suppose, they will lead a more or less unhappy married life, and we are left with the memory of Giles's goodness and the trees which will live on after his death.

This was the last time that Hardy wrote about this kind of hero. The men in his later novels are much more complicated, much less straightforwardly *good* than Giles is, and they don't share his close intimacy with the natural world. What happens to a girl of the same type as Marty South, when her values collide with the Victorian moral code, is shown in detail in *Tess of the d'Urbervilles*.

Angel Clare

Tess Durbeyfield is like Marty (and Gabriel and Giles) because she is happily adjusted to her environment. 'A fresh and virginal daughter of Nature' is what she first seems to Angel Clare. When she is working as a milkmaid at Talbothays Dairy Hardy emphasizes, in some marvellous passages, that she and Angel are leading a kind of life which is not only precious in itself, but essential:

> They met continually; they could not help it. They met daily in that strange and solemn interval, the twilight of the morning, in the violet or pink dawn; for it was necessary to rise early, so very early, here. Milking was done betimes, and before the milking came the skimming, which began at a little past three.... The spectral, half-compounded, aqueous light which pervaded the open mead, impressed them with a feeling of isolation, as if they were Adam and Eve. ... At that preternatural time hardly any woman so well endowed in person as she was likely to be walking in the open air within the boundaries of his horizon; very few in all England. Fair women are usually asleep at midsummer dawns. She was close at hand, and the rest were nowhere.

(XX)

The Crown Inn, Marnhull, Dorset (The Pure Drop, Marlott, in 'Tess of the D'Urbervilles').

Like Gabriel, watching his flock under the stars, Tess and Angel are awake and caring for the animals at a time when most people are in bed. Hardy makes the same point when they deliver milk to the London train, for 'strange people that we have never seen...who don't know anything of us, and where it comes from: or think how we two drove miles across the moor tonight in the rain that it might reach 'em in time'.

But Tess is not a simple character, a girl like Thomasin in *The Return of the Native* whose life is an open book. Angel doesn't know, perhaps because he doesn't understand the roughness of life in the English villages, that she has been seduced and had an illegitimate baby at the age of sixteen. And Tess is unable to be really happy at Talbothays,. as all her instincts tell her to be, because she cannot forget that in the eyes of the world she is a fallen woman:

> Her face had latterly changed with changing states of mind, continually fluctuating between beauty and ordinariness, according as the thoughts were gay or grave. One day she was pink and flawless; another pale and tragical. When she was pink she was feeling less than when pale; her more perfect beauty accorded with her less elevated mood; her more intense mood with her less perfect beauty.

(XVI)

This reminds one of the description of Clym Yeobright's face, where his natural good looks and cheerfulness are being undermined because he cannot stop worrying. Not that Hardy is arguing that people ought *not* to worry; on the contrary he seems to think that under the conditions of modern life they can hardly help it. For modern society is diseased, often cruel and inhuman, and the conventions it lays down are in many important ways *unnatural*. Tess has been 'made to break an accepted social law', but not any law that exists in nature. And it is the conflict between natural human feelings and social conventions which, in the end, destroys her, a conflict which is acted out in the mind of the man she loves, Angel Clare.

Angel is one of the most interesting heroes whom Hardy had so far attempted to draw. He has given up the faith of his father and brothers and become an advanced thinker, who wishes to use his education 'for the honour and glory of man'. Shut out from the university because of his agnosticism (like Hardy), he comes to live at Talbothays to study farming. Like Clym, he has taken a step downwards from his own class by doing this, and the dairyman's wife treats him as a gentleman, making him eat at a different table from everyone else. Again like Clym, he finds that living close to nature makes him surprisingly cheerful:

Unexpectedly he began to like the outdoor life for its own sake...
He became wonderfully free from the chronic melancholy which
is overtaking the civilised races with the decline of belief in a
beneficent Power.

...He grew away from old associations, and saw something new
in life and humanity. Secondarily, he made close acquaintance
with phenomena which he had before known but darkly—the
seasons in their moods, morning and evening, night and noon,
winds in their different tempers, trees, waters and mists, shades
and silences, and the voices of inanimate things.

(XVIII)

Together with this new awareness of nature goes a new awareness of
human beings; he stops thinking of the dairy workers as comic
yokels and begins to like and respect them as people—'much to his
surprise he took, indeed, a real delight in their companionship'.
The change in his attitudes, brought about by working in the dairy
for a while, is responsible for his falling in love with Tess, who is
obviously not the sort of girl his family wants or expects him to marry.
What causes him to reject her is not his natural feelings, but the
residue of prejudice left by his upbringing: 'With all his attempted
independence of judgement this advanced and well-meaning young
man, a sample product of the last five-and-twenty years, was yet the
slave to custom and conventionality when surprised back into his
early teachings.' (XXXIX)

This is one of the most tragic dilemmas in all Hardy's novels, and
one which he was to explore still more deeply in *Jude the Obscure*. It is
not an easy thing to be ahead of one's time, at any rate not in Victorian
England; the most sincere convictions are liable to crack under a
personal shock. Angel leaves Tess after she tells him about her past,
even though he knows that she is at least as pure as he is, calling her
with cruel snobbishness 'an unapprehending peasant woman'. Worse
still, he lets her think that he has gone for good, until in despair she is
forced back to her original seducer. By the end of the novel, after she
has been hanged, he has been reduced, like Clym, to a 'mere yellow
skeleton', who is doomed to be haunted by guilt for the rest of his life.

Society, Hardy seems to be saying in the most bitter novel he had
yet written, has its values turned upside down. Tess was abused as
'a little harlot' in many London drawing-rooms, as in the book
she is condemned as a murderess. Angel, on the other hand, has not
done anything legally wrong. Yet in fact he knows himself to be much
more guilty than she, perhaps even more guilty than Alec d'Urberville, and in the end he could easily have said, like Clym, 'My great
regret is that for what I have done no man or law can punish me'.

Jude Fawley

Jude the Obscure, Hardy's last novel, is more bitter still. By this time he seems to have felt even more certain that something was deeply wrong with the society he lived in, and this feeling is expressed through the surprisingly modern parable of a young working man who wants to go to Oxford, and fails. Like Angel and Clym, Jude has left his own class without joining another one, but, unlike them, he is hoping to *rise* in the world. This is not only ambition, although that has something to do with it; it is much more the yearning for a life which is intellectually and morally *better* than the one he is expected to lead. Hardy makes it clear that no sensitive person could endure life in Marygreen. Nature is much grimmer here than in his earlier novels; Jude's job is scaring birds in a lonely ploughed field and when he lets himself show sympathy for them the farmer beats him. He has no parents and there are no village traditions (such as the Mellstock choir) to which he can attach himself, for the old landmarks have been pulled down and he knows next to nothing about his ancestors who are buried in the dismantled graveyard. One of the most moving passages in the entire novel comes near the end, when he goes into the ugly new church which has been raised on a different site from the old one: 'Everything was new, except a few pieces of carving preserved from the wrecked old fabric, now fixed against the new walls. He stood by these: they seemed akin to the perished people of that place who were his ancestors and Sue's.' (VI, viii)

Jude's alienation has gone so far that the one light on the bleak horizon appears to be Christminster, the university city, based on Oxford, on the extreme border of Hardy's Wessex:

> It had been the yearning of his heart to find something to anchor on, to cling to—for some place which he could call admirable. Should he find that place in this city if he could get there? Would it be a spot in which, without fear of farmers, or hindrance, or ridicule, he could watch and wait, and set himself to some mighty undertaking like the men of old of whom he had heard?
>
> (I, iii)

Like all true Hardy heroes, Jude wants to find something greater than himself to which he can give himself totally. In earlier novels, this had meant productive work on the land; in others it meant the cause of progress or learning (the young hero of *Two on a Tower*, for example, is completely committed to studying the stars). Jude belongs to a generation for whom work on the land has become irrelevant; instead he strains himself to the limit in the struggle to

Balliol College, Jude's Biblioll, c.1900.

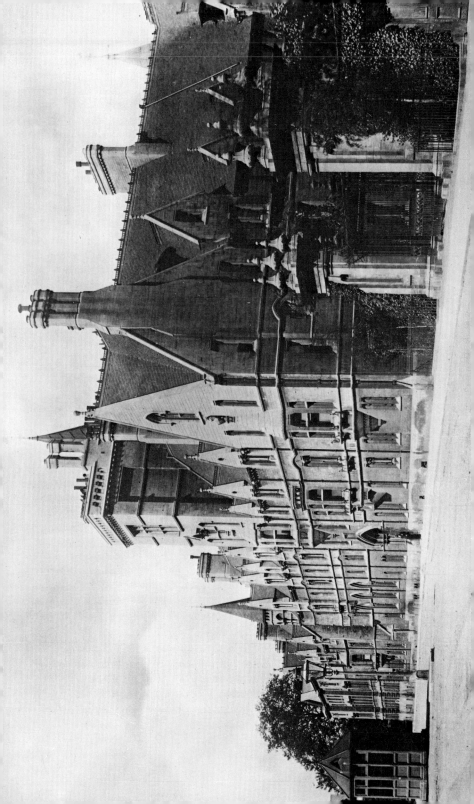

be a learned man who can find a home in the Christminster colleges. But the reality of Christminster, as he finds out when he actually gets there, is that of a bigoted, cruel and sordid city. The university establishment is satirized throughout the story. Colleges have names like Biblioll and Sarcophagus; horses are kicked in the stomach outside the college gates and there are 'two nations' inside the same city: the learned doctors and clergymen, and the ordinary people of Christminster who have no idea what it's all about. This means that the university is closed to those, like Jude, who could benefit most from it, because he was born into the wrong class. When he makes his moving speech to the Christminster crowd about the failure of his dream, Hardy emphasizes that Jude is more intelligent, and more moral, than the gentlemen in the university:

> 'Well preached!' said Tinker Taylor. And privately to his neighbours: 'Why, one of them jobbing pa'sons swarming about here, that takes the services when our head Reverends want a holiday, wouldn't ha' discoursed such doctrine for less than a guinea down! Hey? I'll take my oath not one o' 'em would! And then he must have had it wrote down for 'n. And this only a working man!'
>
> (VI, i)

(Not surprisingly, the policeman in attendance tells Jude, 'Keep yer tongue quiet, my man'.)

When Jude first comes to Christminster he has, as he says himself, 'a neat stock of fixed opinions', but these are gradually eroded under the pressure of the life he leads and the influence of his cousin Sue, an extraordinarily bright and clever girl with whom he falls in love. These 'fixed opinions' were those of most conventional Victorians, and included respect for Oxford University in its contemporary form, the Anglican Church, the institution of marriage and so on. After Jude has realized that the University is closed to the working class, that the Church is indifferent to ordinary human problems and that marriage to the wrong person can be a torment, Hardy says that his experiences have 'enlarged his own views of life, laws, customs and dogmas'. The opposite happens to Sue. The girl whose intellect 'scintillated like a star' cannot hang on to her independence of mind when tragedy strikes her, and she goes back to the husband whom she should never have married, even forcing herself to do 'the ultimate thing'. Jude, dying of exposure and neglect in what was his holy city, Christminster, says:

> 'It takes two or three generations to do what I tried to do in one. . . . As for Sue and me. . . . when our minds were clear, and our love of truth fearless—the time was not ripe for us! Our ideas were fifty years too soon to be any good to us. And so the resistance they met with brought reaction in her, and recklessness and ruin on me!'
>
> (VI, x)

Like another seeker for truth, Clym Yeobright, they were unfortunate in being born too far ahead of their time. Hardy had spent most of his life looking for the truth and various things he wrote, including the poem 'Wessex Heights' (see also p. 138) show that he understood this state of mind only too well. It is not really surprising that Sue breaks and Jude dies, because, again like Hardy, they are both ultra-sensitive, and the pressures on them are more than most people could bear. Just as nobody can understand why the 'obscure' Jude wishes to go to Oxford, or why he and Sue cannot shake down with the people they marry, or why Phillotson refuses to do the proper thing when his wife wants to leave him, so the public couldn't understand what Hardy meant by writing a novel like *Jude*. The attacks on the book, some of them violent and unscrupulous, upset Hardy so much that he wrote no more novels after this, though not for this reason alone.

Jude has nothing to fall back on after Sue leaves him; not God, and not nature, which in many of Hardy's earlier novels was seen as a comforting and strengthening force. Indeed in this novel Hardy says that nature's law is 'mutual butchery', and comments sadly on 'the scorn of Nature for man's finer emotions, and her lack of interest in his aspirations'. And yet these emotions, and these aspirations, are still facts, and Jude is no less of a hero to Hardy because he has failed in almost everything that he set out to do. We don't feel that Giles has failed, at the end of *The Woodlanders*, because it is still possible for Marty to say, 'you was a good man, and did good things'. *Jude* may be related to a group of novels on the theme of growing-up such as *Great Expectations, Mill on the Floss* and (into the future) Joyce's *Portrait of the Artist* and, most strongly, D.H. Lawrence's *Sons and Lovers*. Perhaps the Hardy version of the strains of an education and the aches of maturity borrows a little of its bitterness from feelings arising from his visits to Cambridge in Moule's day. Nevertheless, let down by every person and institution as Jude is, a most unheroic hero whom we might later meet again in novels by such writers as Lawrence, Huxley, Waugh or William Golding, he remains constant in his beliefs and feelings to the last. This independence of the world's opinion was the quality that Hardy understood as valuable and permanent. In his own case as a writer and not a manual worker he returns to this theme in the most important poem, 'Wessex Heights' (see p. 138) in which he shows that the greatest treason is to be false to oneself. This the unhappy Jude is not.

The Mayor of Casterbridge

by Thomas Hardy.

Author of "Far from the Madding Crowd", "a Pair of Blue Eyes", &c.

Chapter I.

One evening of late summer, ~~when~~ before the present century had ~~nearly~~ reached ~~its~~ middle-age, a young man & woman, the latter carrying a child, were approaching the large village of Weydon=Priors on foot. They were plainly but not ill clad, though the thick ~~coating~~ hour of dust which had accumulated on their shoes & clothing from an obviously long journey ~~added a~~ lent a disadvantageous / shabbiness

Hardy's original of opening page of manuscript.

5 'The Mayor of Casterbridge'

Hardy was at the height of his powers when he began work on *The Mayor of Casterbridge* at the age of forty-four. He had written ten novels up to then, but only one, *The Return of the Native*, written seven years before, was a masterpiece. Since that time, he had produced some inferior books. But by 1884 he could afford to have a house built in Dorchester, the town he called Casterbridge, and most of the novel was written there, as were *The Woodlanders*, *Tess of the d'Urbervilles*, and *Jude the Obscure*.

It seems to have had a good effect on his work. *The Mayor of Casterbridge* is a magnificent novel, some would say the finest he ever wrote, although Hardy himself was not entirely happy about it:

> It was a story which Hardy fancied he had damaged more recklessly as an artistic whole, in the interest of the newspaper in which it appeared serially, than perhaps any other of his novels, his aiming to get an incident into each week's part causing him in his own judgment to add events to the narrative somewhat too freely.
>
> (*Life*, 174)

The readers were not entirely happy either, for different reasons. Some felt that it was less good than *Far from the Madding Crowd*, which everybody liked best at that time. Perhaps because it was one of the more cheerful of Hardy's books. And it was very nearly turned down by the publisher on the grounds that 'the lack of gentry among the characters made it uninteresting—a typical estimate of what was, or was supposed to be, mid-Victorian taste' (*Life*, 180).

Perhaps it is just because of its differences from Hardy's other novels that *The Mayor of Casterbridge* is so popular today. It would not have been easy to fit either Henchard or Farfrae into the last chapter, on Hardy's heroes. We saw there that Hardy usually wrote about men like Gabriel Oak, who represented his ideal of the countryman, or about men like himself, deeply troubled intellectuals like Clym Yeobright or Jude. Neither Henchard nor Farfrae is at all like this, and it is one of the triumphs of Hardy's art that he could write so convincingly about men so unlike himself. They are unlike each other,

The next two illustrations of scenes from the book are the melodramatic prints appearing in the serialized version and not reprinted afterwards. They were passed by the author before printing and catch the superficial tone of the personal exchanges in a characteristic manner.

"*I don't drink now — I haven't since that night.*"

"'*Now,*' *said Henchard between his gasps,* '*Your life is in my hands.*'"

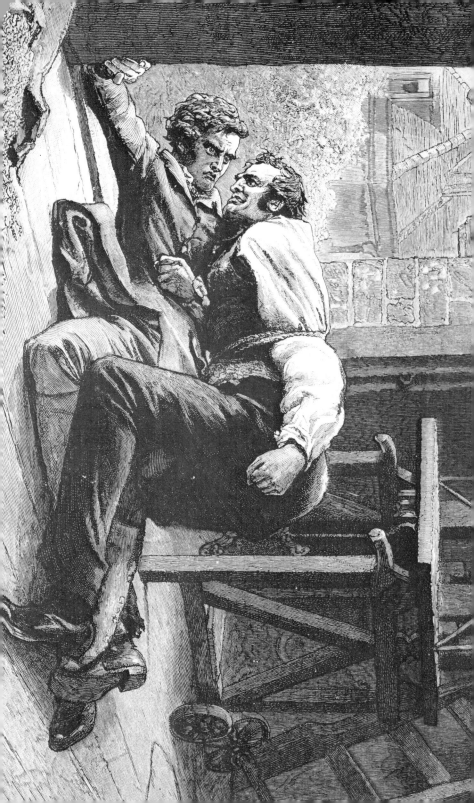

too; in fact the difference goes so deep that it leads to a struggle which can only end in death. Henchard is a giant with black whiskers and eyes 'which always seemed to have a red spark of light in them,' a man of tremendous and sometimes frightening strength who can wrench a bull's head 'as if he would snap it off'. Farfrae is 'ruddy and of a fair countenance, bright-eyed, and slight in build'. Henchard rushes from one extreme to another, in trade and in his emotional life; Farfrae has a cool scientific attitude to trade and to people as well. At the same time he charms everyone he comes into contact with: 'The curious double strands in Farfrae's thread of life—the commercial and the romantic—were very distinct at times. Like the colours in a variegated cord those contrasts could be seen intertwisted, yet not mingling.' (XXIII)

We see something of the basic differences between them when Henchard tells Farfrae about 'the gloomy fits I sometimes suffer from, on account o' the loneliness of my domestic life, when the world seems to have the blackness of hell, and, like Job, I could curse the day that gave me birth'. Farfrae replies, 'Ah, now, I never feel like it', and it is, and is meant to be, a significant point. Hardy *had* felt like that, and this is one reason for the deep sympathy and identification with Henchard which runs right through the book. Not that he glosses over his hero's faults; quite the opposite. Henchard is so *obviously* wrong, most of the time; Farfrae so *obviously* blameless and sweetly reasonable. Yet there is no doubt at all about which Hardy likes best. And such is the genius of his art that we begin to see unsuspected qualities of generosity and goodness in the Mayor, and something unpleasantly cold and scheming about his young rival.

The novel opens dramatically with the splendid scene in which Henchard sells his wife and child to the sailor. Hardy used to say that a novelist could not expect people to read him unless he told them something unusual enough to be worth hearing, and this first chapter is one of the most compelling he ever wrote. Strange though it may seem now, and did seem then to his London readers, it was not at all uncommon for poor and uneducated men to sell their wives, right up to the end of the nineteenth century. It was done in public, with a halter round the woman's neck, and most people firmly believed that it was legal. Susan Henchard does, and Hardy remarks that she was not the first or last woman to do so. Henchard is not so simple; he is a skilled labourer and a comparatively well-educated man (we first see him absorbed in reading a ballad-sheet) who only sells his wife because he is drunk. But before that he has already begun to resent her, not because he wants another wife but because she and the child are holding him back from getting on: 'I haven't more than fifteen shillings in the world, and yet I am a good experienced man in my line. I'd challenge England to beat me in the fodder business; and if I were a free man again I'd be worth a thousand pound before I'd done o't.' (I). This is the introduction to one of the great central themes of the novel: ambition, and its effects on human relationships. Henchard wants to get rid of his wife and child because he thinks they are preventing him from making a fortune.

Later in the novel we meet another young man, Donald Farfrae, who has left Scotland because he is motivated by the same dream of getting some of 'the prizes of life'. And, in her own way, Elizabeth-Jane wants this too—her mother's main reason for going back to Henchard is to 'advance Elizabeth'. For, more than any other Hardy novel, *The Mayor of Casterbridge* is about the great Victorian myth of 'getting on'. In *The Return of the Native* he had shown how the idealistic Clym Yeobright deliberately chooses to go *back* in the world in order to help people; in this novel the ruthless materialist Henchard sacrifices his closest human ties to ambition. In Victorian terms, he is perfectly right. Not that the orthodox economic thinkers would have condoned actual wife-selling, but they would certainly have said that Henchard was very foolish to get married for love at eighteen. It was everywhere preached during the nineteenth century that if you were poor it must be your own fault. Anybody could become rich if he saved every penny, did not drink, and above all, did not encumber himself with dependents—the Reverend Thomas Malthus had preached that the working classes should abstain from having children, and this was a widely influential view. As always, there were just enough people who did rise from the depths and become millionaires to make this view of life plausible. Samuel Smiles's little book *Self-Help* (1859) is full of the stories of such people, and it became a kind of Bible to many thousands who tried to do the same thing. But there was always another strand in Victorian thinking which sensed that this philosophy was destructive to the deepest human values. Dickens had explored its damaging effects in *Great Expectations*, and Hardy, in *The Mayor of Casterbridge*, did the same thing.

It was a paradox that he of all people should be critical of the idea of 'getting on in the world'. He himself had risen in the last twenty years from an obscure young architect to a famous novelist (and had put off marriage, for financial reasons, until he was thirty-four). This involved a good deal of writing and social mixing which he disliked, and it says in the *Life* that at this time he regarded his novels as 'mere journeywork'. When he was a very old man 'he said that if he had his life over again he would prefer to be a small architect in a country town, like Mr Hicks at Dorchester, to whom he was articled' (*Life*, 443). Perhaps he was in a unique position to sympathize with Henchard and yet to see that his ambition would not, in the end, bring him what he cared about most.

When we next see Henchard, some twenty years later, he has done exactly what he said. He has been a great success in 'the fodder business'—the selling of oats, roots and corn. Now he is the Mayor of

Casterbridge, complete with gold chain and diamond studs, and his wife first sees him through the window of the 'chief hotel' where he is presiding at a great public dinner. She is out in the street, with the rest of the people who haven't been invited, and there is a great contrast between the two groups. Hardy shows the dinner-guests 'searching for tit-bits, and sniffing and grunting over their plates like sows nuzzling for acorns' and finally drinking themselves into a stupor. Whereas the poor people outside the window have to live on the bad bread which Henchard has sold them, 'They can blow their trumpets and thump their drums, and have their roaring dinners, . . . but we must needs be put-to for want of a wholesome crust'. These are the people who shout back rudely at Henchard when he is making his speech at the grand dinner, and later on we are to hear much more about them. The tensions which are to destroy Michael Henchard exist already. For Casterbridge is by no means so pleasant a place as it seems. Our first impression is one of 'great snugness and comfort':

> The front doors of the private houses were mostly left open at this warm autumn-time, no thought of umbrella stealers disturbing the minds of the placid burgesses. Hence, through the long, straight entrance passages thus unclosed could be seen, as through tunnels, the mossy gardens at the back, glowing with nasturtiums, fuchsias, scarlet geraniums, 'bloody warriors', snap-dragons, and dahlias, this floral blaze being backed by crusted grey stone-work from a yet remoter Casterbridge than the venerable one visible in the street.
>
> (IX)

But alongside this cosy picture Hardy shows us aspects of Casterbridge which are altogether more sinister. We hear from the talk in the Three Mariners that it is 'an old, hoary place of wickedness', and that 'when you take away from among us the fools and the rogues, and the lammigers, and the wanton hussies, and the slatterns, and such-like, there's cust few left'. We hear about the 'red-robed judge' who sentences sheep-stealers, about hangings, and about the grisly history of the Amphitheatre where a woman was once burned to death. And gradually we get some idea of the precariousness of Henchard's position, which at first seemed so secure.

He is a lonely man, for all his wealth and power, and this is why he is so keen to get Farfrae to stay with him, for he has no real friends in the town. He begins to be undermined at a very early stage, after he has married his wife again (for the child's sake) and taken Farfrae on as his assistant. It is largely his own fault. We see him antagonize Farfrae by his callous treatment of Abel Whittle, even though, as we learn afterwards, he has 'kept Abel's old mother in coals and snuff all the previous winter', which shows that fundamentally he is far from being the bully he seems. But his uncontrollable temper drives

Farfrae away from him, just as it had driven Susan away when he was young. After he had broken up their friendship 'his heart sank within him at what he had said and done'. His problem is that he craves for affection, but can only give it in bouts and spurts. When his wife has died he feels a passionate need for Elizabeth, only to turn against her when he knows that she is really the sailor's child. 'Being uncultivated himself' he is particularly sensitive to what he thinks is common about her behaviour, such as speaking the dialect or being kind to servants. He tells her that she will 'disgrace him to the dust'. Yet he could have learned from Farfrae that the best way to deal with people is by considering their feelings. It turns out that he has offended his colleagues on the Corporation and so is not to be kept on as an alderman, while at the same time, Farfrae is taken on to the Council.

What happens next is financial ruin. Hardy has already shown how the Mayor has entered into a 'war of prices' and 'mortal commercial combat' with Farfrae. This may seem an overdramatic way of describing the rivalry of two corn merchants in a small country town, but, in this novel, Casterbridge *is* the world of commerce, and the struggle between Henchard and Farfrae is just what was happening in the City of London on an infinitely larger scale. There is no room for human kindness in this atmosphere of fierce competition. Farfrae does not want to take away Henchard's customers, but he finds that he has to, in sheer self-defence. In the end his own recklessness and the changeable weather bring Henchard down. Hardy tells us in the Preface that the novel was partly inspired by events in 'the real history of the town called Casterbridge', including the uncertain harvests in the 1840s in which it is set. In those days, before the repeal of the Corn Laws, a bad harvest could mean starvation for the poor and ruin for those who traded in grain. Henchard finds that 'a man might gamble upon the square green areas of fields as readily as upon those of a card-room'. On the other hand Farfrae, the born capitalist, works out a strategy for dealing with the weather which makes him a handsome profit. This is the end of their 'war of prices'. The penniless young singer of the early chapters is all set to become the leading man in town, while the rich Mayor of Casterbridge is humbled to the dust.

Hardy points out more than once that Henchard is incapable of seeing that the best move he could make would be to encourage Farfrae's interest in Elizabeth-Jane. She is obviously the ideal wife for him. They are both sensible, 'moderate' sort of people, eager to get on in the world and very, very respectable (they are both a little shocked by the hard-bitten types in the Three Mariners in Chapter VIII). But this means that neither of them is likely to get carried away by a great passion. Elizabeth tries to stifle her feelings for Farfrae, because they seem 'one-sided, unmaidenly, and unwise', and Farfrae apparently has only a very mild liking for her: 'An exceptionally fortunate business transaction put him on good terms with everybody, and revealed to him that he could undeniably marry if he chose. Then who so pleasing, thrifty, and satisfactory in every way as Elizabeth-Jane?' (XXIII).

It is in this frame of mind that he meets and falls in love with Lucetta, the girl from Jersey who has compromised herself with Henchard before the real story begins. The chapters which deal with her and her two lovers are very much weaker than the rest of the book. It is not only that Hardy is vague about her past life (we are never told exactly what she and Henchard got up to in Jersey); it is that whenever she appears the writing becomes slack, conventional, and at times melodramatic:

> 'I am greatly obliged to you for all that,' said she, rather with an air of speaking ritual. The stint of reciprocal feeling was perceived, and Henchard showed chagrin at once—nobody was more quick to show that than he.
> 'You may be obliged or not for't. Though the things I say may not have the polish of what you've lately learnt to expect for the first time in your life, they are real, my lady Lucetta.'
> 'That's rather a rude way of speaking to me,' pouted Lucetta, with stormy eyes.
>
> (XXV)

This is infinitely less convincing than the speech of the corn merchants and agricultural workers of Casterbridge, which Hardy gives in so much loving detail. He was not nearly so interested in society women, although he knew the type well enough from his visits to London. Lucetta's story is never really integrated with the rest of the novel, and this is its one major flaw.

She is an obvious *femme fatale*, with none of the quiet integrity of Henchard's dead wife, whom she patronizes: 'Poor woman, she seems to have been a sufferer, though uncomplaining, and although weak in intellect not an imbecile'. Although she seems to have an instantaneous effect on every man she meets, quite cutting Elizabeth out, there is little in her beneath the attractive surface. 'How folk do worship fine clothes!' says one of the townspeople, during the Royal visit, making the point that Elizabeth is, in fact, the better-looking woman. At quite an early stage Hardy suggests that Lucetta's personality is, to a great extent, created by *clothes*:

> Entering her friend's bedroom Elizabeth saw the gowns spread out on the bed, one of a deep cherry colour, the other lighter— a glove lying at the end of each sleeve, a bonnet at the top of each neck, and parasols across the gloves, Lucetta standing beside the suggested human figure in an attitude of contemplation.

'I wouldn't think so hard about it,' said Elizabeth, marking the intensity with which Lucetta was alternating the question whether this or that would suit best.

'But settling upon new clothes is so trying,' said Lucetta. 'You are that person' (pointing to one of the arrangements), 'or you are that totally different person' (pointing to the other), 'for the whole of the coming spring: and one of the two, you don't know which, may turn out to be very objectionable.'

It was finally decided by Miss Templeman that she would be the cherry-coloured person at all hazards.   (XXIV)

In the short term Lucetta is a great success. Farfrae marries her, and Henchard is forced to accept the fact that he has lost to the Scotsman all along the line. This is when we first see him standing on the remoter of the two bridges, with the thought of suicide beginning to shape in his mind. Their old positions have been reversed now: 'Here be I, his former master, working for him as man, and he the man standing as master, with my house and my furniture and my what-you-may-call wife all his own' (XXXII).

This marriage is broken up by a group we have heard of already, the poorest and most degraded of the people of Casterbridge. Earlier we saw them outside the windows of the King's Arms, where the Mayor and Corporation were dining, complaining about Henchard's bad bread. We've also caught some idea from the conversation in the Three Mariners (which caters for a slightly lower class of people) of the toughness of Casterbridge life, with its 'hard winters, and so many mouths to feed, and God-a'mighty sending his little taties so terrible small to fill 'em with'. In chapter XXXVI we are introduced to a third inn, Peter's Finger, which 'bore about the same social relation to the Three Mariners as the latter bore to the King's Arms', and which he describes as the *church* of Mixen Lane. This lane (Mill Lane, in reality) was one of the worst parts of old Dorchester, and the scene of one of the last cholera epidemics in England in 1854. Hardy calls it 'a mildewed leaf in the sturdy and flourishing Casterbridge plant', and he hints that it has been the scene of vice, theft and slaughter. Some of the people of the slum are poachers, some are prostitutes, others have drifted from the countryside after losing their livelihood, like the old furmity-woman who commits a crime against the church wall. All of them are delighted to have the chance of getting at Lucetta, as 'one that stands high in this town'. And Farfrae has also grown less popular since he went up in the world

As the Mayor and man of money, engrossed with affairs and ambitions, he had lost in the eyes of the poorer inhabitants something of that wondrous charm which he had had for them as a light-hearted penniless young man, who sang ditties as readily as the birds in the trees.

The skimmity-ride is planned for the evening after a certain Royal Personage has paid a flying visit to Casterbridge. 'As a wind-up to the Royal visit the hit will be all the more pat by reason of their great elevation today.' This visit is based on historical facts, but Hardy has integrated it skilfully with the novel's main theme of rising in the world. There is a strong implication that the whole affair is ridiculous; an absurd waste of energy and emotion over a person who only stays in the town for a few minutes. While the Council prepare to have an impressive ceremony,

> Solomon Longways, Christopher Coney, Buzzford, and the rest of that fraternity, showed their sense of the occasion by advancing their customary eleven o'clock pint to half-past ten; from which they found a difficulty in getting back to the proper hour for several days.

Everybody 'shone in new vesture according to means' except Henchard, and for this reason Lucetta pretends not to see him 'as gaily dressed women will too often do on such occasions'. She is absorbed in Farfrae, who is wearing 'the official gold chain with great square links, like that round the Royal unicorn'; she even dreams that he may get knighted. Yet already the plot is being hatched which will pull down Lucetta, and show up the emptiness of her social pretensions. 'I do like to see the trimming pulled off such Christmas candles,' as one of the Casterbridge women remarks.

This helps us to understand Hardy's instinctive sympathy when Henchard staggers on to the scene, half-drunk, shabbily dressed, and waving his home-made Union Jack at the Illustrious Personage. For what Henchard desperately needs is some sort of recognition of his own importance, and this is coldly refused him by Farfrae and Lucetta. 'She has supplicated to me in her time, and now her tongue won't own me nor her eyes see me!' When Farfrae pushes him out of the way of the Royal carriage 'he could hardly realize such an outrage from one whom it had once been his wont to treat with ardent generosity'. Farfrae is shocked that Henchard should have 'insulted Royalty', whereas Henchard is concerned with the much deeper human outrage against his feelings from the people he has loved. 'Royalty be damned', as he says. This is what leads to his crazy assault on Farfrae, with one arm tied 'to take no advantage'. But it is obvious that he will never be able to kill him; when Farfrae appears, singing a song about *friendship*, he weakens: 'Nothing moved Henchard like an old melody. He sank back. "No; I can't do it!" he gasped. "Why does the infernal fool begin that now?"' And afterwards, when he has Farfrae in his power:

> Henchard looked down upon him in silence, and their eyes met. 'O Farfrae!—that's not true!' he said bitterly. 'God is my witness

that no man ever loved another as I did thee at one time. . . . And now—though I came here to kill 'ee, I cannot hurt thee! Go and give me in charge—do what you will—I care nothing for what comes of me!'

(XXXVIII)

It is the events of this day and the next night and morning which at last bring about a moral crisis in Henchard. Up till now he has constantly been wavering between the best and the worst in his own nature; threatening to ruin Lucetta, and then finding that after all he can't do it; rejecting Elizabeth-Jane, and then softening. After he has threatened to kill Farfrae, he has one of these violent revulsions of feeling and tries to bring him back to see Lucetta before it is too late. But nobody will believe him now, and Lucetta dies:

Besides the watchman who called the hours and weather in Casterbridge that night there walked a figure up and down Corn Street hardly less frequently. It was Henchard's, whose retiring to rest had proved itself a futility as soon as attempted; and he gave it up to go hither and thither, and make inquiries about the patient every now and then. He called as much on Farfrae's account as on Lucetta's, and on Elizabeth-Jane's even more than on either's. Shorn one by one of all other interests, his life seemed centring on the personality of the stepdaughter whose presence but recently he could not endure. To see her on each occasion of his inquiry at Lucetta's was a comfort to him.

The last of his calls was made about four o'clock in the morning, in the steely light of dawn. Lucifer was fading into day across Durnover Moor, the sparrows were just alighting into the street, and the hens had begun to cackle from the outhouses. When within a few yards of Farfrae's he saw the door gently opened, and a servant raise her hand to the knocker, to untie the piece of cloth which had muffled it. He went across, the sparrows in his way scarcely flying up from the road-litter, so little did they believe in human aggression at so early a time.

'Why do you take off that?' said Henchard.

She turned in some surprise at his presence, and did not answer for an instant or two. Recognising him, she said, 'Because they may knock as loud as they will; she will never hear it any more.'

(XL)

This marvellous passage shows the beginning of a profound change in Henchard. Lucetta has faded out of life, almost as swiftly and silently as Susan did earlier; Farfrae is hopelessly alienated, and Elizabeth is the only channel for his affection, though this may not last, as her real father wants her back now. It is after he has told his futile lie to Newson that he goes out to drown himself in Ten Hatches

Weir. Then it seems as if an 'appalling miracle' has been worked to save him; he sees his own effigy floating in the water and this shocks him out of his plan, although it is only an accident:

> Despite this natural solution of the mystery Henchard no less regarded it as an intervention that the figure should have been floating there. Elizabeth-Jane heard him say, 'Who is such a reprobate as I? And yet it seems that even I be in Somebody's hand!'
>
> (XLI)

Of course, as Hardy says, this is not the real answer: 'The emotional conviction that he was in Somebody's hand began to die out of Henchard's breast as time slowly removed into distance the event which had given that feeling birth.' It is human, not divine love which Henchard wants, and he gets this for a short time and in a watered down form from Elizabeth-Jane. It cannot be more than that, for he has 'frozen up her precious affection when originally offered'. Economically things improve for him; his little seed and root shop is making a profit. But he doesn't want the shop without Elizabeth, and when he knows that she is about to find him out he leaves Casterbridge, dressed in working clothes as he was when he came there 'for the first time nearly a quarter of a century before'. Yet even after that he cannot keep far away from Elizabeth: 'O you fool! All this about a daughter who is no daughter of thine!'

At the same time that he has become conscious of his love for a girl who is, strictly speaking, nothing to him, he has lost his ambition. The world has become a 'mere painted scene to him', one which he wouldn't be sorry to leave:

> Very often, as his hay-knife crunched down among the sweet-smelling grassy stems, he would survey mankind and say to himself: 'Here and everywhere be folk dying before their time like frosted leaves, though wanted by their families, the country, and the world; while I, an outcast, an encumberer of the ground, wanted by nobody, and despised by all, live on against my will!'
>
> (XLIV)

Hardy is here using the traditional, biblical images of leaves and grass to express the vulnerability of human beings. Henchard is reaping the grass before its time, and death, too, has been visualized throughout the centuries as a Reaper who cuts off human lives in the same meaningless way. Henchard feels that he cannot die, because of the irony of things. But he does die before his time, and without any obvious reason; perhaps the truth is that he dies of a broken heart. When he comes back for Elizabeth's wedding he is made to feel, more than ever, that he is unwanted. Just as she and Farfrae once looked in from the outside at him, when he was the Mayor of Caster-bridge and presided at dinners in the King's Arms, so he is now the outsider looking in at them. Elizabeth's cold words are all he needs. Frozen out of Casterbridge, he goes out on to Egdon Heath, 'that ancient country whose surface never had been stirred to a finger's depth, save by the scratchings of rabbits, since brushed by the feet of the earliest tribes'. Once he is cut off from civilization, he dies.

Throughout the novel Hardy seems to be making the point that the only way to live in a community is not to ask for too much from it. Farfrae and Elizabeth-Jane can be happy because they have the knack of 'making limited opportunities endurable', through 'the cunning enlargement of those minute forms of satisfaction that offer themselves to everybody not in positive pain'; Henchard dies because he has no idea of how to do this. Yet the community which elects Farfrae as Mayor seems, like Farfrae himself, cold and narrow. In the end, the most compassionate person in Casterbridge is not Elizabeth but a half-witted labourer, Abel Whittle, and the way in which he cares for ·Henchard in the last days of his life shows up, though he doesn't know it, Elizabeth's moral failure.

Hardy continually stresses that man, like the leaves and grass, has only a short time on earth, and that everything he has worked for can be destroyed in a moment. In a cancelled passage, he shows the dying Mrs Henchard sitting in an avenue of trees on an autumn day, and talking to Lucetta.

> Old Solomon Longways, with a long white wooden rake, was scraping together the yellow, brown, and green leaves which had fallen, and heaping them into a deep wheelbarrow; they were insinuating visitors, those autumn leaves, sailing down the air into chimneys, green-houses, and roof gutters, even finding their way, in some mysterious manner, as far as the Town Pump.... Upon her shoulders, as upon his wife's, an occasional red leaf rested as it floated down.

The leaves symbolize the fragility of Mrs Henchard's life, even though they are real leaves, and realistically observed. And Hen-chard's commercial empire is equally fragile.

> Afterwards she was passing by the corn-stores and haybarns which had been the headquarters of his business. She knew that he ruled there no longer; but it was with amazement that she regarded the familiar gateway. A smear of decisive lead-coloured paint had been laid on to obliterate Henchard's name, though its letters dimly loomed through like ships in a fog. Over these, in fresh white, spread the name of Farfrae.

(XXXI)

The same theme of the blotting out of names is taken up again in chapter XXXIII, where Henchard makes the choir sing a psalm which is directly aimed at Farfrae:

A swift destruction soon shall seize
On his unhappy race;
And the next age his hated name
Shall utterly deface.

This is adapted from the Authorised Version: 'Let his posterity be cut off; and in the generation following let their name be blotted out' (Psalm 109, 13). It is exactly what happens to Henchard, for he leaves no posterity and his last wish is that his own name shall be forgotten:

'That Elizabeth-Jane Farfrae be not told of my death, or made to
    grieve on account of me.
'& that I be not bury'd in consecrated ground.
'& that no sexton be asked to toll the bell.
'& that nobody is wished to see my dead body.
'& that no murners walk behind me at my funeral.
'& that no flours be planted on my grave.
'& that no man remember me.'

(XLV)

In this Last Will and Testament, Henchard clearly rejects the pomp and ceremony which surround a mayor's funeral. And in doing this, he also rejects the ambition to which he has given twenty years of his life. In a world where life is necessarily short, and which is dominated by the values of industrial capitalism, Hardy suggests that the one thing which really matters is solidarity between people. Henchard knows that it is not enough to be a property owner, Justice of the Peace, and Mayor of Casterbridge; morally he is a changed man when he dies. And, strangely enough, the sailor's bastard daughter becomes the wife of the next Mayor. Elizabeth, narrow and rather prudish in the beginning, has also learned a good deal by the end of the novel, and it is only because of this, Hardy feels, that she has the right to be happy. For, in the future, she will be more compassionate than she was to Henchard. 'Her strong sense that neither she nor any human being deserved less than was given, did not blind her to the fact that there were others receiving less who had deserved much more.'

6 Selected Poems

Hardy's first book of verse, *Wessex Poems*, was published three years after his last novel, *Jude the Obscure*. For the remaining thirty years of his life he wrote nothing but poetry, and most of the best of his poems belong to these years. But in fact he had always thought of himself as a poet in the first instance, although he had written novels to earn a living:

> The change, after all, was not so great as it seemed. It was not as if he had been a writer of novels proper, and as more specifically understood, that is, stories of modern artificial life and manners showing a certain smartness of treatment. He had mostly aimed at keeping his narratives close to natural life and as near to poetry in their subject as the conditions would allow, and had often regretted that those conditions would not let him keep them nearer still.
>
> (*Life*, 291)

As he grew older he talked about his novels with a touch of contempt which many of his admirers found hard to understand. It seems that his novel-writing period held painful memories for him, partly because it involved mixing in society and the fear that he might be driven to writing 'society novels', partly because it had brought down so many attacks on his head:

> Poetry. Perhaps I can express more fully in verse ideas and emotions which run counter to the inert crystallised opinion—hard as a rock—which the vast body of men have vested interests in supporting. To cry out in a passionate poem that (for instance) the Supreme Mover or Movers, the Prime Force or Forces, must be either limited in power, unknowing, or cruel—which is obvious enough, and has been for centuries—will cause them merely a shake of the head; but to put it in argumentative prose will make them sneer, or foam, and set all the literary contortionists jumping upon me, a harmless agnostic, as if I were a clamorous atheist, which in their crass illiteracy they seem to think is the same thing. If Galileo had said in verse that the world moved, the Inquisition might have let him alone.
>
> (*Life*, 284–5)

Altogether nearly a thousand of his poems have survived (apart from *The Dynasts*), some written when he was a young man and many others when he was over eighty, for he kept on working almost to the end. It has never been easy for the critics to agree about these poems. His reputation has been growing steadily, but few of his admirers have read *everything* he wrote, and it is generally thought that the majority of these poems are negligible, apart from some twenty or thirty which can be called truly great. But although certain poems ('The Darkling Thrush', for example) have been praised by almost everybody, there is no general agreement about which are the best twenty.

It is possible to argue that nearly everything Hardy wrote can be read with profit. Indeed, Philip Larkin claims exactly this. He was a very versatile poet, experimenting with many different metres and almost as many different subjects, and, if we trace his development from youth to old age, we shall find many poems that are masterpieces and a good many so-called failures that are at least interesting.

Early poems

We noted in chapter 1 that, although Hardy wrote several poems as a young man, none was published until very much later. This was probably because he had no pull in London literary circles of that time, for they were at least as good as many others that got into print. Like most young poets, he began by imitating other people. Some of his 'Shakespearean' sonnets, later published in *Wessex Poems*, were not at all bad as imitations, and there is a still earlier poem, 'Domicilium', which shows very clearly the influence of Wordsworth. It is a description of his father's cottage, and is the earliest thing he is known to have written:

Domicilium

It faces west, and round the back and sides
High beeches, bending, hang a veil of boughs,
And sweep against the roof. Wild honeysucks
Climb on the walls, and seem to sprout a wish
(If we may fancy wish of trees and plants)
To overtop the apple-trees hard by.

Red roses, lilacs, variegated box
Are there in plenty, and such hardy flowers
As flourish best untrained. Adjoining these
Are herbs and esculents; and farther still
A field; then cottages with trees, and last
The distant hills and sky.

Behind, the scene is wilder. Heath and furze
Are everything that seems to grow and thrive
Upon the uneven ground. A stunted thorn
Stands here and there, indeed; and from a pit
An oak uprises, springing from a seed
Dropped by some bird a hundred years ago.

In days bygone—
Long gone—my father's mother, who is now
Blest with the blest, would take me out to walk.
At such a time I once inquired of her
How looked the spot when first she settled here.
The answer I remember. 'Fifty years
Have passed since then, my child, and change has marked
The face of all things. Yonder garden-plots
And orchards were uncultivated slopes
O'ergrown with bramble bushes, furze and thorn:
That road a narrow path shut in by ferns,
Which, almost trees, obscured the passer-by.

'Our house stood quite alone, and those tall firs
And beeches were not planted. Snakes and efts
Swarmed in the summer days, and nightly bats
Would fly about our bedrooms. Heathcroppers
Lived on the hills, and were our only friends;
So wild it was when first we settled here.'

DATE. Hardy tells us that this was written between 1857 and 1860, when he was a teenager and apprenticed to John Hicks. It is published in the *Life* (p. 4).

STYLE. Hardy himself calls this poem Wordsworthian, and indeed this is obvious. The blank verse he uses here is similar to that in *The Prelude* and 'Michael', and other early poems by Wordsworth, who died only a few years before Hardy began to write. Except in *The Dynasts*, he hardly ever used blank verse again. 'Domicilium' has the deliberate simplicity of many of Wordsworth's poems, as well as his occasional ponderous naïveté ('If we may fancy wish of trees and plants'); it also shares his preoccupation with nature. Like Wordsworth, Hardy grew up in a lonely place, where human beings seemed almost closer to the land than to each other, and although he did not go on imitating the older poet for much longer, his mind was to be coloured by many of the same images (see chapter 3). It may be added that Wordsworth, at least in his great period, would certainly have disapproved of a poet who called honeysuckles 'honeysucks'.

SUBJECT. The poem is almost straight description. It gives, Hardy said 'with obvious and naïve fidelity the appearance of the paternal homestead' (*Life*, 4). He builds up a good clear contrast between the cottage garden with its herbs and flowers and the uncultivated heath in the background, which once came right up to the house. This heath will be familiar to Hardy's readers. We hear about snakes, heathcroppers, and narrow paths 'shut in by ferns' in *The Return of the Native*, and also about the backbreaking work of reclaiming waste ground. We can also see in this poem the strong sense of history which Hardy showed in almost everything he wrote—the main description is of the heath fifty years before he was born, and oaks grow from a seed 'dropped by some bird a hundred years ago'. In the same way, Giles in *The Woodlanders* is interested in how the trees will grow fifty years after he dies. For a teenage boy this was a remarkable poem. It showed that he could not only master another poet's style, but also write good descriptive verse of his own, and with traces of what were later to become his characteristic ideas. Like most of Wordsworth's, this is a serene piece of writing. It is not just commonplace expressions like 'blest with the blest' which give it its calm and happy atmosphere; it is the whole conception of nature as a benevolently peaceful force and as one which can be humanized.

When we look at the poems which Hardy wrote in London a few years later, we find that his outlook had changed a good deal. By this time he would probably have thought that 'Domicilium' was sentimental. We know little about his emotional life during the London years, but it was probably not very happy. He had seen the extremes of poverty both in the countryside and in the city; he had also met prostitutes face to face. His political views had altered from Liberal to Radical, and his poetry had developed a sharp cutting edge. The next poem we look at, 'The Ruined Maid', is a disillusioned and angry one; very much the work of the young man who was soon to write *The Poor Man and the Lady*:

The Ruined Maid

'O 'Melia, my dear, this does everything crown!
Who could have supposed I should meet you in Town?
And whence such fair garments, such prosperi-ty?'—
'O didn't you know I'd been ruined?' said she.

—'You left us in tatters, without shoes or socks,
Tired of digging potatoes, and spudding up docks;
And now you've gay bracelets and bright feathers three!'—
'Yes: that's how we dress when we're ruined!' said she.

—'At home in the barton you said 'thee' and 'thou',
And 'thik oon' and 'theäs oon' and 't'other'; but now
Your talking quite fits 'ee for high compa-ny!'—
'Some polish is gained with one's ruin', said she.

—'Your hands were like paws then, your face blue and bleak
But now I'm bewitched by your delicate cheek,
And your little gloves fit as on any la-dy!'—
'We never do work when we're ruined', said she.

—'You used to call home-life a hag-ridden dream,
And you'd sigh, and you'd sock; but at present you seem
To know not of megrims or melancho-ly!'—
'True. One's pretty lively when ruined,' said she.

—'I wish I had feathers, a fine sweeping gown,
And a delicate face, and could strut about Town!'—
'My dear—a raw country girl, such as you be,
Cannot quite expect that. You ain't ruined,' said she.

                                                    (*CP*, 145)

DATE. This was written in 1866, but not published until some forty years afterwards, perhaps because Hardy's untypical treatment of this Victorian theme would have upset the Victorians too much.

STYLE. The slow, reflective blank verse of 'Domicilium' has been exchanged for the hard-hitting metre of the popular London ballads, the stress falling emphatically on the last word of each line. The *meaning*, in this poem, is given much more importance than the sound. It is also interesting as one of the few poems in which Hardy tries to reproduce the dialect of Wessex (he wrote another, the same year, called 'The Bride-Night Fire' *CP*, 63). We have already discussed the influence of William Barnes, who was then still living, and it is clear that Hardy was trying to imitate the style, if not the spirit, of his work at this time.

BACKGROUND. During his London years Hardy must have got used to the sight of prostitutes, resplendent in feathers and fine clothing, on every city street. He must also have known about the thousands of young girls who were leaving Dorset and the country districts to come up to 'Town', for it was always the girls who were the first to go. They despised the young men who stayed to work on the land, and they wanted a more exciting and colourful life. Some of them went into 'service' or into the factories; some, inevitably, drifted into being what the Victorians called 'fallen women'. This is the background to the dialogue between the 'raw country girl' who has just come to London to seek her fortune and her friend, 'Melia, the 'ruined maid'. ('Maid' is simply the Dorset dialect word for 'girl', but of course it carries associations of purity and innocence.)

SUBJECT. The girl from the country speaks in broad Dorset; she has been used to working in the 'barton' (farmyard) and grubbing up potatoes and weeds. 'Melia, on the other hand, is elegant, idle, and expensively dressed. It is because she could not stand the kind of life the other girl describes so vividly that she has become a prostitute; Hardy was always scathing about people who supposed that life in the villages was all a matter of roses round the cottage door. In this poem he explores the situation with considerable wit and gaiety, very unlike the majority of writers who showed prostitutes as doomed, tragic figures, who could never recover from the loss of their innocence. And he poses some interesting questions. Is it not better to live luxuriously as a 'fallen woman' than to exist 'in tatters, without shoes or socks', as 'Melia did on the farm? Will the other girl, too, elect to be a 'ruined maid' when she has learned a bit more?

CONCLUSION. We need not suppose that this poem is quite as subversive of orthodox Victorian morality as it may at first sound. Hardy did believe that a woman who sold her body was, in a very real sense, 'ruined'; when Tess Durbeyfield finally consents to live with Alec he shows that it is because she no longer cares what becomes of her; that she has traded her identity as a human being for a life of leisure and fine clothes. But for her, as for the heroine of this poem, it was a choice between that and a lifetime spent 'digging potatoes, and spudding up docks'. One cannot blame these girls, Hardy appears to be saying. It is society which has made them like this.

Hardy's black period

During his years as a novelist Hardy went on writing poems, but few of them are among his greatest. In the black period which followed the publication of *Jude the Obscure* he turned exclusively to poetry again, and the bitterness of the years 1895–6 is crystallized in two of the longer poems, 'In Tenebris' and 'Wessex Heights'. The first of these is a group of three poems, apparently loosely related, but sharing a common feeling of pain, loneliness and deprivation.

In Tenebris

'Percussus sum sicut foenum, et aruit cor meum.'

Wintertime nighs;
But my bereavement-pain
It cannot bring again:
Twice no one dies.

Flower-petals flee;
But, since it once hath been,
No more that severing scene
Can harrow me.

Birds faint in dread:
I shall not lose old strength
In the lone frost's black length:
Strength long since fled!

Leaves freeze to dun;
But friends can not turn cold
This season as of old
For him with none.

Tempests may scath;
But love can not make smart
Again this year his heart
Who no heart hath.

Black is night's cope;
But death will not appal
One who, past doubtings all,
Waits in unhope.

(*CP*, 153)

DATE. This was probably written in 1895, but was not published until 1902.

STYLE. This is one of Hardy's most perfect lyrics, in spite of the fact that it is so dark in feeling. The very short lines emphasize the feeling of starkness (what could be more abrupt and factual than 'Wintertime nighs'?) which is powerfully brought home in the last line of each verse. Hardy seems to be raising a series of moderately hopeful images, only to dash them. He will not lose his strength or his friends because he no longer has any; he does not suffer from doubt because he has no hope. Each verse is a self-contained unit which goes through a dialectical process; nature is bleak; this does not frighten the poet, because, and here the shock comes, things are bleaker within his own soul.

IMAGERY. 'In Tenebris' means 'in the darkness', and the Latin motto from Psalm 102 means, 'My heart is smitten, and withered like grass'. These images of darkness and of the death of nature are repeated all the way through the poem. Frost, and of course night, is 'black'; flowers and leaves die and birds 'faint in dread'. And, as argued in the chapter on *The Mayor of Casterbridge*, leaves and grass are a symbol of the frailty of human beings; Hardy tells us in the first verse that someone has died and the 'severing scene' in the next verse may be the same thing, or may refer to his estrangement from his wife.

CONCLUSION. There seems to be no chink of hope in this poem, and indeed the climactic word 'unhope' (one of the eccentric constructions which Hardy was fond of) deliberately rules it out. The speaker is only not suffering because his heart is dried up and he can suffer no more. But to print this poem in isolation, as is sometimes done, gives a wrong impression. It has to be seen as part of the whole cycle.

In Tenebris II

'Considerabam ad dexteram, et videbam; et non erat qui
    cognosceret me.
Non est qui requirat animam meam.'

When the clouds' swoln bosoms echo back the shouts of
    the many and strong
That things are all as they best may be, save a few to be
    right ere long,
And my eyes have not the vision in them to discern what to
    these is so clear,
The blot seems straightway in me alone; one better he
    were not here.

The stout upstanders say, All's well with us: ruers have
    nought to rue!
And what the potent say so oft, can it fail to be somewhat
    true?
Breezily go they, breezily come; their dust smokes around
    their career,
Till I think I am one born out of due time, who has no
    calling here.

Their dawns bring lusty joys, it seems; their evenings all
    that is sweet;
Our times are blessed times, they cry: Life shapes it as is
    most meet,
And nothing is much the matter; there are many smiles to
    a tear;
Then what is the matter is I, I say. Why should such a one
    be here?

Let him in whose ears the low-voiced Best is killed by the
   clash of the First,
Who holds that if way to the Better there be, it exacts a full
   look at the Worst,
Who feels that delight is a delicate growth cramped by
   crookedness, custom and fear,
Get him up and be gone as one shaped awry; he disturbs
   the order here.

(CP, 154)

DATE. Hardy dated this poem 1895–6. The motto, from Psalm 142, is:
'I looked on my right hand, and beheld, but there was no man that
would know me. No man cared for my soul.'

STYLE. This poem is written in a completely different way from the
first part of 'In Tenebris'. It is not just a matter of very long lines
rather than very short ones; the whole method is different. Instead
of dramatizing his feelings through a series of poetic images, Hardy
tries to argue them out in the form of a dialogue with those who see a
different world from the one that he sees. He also gives us some idea,
in this second poem, of why he is suffering, and it is from a much
more complex cause than bereavement.

SUBJECT. There cannot be much doubt about what Hardy is describing: the reception of *Jude the Obscure* and the way he and his ideas
were abused. This might not have been very painful for someone
who enjoyed controversy and could give back as good as he got; for
Hardy, who was not like that at all, the whole experience was a
nightmare. Having tried to write an honest novel about what seemed
to him to be universal problems, he found himself abused on all
sides as morbid. The ideas which Hardy expresses in this poem have
been discussed at length in Chapter 3. It will be seen that the
poet is not saying that the world is necessarily a bad place; merely
that evils do exist and always have done since the earliest times (the
'clash of the First' refers to the biblical legend in which Abel is killed
by Cain). 'Delight' again, is by no means impossible, but it is 'a
delicate growth cramped by crookedness, custom, and fear'. This
means that people will have to struggle for it if they want to get it,
and that, in certain social conditions, they may fail. If one thinks of
the prejudices and the outworn conventions which ruin people's lives
in *Jude the Obscure* and *Tess of the d'Urbervilles* one begins to understand
what he means. Hardy is asking that human beings should be honest
about the imperfect state of the world they live in, rather than insisting
(as many of the brasher Victorians did) that everything was for the
best in the best of all possible worlds. He was always upset when he
was accused of being unnecessarily gloomy. In later years he often
quoted the line 'if way to the Better there be, it exacts a full look at the

Worst', as a truer statement of his feelings, and in the Preface to *Late Lyrics and Earlier*, published in 1922, he said that his philosophy could be called 'evolutionary meliorism'. But in spite of his own clear statements, the myth that Hardy was an incurable pessimist persists to this day.

In Tenebris III

'Heu mihi, quia incolatus meus prolongatus est! Habitavi cum habitantibus Cedar; multum incola fuit anima mea.'

There have been times when I well might have passed and the
    ending have come –
Points in my path when the dark might have stolen on me, artless,
    unrueing —
Ere I had learnt that the world was a welter of futile doing:
Such had been times when I well might have passed, and the
    ending have come!

Say, on the noon when the half-sunny hours told that April was
    nigh,
And I upgathered and cast forth the snow from the crocus-border,
Fashioned and furbished the soil into a summer-seeming order,
Glowing in gladsome faith that I quickened the year thereby.

Or on that loneliest of eves when afar and benighted we stood,
She who upheld me and I, in the midmost of Egdon together,
Confident I in her watching and ward through the blackening
    heather,
Deeming her matchless in might and with measureless scope
    endued.

Or on that winter-wild night when, reclined by the chimney-nook
    quoin,
Slowly a drowse overgat me, the smallest and feeblest of folk there,
Weak from my baptism of pain; when at times and anon I awoke
    there –
Heard of a world wheeling on, with no listing or longing to join.

Even then! while unweeting that vision could vex or that knowledge
    could numb,
That sweets to the mouth in the belly are bitter, and dark, and
    untoward,
Then, on some dim-coloured scene should my briefly raised curtain
    have lowered,
Then might the Voice that is law have said 'Cease!' and the
    ending have come.

(CP, 155)

DATE. 1896. The motto is translated in the Authorized Version of Psalm 120 as, 'Woe is me that I sojourn in Mesech, that I dwell in the tents of Kedar! My soul hath long dwelt with him that hateth peace.'

STYLE. In this third part of the poem Hardy adopts a third kind of rhythm to express what he wants to say. The very long and slowly moving lines help to create the mood of the poem, which is reminiscent, elegiac and sad. It is an impressive piece of work, but the language has certain faults. Hardy had a weakness for archaic words like 'overgat' (overcame), and 'unweeting' (unknowing), which still makes parts of his work, and especially his poetry, difficult to read. The alliteration is too obvious in places; 'winter-wild' is a beautiful construction but 'glowing in gladsome faith' and 'matchless in might and with measureless scope endued' sound artificial and forced. The best lines are the very simple ones where the words are all short and natural, 'Such had been times when I well might have passed, and the ending have come!'

SUBJECT. This is very different from the first part of 'In Tenebris', a brief lyrical statement on one man's condition, and from the second part, which, however sad in its tone, is still *arguing*, still defending a position. This is a 'dim-coloured' poem, which makes few direct statements, merely guides the reader back gradually into the past. Hardy is looking back at the times when he might have died as a child (as many did). Almost certainly he was thinking of how he was left for dead as a baby, and also about how for many years he was a small and very frail boy—'weak from my baptism of pain'. It might have been better to have died then because he would not have discovered the full suffering and complexity which is involved in being an adult—when he says that 'knowledge could numb' he is referring to the pain of having to *think*, which seemed to him and to so many other Victorians to force on him an intolerable weight of responsibility. Neither in this poem, nor in the *Life*, does he pretend that his childhood was always happy, but at least, he seems to be saying, it offered him security of a kind. It was rather like being able to sit by the fire while the winter winds were raging outside. A small child can derive a real joy from helping to cultivate a garden, because it seems to him that he can control his environment with no real effort, 'glowing in gladsome faith that I quickened the year thereby'. In the same way, he notes that he did not mind being stranded on Egdon Heath after dark, because he was with his mother who 'upheld' him—and, to a child, the mother seems all-powerful. But now he cannot rely on anyone to guide him through the world, which he has come to see as 'a darkling plain', where each man is alone. He is not *wishing* that he had died at that time; he is simply reflecting on the infinite uncertainty of human life and considering how much more complex his own life has become since he was a child.

CONCLUSION. The third part of 'In Tenebris' has affinities with some of Hardy's other poems. 'To an Unborn Pauper Child' describes his fears for the future of a child which is going to be born into poverty, his desire to protect it, and his unhappiness in realizing that the child which has no knowledge of the world as yet will eventually have to find out what suffering is. 'The Oxen' is about his childish belief that the animals went on their knees on Christmas Eve, and more importantly how he wishes that he could believe in it still.

As was said above, 'In Tenebris' (whose sections seem to have been written at different times) is not totally unified. The first part belongs with the best of Hardy's short poems, which are more important for their lyricism than for their meaning; the second and third parts are very closely related to Hardy's thinking on pessimism and agnosticism. They can usefully be read with the discussion of this subject in Chapter 3.

Hardy wrote one more great poem during his black period:

Wessex Heights

There are some heights in Wessex, shaped as if by a kindly
    hand
For thinking, dreaming, dying on, and at crises when I stand,
Say, on Ingpen Beacon eastward, or on Wylls-Neck westwardly,
I seem where I was before my birth, and after death may be.

In the lowlands I have no comrade, not even the lone
    man's friend—
Her who suffereth long and is kind; accepts what he is too
    weak to mend:
Down there they are dubious and askance; there nobody
    thinks as I,
But mind-chains do not clank where one's next neighbour
    is the sky.

In the towns I am tracked by phantoms having weird
      detective ways—
Shadows of beings who fellowed with myself of earlier days:
They hang about at places, and they say harsh heavy
      things—
Men with a wintry sneer, and women with tart disparagings.

Down there I seem to be false to myself, my simple self that
      was,
And is not now, and I see him watching, wondering what
      crass cause
Can have merged him into such a strange continuator as this,
Who yet has something in common with himself, my
      chrysalis.

I cannot go to the great grey Plain; there's a figure against
      the moon,
Nobody sees it but I, and it makes my breast beat out of tune;
I cannot go to the tall-spired town, being barred by the
      forms now passed
For everybody but me, in whose long vision they stand
      there fast.

There's a ghost at Yell'ham Bottom chiding loud at the
      fall of the night,
There's a ghost in Froom-side Vale, thin-lipped and vague,
      in a shroud of white,
There is one in the railway train whenever I do not want
      it near,
I see its profile against the pane, saying what I would not
      hear.

As for one rare fair woman, I am now but a thought of hers,
I enter her mind and another thought succeeds me that
      she prefers;
Yet my love for her in its fullness she herself even did not
      know;
Well, time cures hearts of tenderness, and now I can let her
      go.

So I am found on Ingpen Beacon, or on Wylls-Neck to the
      west,
Or else on homely Bulbarrow, or little Pilsdon Crest,
Where men have never cared to haunt, nor women have
      walked with me,
And ghosts then keep their distance; and I know some
      liberty.

                                   (CP, 300)

DATE. 1896. Hardy did not publish it until many years afterwards.

GEOGRAPHY. The heights which Hardy names all stand in different parts of 'Wessex'. Ingpen Beacon is near Basingstoke, Wylls-Neck in Somerset, and Bulbarrow and Pilsdon in Dorset. The 'tall-spired town' is Salisbury (Hardy's Melchester) and 'the great grey plain' may be either Salisbury Plain or Egdon Heath.

REFERENCES. J.O. Bailey (in *The Poetry of Thomas Hardy*) has conjectured that 'the forms now passed' who bar the poet from going to Salisbury may be the long-dead church officials who (it is said) prevented him from studying theology there. According to Florence Hardy, all the people mentioned in the poem were actual women. They cannot all be identified with any certainty, but one of the ghosts in the sixth verse may be that of Tryphena Sparks. It seems definite that the 'one rare fair woman' who never knew how much Hardy loved her was Mrs Florence Henniker, whom he had met and been deeply attracted to three years before.

STYLE. Again Hardy uses the long reflective line to create the mood of this poem. Although some parts are difficult to understand immediately, the poem has always had a strong appeal, perhaps because it describes emotions which are almost universal.

SUBJECT. ' "Wessex Heights" will *always* wring my heart,' Florence Hardy wrote, soon after she married the poet, 'for I know when it was written, a little while after the publication of *Jude*, when he was so cruelly treated.' 1896 was the year when *Jude the Obscure* was being attacked in every newspaper in the country, and when Hardy was literally afraid to go out of doors in case he was stopped and abused for writing an immoral book. We can see how bitter this experience was when we read the third verse of 'Wessex Heights', where he feels that he is being followed about by ghostly detectives:

> They hang about at places, and they say harsh heavy things—
> Men with a wintry sneer, and women with tart disparagings.

'In the towns' he is tormented by the feeling that everybody is watching him, and that he is hopelessly different from other people. 'Nobody thinks as I'—he had discovered this when his novel was published, and it made him feel that his critics (like those in 'In Tenebris II') were wearing 'mind-chains' which made them unable to break with their preconceived ideas. He is desperately lonely. He has no friends at all—not even his wife, it's worth noting—and indeed we know now that Emma had tried to suppress *Jude* and that their marriage had become impossible by the time Hardy

'Homely Bulbarrow' near Blandford, one of Hardy's favourite heights.

wrote 'Wessex Heights'. But he is not only at odds with other people, but also with himself:

> Down there I seem to be false to myself, my simple self that was,
> And is not now, and I see him watching, wondering what crass cause
> Can have merged him into such a strange continuator as this,
> Who yet has something in common with himself, my chrysalis.

Perhaps these are the most interesting lines in the poem, for they reveal that Hardy was very often a prey to inward guilts and tensions, the feeling that he had been 'false to himself'. On the Wessex hills, which had been familiar to him since his earliest childhood, he may indeed have felt that his life had developed in all the wrong ways. He had made the wrong marriage, got into the wrong social set, and spent the greater part of his life doing uncongenial work. His 'simple self' which had known of nothing better than life in Wessex must have seemed very far removed from what he had become.

'I will lift up mine eyes to the hills, from whence cometh my help', says a Psalm which Hardy knew very well. It seemed to him, during the crises in his life, that if he could get away on to the hills 'where one's next neighbour is the sky' his real values would come back into perspective. It was not that he disliked other people, as this poem may suggest at a first reading, but he did very often feel the need to escape from a society with which he was deeply out of sympathy. His work shows time and again that, like Wordsworth, and like his own hero, Clym Yeobright, he found that nature could be a soothing and strengthening force.

POSTSCRIPT. It is worth noting that some of the images in this poem are very like the images in *Jude the Obscure*, which of course had only been written a short time before. There are several places, 'in the lowlands,' where Hardy literally finds it too painful to go. Jude has the same fear of reviving memories, 'We mustn't go to Alfredston, or to Melchester, or to Shaston, or to Christminster' (V, vi). Like Jude when he first enters Christminster, Hardy is surrounded by 'phantoms' which appear more real to him than solid flesh-and-blood people. 'I am neither a dweller among men nor ghosts', Jude says (VI, ix), and Hardy in 'Wessex Heights' has the same feeling. In the line, 'I seem where I was before my birth, and after death may be', he looks forward to becoming a disembodied spirit himself.

Turn of the century poems

As we have seen, Hardy turned exclusively to poetry after the attacks on his last novel, and this was not only because he had always preferred this particular art form but also because he hoped to be able to 'express more fully in verse ideas and emotions which run counter to the inert crystallised opinion—hard as a rock—which the vast body of men have vested interests in supporting'. On the whole he was happy to have made the change; he quickly became recognized as a distinguished poet, and in any case the climate of opinion was becoming more tolerant as the old century gave way to the new. But he did not always escape criticism when he included heterodox ideas in his poems. In 1907 he had great difficulty in publishing a narrative poem, 'A Sunday Morning Tragedy', which tells the story of a girl who tries to procure an abortion and dies. He wrote this without any thought of sensationalism, for he had been worried by the growth of this practice and the 'false shame' which led to it, but every magazine in London refused to publish the poem on the now familiar grounds that they had to think of their subscribers. But Hardy was finding friends by this time, and a group of literary men, including Ford Madox Ford, founded the *English Review* on purpose to print it.

Three poems are studied in this section; one of them very popular, two rather unpopular, and in each case this can be traced back to their uplifting, or subversive, views. In the case of the little group of poems he wrote about the South African War (1899–1902), Hardy was fairly conscious of writing from a minority point of view. Most people in England approved of the sending of British troops to fight the Boers or Dutch settlers; Hardy was much more doubtful about the ultimate wisdom of hanging on to the Empire. Afterwards, he was able to write about these poems, 'I am happy to say that not a single one is Jingo or Imperial—a fatal defect according to the judgment of the British majority at present, I dare say' (letter to Florence Henniker, printed in *One Rare Fair Woman*, ed. Evelyn Hardy and F.B. Pinion, 1972). He refused to glorify the troops, as so many hack writers were doing; instead he wrote out of a deep sense of what a younger poet, Wilfred Owen, was later to call 'the pity of war'.

A Christmas Ghost-Story

South of the Line, inland from far Durban,
A mouldering soldier lies—your countryman.
Awry and doubled up are his grey bones,
And on the breeze his puzzled phantom moans
Nightly to clear Canopus, 'I would know
By whom and when the All-Earth-gladdening law
Of Peace, brought in by that Man Crucified,
Was ruled to be inept, and set aside?
And what of logic or of truth appears
In tacking 'Anno Domini' to the years?
Near twenty-hundred liveried thus have hied,
But tarries yet the cause for which He died.'

(*CP*, 82)

DATE. This was dated Christmas Eve 1899, and appeared in the *Westminster Gazette* on the previous day. The incongruity between war and Christmas seems to have been the germ of the poem in Hardy's mind. In the original version only the first eight lines appeared; the last four were written afterwards.

STYLE. This is a dramatic poem and one which is meant to shock the reader—the second line is a distinctly startling one and the couplets, with their heavy stress on the last syllable, reinforce the impression that the poet wants to make people *think*. At the same time the poem is not merely an argument, but also a very beautiful and haunting conception. Hardy uses the method of the classical poets and Dante in making ghosts speak to the living to warn them; it was a method which was also to be used by poets about the Great War.

SUBJECT. There is nothing romantic in the way Hardy writes. The soldier is 'mouldering'; his bones are twisted and grey. We are made to feel the full ugliness of death before we get to the poem's message, that the so-called Christian nations are utterly hypocritical in their attitude to war. We use the label 'Anno Domini'—in the year of the Lord—yet, nearly two thousand years after Christ, there is no peace on earth. This was a point often made by Tolstoy, who, like Hardy, had mixed feelings about the Christian Church.

POSTSCRIPT. An ultra-patriotic newspaper editor attacked the poem for its pacifism, and accused Hardy of not saying anything about the soldier's courage. Hardy replied in a letter that a ghost could not be expected to be patriotic, 'His views are no longer local; nations are all one to him; his country is not bounded by seas, but is co-extensive with the globe itself, if it does not even include all the inhabited planets of the sky' (*PW*, 201). It can be seen from the section on Hardy's politics in chapter 3 that this was the only kind of patriotism which he really admired. The ghost, like the one in Owen's 'Strange Meeting', is disembodied, unhappy, and puzzled about why it has died. Being 'south of the Line' (the Equator) it lies under one of the southern stars, Canopus. The soldier is 'your countryman', and yet Hardy manages to suggest that he is infinitely far away, and *different*, from the people who read about him in newspapers in England.

In the following year Hardy wrote a very different kind of poem;

The Darkling Thrush

I leant upon a coppice gate
    When Frost was spectre-gray,
And Winter's dregs made desolate
    The weakening eye of day.
The tangled bine-stems scored the sky
    Like strings of broken lyres,
And all mankind that haunted nigh
    Had sought their household fires.

The land's sharp features seemed to be
    The Century's corpse outleant,
His crypt the cloudy canopy,
    The wind his death-lament.
The ancient pulse of germ and birth
    Was shrunken hard and dry,
And every spirit upon earth
    Seemed fervourless as I.

At once a voice arose among
    The bleak twigs overhead
In a full-hearted evensong
    Of joy illimited;
An aged thrush, frail, gaunt, and small,
    In blast-beruffled plume,
Had chosen thus to fling his soul
    Upon the growing gloom.

So little cause for carolings
    Of such ecstatic sound
Was written on terrestrial things
    Afar or nigh around,
That I could think there trembled through
    His happy good-night air
Some blessed Hope, whereof he knew
    And I was unaware.

(*CP*, 137)

DATE. This poem was first published in the last days of 1900, under the title 'By the Century's Deathbed'.

STYLE AND LITERARY BACKGROUND. Nobody else could conceivably have written this poem, yet it owes a good deal to two masterpieces by the younger Romantics, Keats's 'Ode to a Nightingale' and

Shelley's 'To a Skylark'. Hardy knew both these poems well, and 'The Darkling Thrush' is written from the same point of view. In all three poems, the bird's song reveals a new, mysterious and joyful world to the poet, who is deeply unhappy and dissatisfied with the world as it is. Keats, listening to the nightingale, wishes to 'leave the world unseen/And with thee fade away into the forest dim',

> Fade far away, dissolve, and quite forget
> What thou among the leaves hast never known,
> The weariness, the fever, and the fret,
> Here, where men sit and hear each other groan;
> Where palsy shakes a few, sad, last gray hairs,
> Where youth grows pale, and spectre-thin, and dies;
> Where but to think is to be full of sorrow
> And leaden-eyed despairs;
> Where Beauty cannot keep her lustrous eyes,
> Or new Love pine at them beyond tomorrow.

Shelley also feels that the skylark is living in a much happier state than human beings can ever reach:

> Yet if we could scorn
> Hate, and pride, and fear;
> If we were things born
> Not to shed a tear,
> I know not how thy joy we ever should come near.

Unhappiness, a feeling of deadness and desolation, is the point from which Hardy begins 'The Darkling Thrush'. The first two verses show a landscape on a winter evening, which mirrors the 'fervourless' state of the poet's mind. In the third verse, and quite unexpectedly, he suddenly hears the thrush 'fling his soul/ Upon the growing gloom'. The language is similar to that of Keats, who imagines the nightingale 'pouring forth thy soul abroad/In such an ecstasy' (the thrush is 'ecstatic' too). Yet the overall impression of this poem is quite different from that of Keat's, or Shelley's. Shelley imagines the singing bird as a 'blithe spirit', 'an unbodied joy', or 'a star of heaven in the broad daylight' (it is significant that he cannot actually *see* it). The nightingale in the Keats ode is also invisible, an ethereal being which was 'not born for death'. Both of them seem unaware that this marvellous music actually comes from a little, ordinary bird. Hardy, on the other hand, can see the bird clearly:

> An aged thrush, frail, gaunt, and small,
> In blast-beruffled plume.

This bird obviously *is* born for death. It is old, frail, and knocked about by the winter winds, yet this does not destroy the core of happiness which makes it sing.

Although, as we noted, some expressions in this poem (including the word 'darkling') were suggested by the Keats ode, this is a deliberately plain and simple piece of work which keeps well clear of the 'poetic' imagery used by the two earlier writers. 'I leant upon a coppice-gate' is so very different, as an opening line, from 'Hail to thee, blithe spirit!' This is characteristic of Hardy's writing. 'For as long as I can remember,' he wrote to Edmund Gosse in 1919, 'it has been my instinctive feeling to avoid the jewelled line in poetry, as being effeminate.'

SUBJECT. We know that the 1890s were a bad time for Hardy, with the attacks on his last two novels and the breakdown of his marriage (and if we didn't know, we could guess it from 'In Tenebris' and 'Wessex Heights'). He must also have felt that the nineteenth century had been a time of terrible human suffering (he had only just finished writing a series of poems about the South African war). Of course this tended to make him feel that the only way to live without being hurt was in a state of 'unhope'. In this frame of mind he becomes aware of the thrush, which is singing joyfully as the landscape grows darker, although there is no apparent reason:

> So little cause for carolings
> Of such ecstatic sound
> Was written on terrestrial things
> Afar or nigh around.

The thrush, then, seems to know about 'some blessed Hope' of which the poet is 'unaware'. Some critics have thought that this 'blessed Hope' must be God. Perhaps, but then Hardy had always believed that human life contained hopeful elements (this poem is never cited by those who call him a pessimist). He had shown how the same thing happened to Tess Durbeyfield, after her 'fall': 'Some spirit within her rose automatically as the sap in the twigs. It was unexpended youth, surging up anew after its temporary check, and bringing with it hope, and the invincible instinct towards self-delight' (XV). It is this 'invincible instinct towards self-delight' which makes the thrush sing, just as it makes the sap rise (Hardy describes how 'the ancient pulse of germ and birth/Was shrunken hard and dry', but we can scarcely doubt that, in spring, it will begin all over again. Hardy's point seems to be that the bleakest of lives can still offer sources of happiness, even if this is only the song of an elderly thrush.

POSTSCRIPT. This has become one of the most popular poems that Hardy ever wrote.

New Year's Eve

'I have finished another year,' said God,
'In grey, green, white, and brown;
I have strewn the leaf upon the sod,
Sealed up the worm within the clod,
And let the last sun down.'

'And what's the good of it?' I said;
'What reasons made you call
From formless void this earth we tread,
When nine-and-ninety can be read
Why nought should be at all?

'Yea, Sire; why shaped you us, "who in
This tabernacle groan"—
If ever a joy be found herein,
Such joy no man had wished to win
If he had never known!'

Then he: 'My labours—logicless—
You may explain; not I:
Sense-sealed I have wrought, without a guess
That I evolved a Consciousness
To ask for reasons why.

'Strange that ephemeral creatures who
By my own ordering are,
Should see the shortness of my view,
Use ethic tests I never knew,
Or made provision for!'

He sank to raptness as of yore,
And opening New Year's Day
Wove it by rote as heretofore,
And went on working evermore
In his unweeting way.

(*CP*, 260)

DATE. First published in January 1907, probably written late in 1906.

STYLE. The first verse is the best in this poem, with its startling opening line and its lovely evocation of the coming of winter, painted in the colours of the English countryside—'grey, green, white and brown' —and of 'the last sun'. It has an easy conversational movement and a simplicity of language which is lost as the poem goes on. ' "I have finished another year," said God', is ordinary English (however surprising it may sound!); so is, ' "And what's the good of it?" I said.' But the third verse is written in Hardy's most elaborate style ('Yea,

148

Sire, why shaped you us') and much of the rest of the poem sounds forced. Words like 'herein', 'as of yore', 'heretofore', 'evermore', and 'unweeting' are examples of the unnatural language which he used too often.

SUBJECT. This is one of several poems in which Hardy deeply shocked the conventional Christians of his time. The speaker is called 'God', and it was a daring idea to write a dialogue between God and the poet in which the poet distinctly comes off better. But this is not a God of love, or one who is closely involved with his creation. His job is to keep the universe ticking over:

> I have strewn the leaf upon the sod,
> Sealed up the worm within the clod,
> And let the last sun down.

He has, apparently, no other interests.

The poet asks God to explain the problem of pain—why human beings are forced to suffer in what the Bible calls 'this tabernacle of flesh'. But God has no answer. He is 'sense-sealed', that is, he only cares about the processes of nature, not the spiritual struggles of human beings (an extraordinary thing, incidentally, to say about God). Perhaps it would be easier to understand this poem if Hardy had called this God *Nature*. He is obviously thinking in terms of a force which keeps the universe going, but which is not conscious or moral, and which, of course, would not be capable of holding a conversation with an individual man!

Hardy often said that he thought the cause of things was 'neither moral nor immoral, but *unmoral*'; at times he went further and imagined a God who resembled a sleepwalker. Sue in *Jude the Obscure* speculates that 'the First Cause worked automatically like a somnambulist, and not reflectively like a sage'.

POSTSCRIPT. Many years later the Catholic poet Alfred Noyes accused Hardy of visualizing a God who enjoyed tormenting human beings, and cited this poem among others to prove his point. Hardy said that he had never believed any such thing, and that 'New Year's Eve' and other poems like it were merely 'fanciful impressions of the moment' (*Life*, 409).

Poems to Emma

Hardy did not write many poems about his first wife until after she died. The shock made his mind go back forty years into the past, to when he had first met her in Cornwall, and, in a sense, he fell in love with her all over again. He went back to see the places they had visited when she was living in St Juliot, and the scenery brought her back very vividly to his mind:

149

Yes: I have re-entered your olden haunts at last;
Through the years, through the dead scenes I have
    tracked you;
What have you now found to say of our past—
Scanned across the dark space wherein I have lacked you?
Summer gave us sweets, but autumn wrought division?
Things were not lastly as firstly well
With us twain, you tell?
But all's closed now, despite Time's derision.

This is a verse from 'After a Journey', one of the finest of the *Poems
of 1912–13*. He seemed to see Emma's ghost in the lonely countryside
of Cornwall, telling him mutely that the years of division had all
been a mistake:

Woman much missed, how you call to me, call to me,
Saying that now you are not as you were
When you had changed from the one who was all to me,
    But as at first, when our day was fair.

'The Voice'

Most of these poems refer to what in another place he called 'our
deep division, and our dark undying pain' ('Had you Wept'). One
of the few which treats this division as if it had not happened is
'Beeny Cliff', which is also one of the best and most immediately
accessible:

Beeny Cliff

I

O the opal and the sapphire of that wandering western sea,
And the woman riding high above with bright hair
    flapping free—
The woman whom I loved so, and who loyally loved me.

II

The pale mews plained below us, and the waves seemed
    far away
In a nether sky, engrossed in saying their ceaseless
    babbling say,
As we laughed light-heartedly aloft on that clear-sunned
    March day.

III

A little cloud then cloaked us, and there flew an irised rain,
And the Atlantic dyed its levels with a dull misfeatured
    stain,
And then the sun burst out again, and purples prinked the
    main.

IV

—Still in all its chasmal beauty bulks old Beeny to the sky,
And shall she and I not go there once again now March is
    nigh,
And the sweet things said in that March say anew there
    by and by?

V

What if still in chasmal beauty looms that wild weird
    western shore,
The woman now is—elsewhere—whom the ambling pony
    bore,
And nor knows nor cares for Beeny, and will laugh there
    nevermore.

(*CP*, 330)

DATE. The poem is subtitled 'March 1870–March 1913'. The subject is two March days, the first in 1870 when Hardy and Emma went to the cliff together, and the second, forty-three years later, when he went back there alone.

PLACE. Beeny Cliff, also known as the Cliff Without a Name, is a few miles from the village of St Juliot. Hardy walked there with Emma while she rode her pony. In his notebook he described the scene:

> Beeny Cliff . . . green towards the land, blue-black towards the sea. Every ledge has a little, starved, green grass upon it: all vertical parts bare. Seaward, a dark-grey ocean beneath a pale green sky, upon which lie branches of red cloud. A lather of foam around the base of each rock. The sea is full of motion internally, but still as a whole. Quiet and silent in the distance, noisy and restless close at hand. (*Thomas Hardy's Notebooks*, 38)

Emma has left her own description of their courtship:

> Scarcely any author and his wife could have had a much more romantic meeting, with its unusual circumstances in bringing them together from two different, though neighbouring counties to this one at this very remote spot, with a beautiful sea-coast, and the wild Atlantic Ocean rolling in with its magnificent waves and spray, its white gulls, and black choughs and grey puffins, its cliffs and rocks and gorgeous sunsettings, sparkling redness in a track widening from the horizon to the shore. All this should be seen in the winter to be truly appreciated. No summer visitors can have a true idea of its power to awaken heart and soul. It was an unforgettable experience to me, scampering up and down the hills on my beloved mare alone, wanting no protection, the rain going down my back often, and my hair floating on the wind. (*Life*, 69)

STYLE. This is one of the most lyrical of Hardy's poems. Here he does not 'avoid the jewelled line', as was his normal practice (he even uses the names of jewels to evoke the mood of the first line) and the alliteration, and the very simple verse form, make it a more traditional, even a more 'Victorian' poem than he usually wrote.

SUBJECT. The subject also is very simple; the contrast between 'then' and 'now'. The first three verses are all set in the past. The brilliant word pictures here make us *see* the cliff, the spring sunshine and the fair-haired girl on her pony, pictures which have shone in the poet's memory for over forty years. They give a clear impression of how happy and easy everything seems for the young lovers. Even the rain only lasts for a few minutes. Emma is riding 'high above' the cliff and the sea; they are both 'aloft' and laughing light-heartedly; the waves seem a long way away. The 'mews' (seagulls) are in the mid-air, lower down. We get the feeling that we are looking up at them from a great distance, and that they cannot see the abyss and the vast Atlantic under their feet. They have no idea, on that first spring day, that youth and happiness do not last for ever. Hardy knows it now, and in the last verse he faces the fact that the 'chasmal beauty' of the coastline means nothing to him now that Emma is gone.

Hardy deliberately simplified this poem by leaving out every hint of his long estrangement from Emma. She is quite straightforwardly 'the woman whom I loved so, and who loyally loved me'. Nothing, in 'Beeny Cliff', is allowed to darken the picture of the two lovers. Time and death are the sole forces they have to fear.

Late Poems

We have seen that Hardy went on writing poetry until about a month before he died. The last three volumes of his work contain several fine poems, but no masterpieces, and it seems better to end this chapter with two of his very greatest poems, which do not belong to his last years, but were both written when he was over seventy-five. When he wrote them the Great War had begun, and he was writing several minor patriotic pieces at the same time, but 'In Time of "The Breaking of Nations"' is probably his ultimate comment on that, or any, war:

In Time of 'The Breaking of Nations'

I

Only a man harrowing clods
  In a slow silent walk
With an old horse that stumbles and nods
  Half asleep as they stalk.

II

Only thin smoke without flame
    From the heaps of couch-grass;
Yet this will go onward the same
    Though Dynasties pass.

III

Yonder a maid and her wight
    Come whispering by:
War's annals will cloud into night
    Ere their story die.

(*CP*, 511)

DATE 1915.

TITLE. The title is taken from a verse in the Old Testament, 'With thee will I break in pieces the nations, and with thee will I destroy kingdoms' (Jeremiah, 51:20).

STYLE. This is a deceptively simple poem; the short lines and apparently ordinary observations hiding the real depth of the thought. Hardy gives each verse a separate number, and at first there seems to be no connection between them. It is only at the end of the poem that we see how these apparently arbitrary and disconnected images form a perfect whole.

SUBJECT. Hardy was, of course, thinking about the Great War when he wrote this poem, but strangely enough it had been suggested forty-five years earlier, when the Franco-Prussian War of 1870 was being fought and Hardy was in Cornwall with Emma:

> On the day that the bloody battle of Gravelotte was fought they were reading Tennyson in the grounds of the rectory. It was at this time and spot that Hardy was struck by the incident of the old horse harrowing the arable field in the valley below, which, when in far later years it was recalled to him by a still bloodier war, he made into the little poem of three verses entitled 'In Time of "The Breaking of Nations" '.
>
> (*Life*, 78–9)

It is not, perhaps, surprising that the idea (like the image of Emma on Beeny Cliff) had lain dormant in his mind for nearly half a century. Throughout his life Hardy had always believed that *written* history, the stories of kings and queens and battles, had at most only a very tenuous connection with the history that really mattered. In *Jude the Obscure* he suggested that the Crossway in Christminster 'had more history than the oldest college in the city' because it had long been a focus and gathering-point for ordinary people 'whom nobody ever thought of now' (II, 21). The man and the old horse

153

ploughing a field, the 'thin smoke without flame' and the two lovers will never get into any history book. Yet they seem to him to have much more reality than the battle which is being fought on the same day in another country. His long poem *The Dynasts* had also studied the relationship between wars and territorial ambitions, and everyday life, and its title is taken up in the word 'Dynasties' in the second stanza. The Franco-Prussian war had wiped out one dynasty; the Great War was to wipe out three, and change the whole course of European history. But the 'maid and her wight' will presumably marry and have children, and this, Hardy suggests, is more important, not only because it is of more human significance, but because it touches eternity.

Afterwards

When the Present has latched its postern behind my tremulous stay,
    And the May month flaps its glad green leaves like wings,
Delicate-filmed as new-spun silk, will the neighbours say,
    'He was a man who used to notice such things'?

If it be in the dusk when, like an eyelid's soundless blink,
    The dewfall-hawk comes crossing the shades to alight
Upon the wind-warped upland thorn, a gazer may think,
    'To him this must have been a familiar sight.'

If I pass during some nocturnal blackness, mothy and warm,
    When the hedgehog travels furtively over the lawn,
One may say, 'He strove that such innocent creatures should come
        to no harm,
    But he could do little for them; and now he is gone.'

If, when hearing that I have been stilled at last, they stand at the
        door,
    Watching the full-starred heavens that winter sees,
Will this thought rise on those who will meet my face no more,
    'He was one who had an eye for such mysteries'?

And will any say when my bell of quittance is heard in the gloom,
    And a crossing breeze cuts a pause in its outrollings,
Till they rise again, as they were a new bell's boom,
    'He hears it not now, but used to notice such things'?

                                                    (*CP*, 521)

DATE 1917. Hardy was seventy-seven when he wrote 'Afterwards' and in some ways it is a deliberate valediction. In the nature of things, he felt, it was not very likely that he had much more time ahead of him (though he did, in fact, live for another ten years).

STYLE. The movement of this poem is slow, gentle, and rather hesitating (perhaps Hardy's own word, 'tremulous', is the best one to use). The images in each verse are the most memorable part of it, and these build up an impression that Hardy is, not exactly confident, but at least hopeful that he will be remembered by a few people, not as a poet or novelist but simply as a loving observer of nature.

SUBJECT. In its quiet way, this is a curiously optimistic poem, and one which is concerned not so much with death as with the possibilities of life. Hardy never actually says this, but each verse gives a different picture of the world he will be leaving, and these pictures are very moving and convincing. The real focus of interest is not himself, but the animals, birds, leaves and stars which he used to 'notice'.

There is a distinct feeling of gaiety in the first verse, that we might not expect in a poem which is 'about' death. 'The May month flaps its glad green leaves like wings,—Hardy sees this happening after he is gone, just as the bells of Christminster rang 'joyously' when Jude was in his coffin, and he does not resent it at all. He only hopes that it may bring him to mind momentarily, because he was 'a man who used to notice such things'. In the rest of the poem there is more evidence that he was, in fact, a keen observer of the world around him. For example, how many of us would think of comparing the flight of a hawk to an *eyelid*? But this image very skilfully evokes the ideas of speed and soundlessness, and it could only have been conceived by one who, like Hardy, was used to noticing almost imperceptible things.

Hardy was fond of hedgehogs, and throughout his life, as we have seen, he campaigned vigorously against cruelty to animals and birds. Many people were amused when, asked for his comments on modern warfare, he suggested that armies should at least stop using horses on the battlefield. In the third verse of 'Afterwards', he recognizes that he could do very little for dumb animals, but, at the same time, holds on to his belief that even a hedgehog has a right to live, and a value and worth of its own.

The fourth verse moves out from the homely image of hedgehogs and moths on the lawn of Hardy's house to the 'mystery' of the starry sky, and the questions it raises in our minds about man's place in the universe, which he had described, long before, in *Far from the Madding Crowd* (though it is characteristic that, in the last verse of all, he should move back from this to the familiar sound of bells from a country church). It is not a religious image; after all those years of searching, Hardy felt that he was still no nearer an answer to 'the eternal question of what Life was, and why we were there'. He can only comment on the everyday things which he does understand, and keep his sense of wonder in the face of the unknown. The poem makes no dogmatic statements. It merely suggests, rather tentatively, that an individual man can make only the faintest of marks on the universe, and that the most he can hope for is to be remembered with kindness by a few people after he dies. It also suggests that there is nothing tragic about this; if anything, it is a happy thing, when the time comes, to be absorbed back into the natural world.

This is what happens to most of us, of course, but it has not in fact happened to Hardy. One of the most modest of men, he would not have thought of claiming, like Shakespeare, 'Not marble nor the gilded monuments/Of princes shall outlive this powerful rhyme', even though in his case it was true. 'Afterwards' is among the small group of Hardy's finest works which make his place in literature secure.

Hardy would be glad to know that in many circles today his poetry is prized more highly than his novels. *The Dynasts* is not much read, but the best of his short poems have found almost as wide an audience as they deserve and are studied in schools and universities as a matter of course. Conventional people did not like them; he was never offered the Poet Laureateship or the Nobel Prize for literature, which, in any case, he would probably not have wished for. In their own day, because of their great difference from popular Victorian poetry with its deliberately 'jewelled lines' and its smug moral certainties, they probably seemed a bit too avant-garde. But the war killed this kind of poetry forever, and young writers, particularly the bitter satirist Siegfried Sassoon, found him very sympathetic to their values. A poet as modern as Ezra Pound could say that he had learned a lot from Hardy, describing his *Collected Poems* as the 'harvest' of the novels. Today there are almost as many critical works on his poetry as on his novels, and several good short selections which make the beginner's task easier. His reputation stands higher than it has ever done; it is even possible for a modern critic, Donald Davie, to argue in a recent work that Hardy has been the greatest single influence on English poetry in this century (although I do not think that this has been proved). The editor of the 1960 Penguin Poets edition writes, 'There have been relatively few poet-novelists in English literature. . . . the only authentic double-firsts in this field are, I believe, Hardy and D.H. Lawrence.'

Part Three
Reference Section

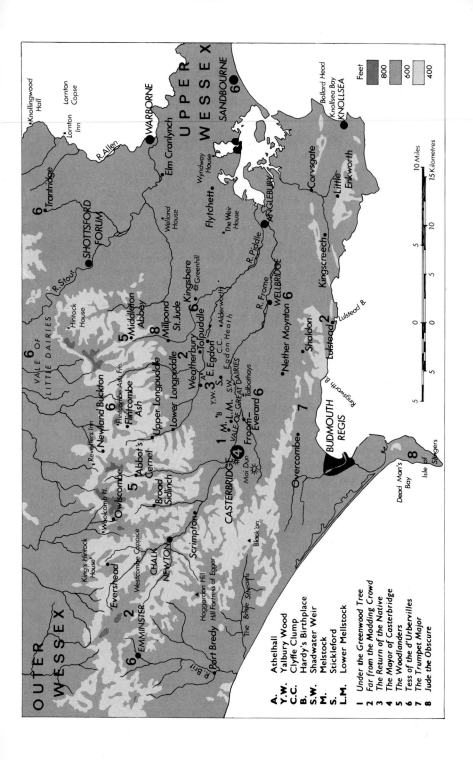

OUTER WESSEX

UPPER WESSEX

Feet
800
600
400

A.   Athelhall
Y.W.   Yalbury Wood
C.C.   Clyffe Clump
B.   Hardy's Birthplace
S.W.   Shadwater Weir
M.   Melstock
S.   Stickleford
L.M.   Lower Mellstock

1   Under the Greenwood Tree
2   Far from the Madding Crowd
3   The Return of the Native
4   The Mayor of Casterbridge
5   The Woodlanders
6   Tess of the d'Urbervilles
7   The Trumpet Major
8   Jude the Obscure

Knollingwood Hall
Lornton Copse
Lornton Inn
WARBORNE
Elm Cranlynch
SANDBOURNE
Bollard Head
Knollsea Bay
KNOLLSEA
R.Allen
Trantridge 6
SHOTTSFORD FORUM
Wyndway House
Flytchett
The Weir House
ANGLEBURY
Corvsgate
Little Enkworth
R.Stour
Welland House
Kingsbere
Greenhill
WELLBRIDGE 6
Kingscreech
R.Piddle
Hintock House
VALE OF LITTLE DAIRIES 6
Middleton Abbey 5
Millpond 8
St.Jude
Tolpuddle
Alderworth
C.C.
Nether Moynton 6
Shaldon
Lulstead B.
Lulstead 2
Revellers Inn
Newland Buckton 6
Flintcombe Ash Fm.
Flintcombe Ash
Upper Longpuddle
Lower Longpuddle
Weatherbury 2
"A" E.Egdon
Y.W. S. SW. Egdon Heath
VALE OF GREAT DAIRIES
Froom-
Everard 6
R.Frome
Talbothays
R.Bil
Port Bredy
EMMINSTER 2 6
King's Hintock House
Woolcomb H.
Evershead
Owlscombe
Westcombe Coppice
Abbot's Cernel
Broad Sidlinch 5
Scrimpton
CHALK NEWTON
Hoggardon Hill
Hill Fortress of Eggar
The Brig Shears
Black'on
Mai Dun
CASTERBRIDGE 1 4
M. "B" 3
A. L.M.
Overcombe 7
BUDMOUTH REGIS
Dead Man's Bay
Isle of Slingers 8
Kingsworth B.

10 Miles
15 Kilometres
0   5   10
5   5
5

Short Biographies

ARCH, JOSEPH, 1826–1919. The son of a shepherd in Warwickshire, Arch worked in the fields scaring rooks as a child. He bought as many books as he could and became a skilled worker and a Methodist lay preacher. The terrible conditions among agricultural labourers made him a radical, and in 1872 he agreed to organize the Warwickshire labourers into a union which soon spread over much of the countryside. It was a miracle to many people that this class had any spirit, and Arch was held responsible for it. He became a kind of bogeyman to the farmers. Although the Union collapsed in the end, it managed to do a great deal for the labourers. In later life Arch went into parliament as a Liberal. His autobiography, *The Life of Joseph Arch* (1898, reprinted 1971) is essential reading for anyone interested in English rural history. Hardy publicly paid tribute to him in his article, 'The Dorsetshire Labourer', for his reasonableness and moderation.

ARNOLD, MATTHEW, 1822–88. Son of Thomas Arnold, the famous headmaster of Rugby. Although he earned his living as an inspector of schools, Arnold was one of the foremost Victorian poets and critics; he also did a great deal for popular education. For a time he was Professor of Poetry at Oxford. He was concerned with the survival of culture, the humanization of English society, and, above all, with the problem of how religion could be adapted to the modern mind. He had been deeply influenced by the Oxford Movement, but felt that a more enlightened form of Christianity must be evolved if it was to survive at all. Hardy (who met him socially in London and who shows him apostrophizing Oxford University in *Jude the Obscure*) disapproved of his efforts. He thought that if religion had to be propped up by 'hair-splitting' like Arnold's it must be in a desperate state.

BARNES, WILLIAM, 1801–86. A Dorset farmer's son, Barnes became first a lawyer's clerk, then a schoolmaster, and finally a clergyman, after he had taken an external degree at Oxford over a period of ten years. He was and is best known for his dialect poetry, although he also wrote poems in ordinary English. A great, though entirely self-educated linguist, he was devoted to old-fashioned forms of speech and according to Hardy thought that a bicycle should have been called a 'wheelsaddle'. A collected edition of his poems was published in 1879 and Hardy edited a selection in 1908. He thought that Barnes's pictures of the Dorset labourers were generally too happy to be realis-

Map of Wessex

tic: this is mostly, but not always, true. Apart from Burns, he was probably the greatest of all our dialect poets.

DARWIN, CHARLES, 1809–82. Generally considered to be rather stupid at school and university, Darwin as a young man accompanied the ship *Beagle* on a voyage round the world as a naturalist. It was in the Galapagos islands off the coast of Ecuador that he made the observations about animal development which led him to work out the theory of evolution. He did not publish his findings as *Origin of Species* until 1859, when he heard that another scientist, Alfred Russel Wallace, had independently reached the same conclusions. A semi-invalid, Darwin kept out of the resulting furore as much as he could. Like Hardy, he was an extremely modest man and hated the notoriety which his work brought him.

ELIOT, GEORGE (Mary Ann Evans), 1819–81. This great novelist is remembered by her pseudonym, used because she feared that a woman's novels would not be taken seriously. By the time Hardy was beginning to be published the secret was out, but she was respected almost universally for her tremendous intellect. She was a member of the small group of advanced intellectuals who wrote for the *Westminster Review*. Hardy considered her to be one of the greatest living thinkers, although he was doubtful whether her novels had anything of value to say about country life.

HARDY, EMMA (née Gifford), 1840–1912. Emma Gifford was born a solicitor's daughter in Plymouth and when Hardy met her she was living with her elder sister, the wife of the rector of St Juliot. Having no money of her own, she encouraged Hardy to keep on with his writing, although this meant that they could not afford to get married for four years. In later life her behaviour became increasingly odd, and Hardy's poem 'The Interloper' expresses the fear that she might be insane. Emma has had a bad press from the critics, but Hardy himself was much more charitable about her memory. Her writings show that she was capable of thinking for herself and had many original ideas.

HARDY, FLORENCE EMILY (neé Dugdale), 1879–1937. Hardy had known Miss Dugdale for several years when he married her in 1914. She was a much more competent and self-effacing person than Emma, and in spite of the great difference in age it was a happy marriage. His poems 'After the Visit' and 'I Sometimes Think' give us an idea of how much she helped him. After his death she arranged and published the *Life*, which was very largely written by Hardy himself, although it appeared under Florence's name.

HARDY, JEMIMA (née Hand), 1813–1904. The novelist's mother. Hardy described her as 'a girl of unusual ability and judgment, and an energy that might have carried her to incalculable issues' (*Early Life*,

9). Her own mother was a widow with a large family and she had a very hard life before she was married. She liked reading, and taught her son to do the same, and she had an impressive knowledge of local traditions. She is thought to have inspired the character of Mrs Yeobright in *The Return of the Native*.

HARDY, THOMAS (the First), 1778–1837. Hardy heard a good deal of family reminiscences about his grandfather, who died three years before he was born. He was said to have been a smuggler, and he and his two sons had practically created the choir at Stinsford Church. His wife, Mary Head, who lived with the family when Hardy was a child, had grown up as an orphan at Great Fawley in Berkshire, the 'Marygreen' of *Jude the Obscure*. Some of her childhood experiences may have been incorporated in the novel.

HARDY, THOMAS (the Second), 1811–92. Hardy's father was a master-mason and a very good violinist. He was a sociable man with no great ambition for himself or his children, and he spent his entire life in the cottage at Higher Bockhampton where he was born. He is buried in Stinsford churchyard with the other members of the Hardy family. Hardy, who was very attached to him, records that 'almost the last thing his father had asked for was water fresh drawn from the well—which was brought and given him; he tasted it and said, 'Yes—that's our well-water. Now I know I am at home' (*Life*, 248).

HENNIKER, HON. FLORENCE, 1855–1923. A society hostess and occasional novelist, married to a Major-General. Hardy met her in Dublin in 1893, after he had secretly become estranged from his wife. She was a charming woman and he was soon very attracted to her, although he realized that there was not much hope for him. They had a good deal in common emotionally, particularly a love of literature and a hatred of cruelty to animals, though Hardy was rather annoyed with her for remaining an orthodox Christian. They worked together on a short story, 'The Spectre of the Real'. In later years their friendship became less emotionally charged. Hardy's letters to her have been collected by F. B. Pinion and Evelyn Hardy in *One Rare Fair Woman*. (1972)

HUXLEY, THOMAS HENRY, 1825–95. Scientist who became the foremost defender of Darwin's theory of evolution. He used to say that he had been named after the Apostle with whom he had the most sympathy, 'Doubting Thomas'. His place in the history of intellectual progress is assured by his thoughtful essays on science and agnosticism. He was a member of the London School Board during the brief time that Hardy was designing buildings for it, and was a distinguished educator. *Man's Place in Nature* (1863) is his chief non-technical book.

MILL, JOHN STUART, 1806–73. One of the most remarkable thinkers of his age, almost worshipped by Hardy as a young man. He was ahead of his time in many ways; during his short career in Parliament he proposed a Bill giving the vote to women which nobody else would vote for, and he becàme very unpopular when he tried to prosecute Governor Eyre of Jamaica for summarily hanging some of the 'natives'. The full extent of his influence on Hardy has probably not yet been traced. His most influential works are *On Liberty* (1859) and *Utilitarianism* (1863).

MOULE, HORACE, 1832–73. The son of a much-loved Dorchester clergyman, Horace Moule was one of the strongest influences on the young Hardy. He helped him to widen his reading, and wrote encouraging reviews of his earliest books. Though a brilliant scholar, it took him many years of intermittent study at Oxford and Cambridge to get his degree. Hardy was shocked when he committed suicide, although his family had known for years that there was a danger of this. A poem, 'Standing by the Mantelpiece', is based on his death. Hardy may well have had this tragedy in mind when he began planning *Jude the Obscure*; it has also been suggested that Moule was a model for the intellectual hero Knight in *A Pair of Blue Eyes*.

NEWMAN, JOHN HENRY, 1801–90. Beginning his career as an Anglican clergyman and a Fellow of Oriel College, Newman was one of the leading spirits in the Oxford Movement which strove to make the Church of England more 'Catholic'. He wrote several of the *Tracts for the Times* which led to the movement being called Tractarian, and his sermons in the University Church had a deep influence on many undergraduates including the young Matthew Arnold. Another of his disciples was the Jesuit poet Gerard Manley Hopkins. When he joined the Catholic Church in 1845 the movement effectively broke up. In 1864, after an attack by Charles Kingsley, he published *Apologia Pro Vita Sua* which won him many admirers in the Anglican as well as the Catholic Church. Horace Moule recommended it to Hardy, who, however, was not convinced. Another distinguished work of Newman's was the *Grammar of Assent* (1870). His chief argument, which Hardy quotes in *Jude the Obscure*, was that 'probabilities which did not reach to logical certainty might create a mental certitude' of the truth of Christianity. Newman was made a cardinal in 1879.

SPARKS, TRYPHENA, 1851–90. Hardy's cousin, a pupil-teacher in Puddletown, with whom he fell in love after he came back from London in 1867. Nothing was known of her until Lois Deacon and Terry Coleman published *Providence and Mr Hardy* in 1966. After such a long space of time, very few facts about her are ascertainable. There are many theories about the relationship, but although we can be almost certain that she meant a good deal to Hardy at one time, and that she had some influence on *Jude the Obscure*, we are not likely ever to know the full truth.

STEPHEN, LESLIE, 1832–1904. Critic and editor of the *Cornhill Magazine*, which published two of Hardy's novels. He was the first editor of the *Dictionary of National Biography*; he also wrote several books, including one on George Eliot which is still widely read. Hardy was deeply influenced by Stephen's agnostic philosophy, and witnessed his formal (and belated) renunciation of the holy orders he had taken at Cambridge as a young man. Stephen is best remembered as the father of Virginia Woolf, who drew a rather cruel portrait of him as Mr Ramsay in *To the Lighthouse*.

SWINBURNE, ALGERNON CHARLES, 1837–1909. Although he was only a little older than Hardy, Swinburne became established as a writer at a very much earlier date. *Poems and Ballads* caused a sensation when it came out in 1866; it was followed by the equally daring *Songs before Sunrise*. Swinburne's early poems were very popular with Hardy's generation—perhaps more popular than they deserved. Hardy often quoted them in his novels. Swinburne was passionately devoted to the idea of liberty, particularly to the crusade for a united Italy which attracted a great deal of sympathy in England. But his radicalism was romantic, not systematic. In his old age he became a Jingo and wrote some bellicose poems about the Boer War, to Hardy's distress. By this time he had written nothing significant for a great many years.

TENNYSON, ALFRED, 1809–92. Poet Laureate after the death of Wordsworth, and raised to the peerage in 1884, Tennyson was very much the Victorians' favourite poet. Hardy had little in common with him as a writer, but found him unexpectedly endearing when he visited him in London. His reputation has shrunk in the twentieth century, but he is likely to survive as a poet. *In Memoriam*, which goes considerably deeper than his later work, is generally accepted as his greatest achievement.

Gazetteer

Everybody has heard of Wessex now; few know that it was Hardy who revived the old name for the south-west of England. His decision to be a local or regional novelist compelled him to limit his scene of action to Dorset and the neighbouring counties only (though it is exclusively in Dorset that most of the Wessex novels are set). He said of this decision:

> The geographical limits of the stage here trodden were not absolutely forced on the writer by circumstances; he forced them upon himself from judgment. I considered that our magnificent heritage from the Greeks in dramatic literature found sufficient room for a large proportion of its action in an extent of their country not much larger than the half-dozen counties here reunited under the old name of Wessex, that the domestic emotions have throbbed in Wessex nooks with as much intensity as in the palaces of Europe, and that, anyhow, there was quite enough human nature in Wessex for one man's literary purpose. So far was I possessed by this idea that I kept within the frontiers when it would have been easier to overleap them and give more cosmopolitan features to the narrative.   (General Preface to the Novels and Poems)

The map which can be found in almost all editions of Hardy's novels ('Fictitious names as Exonbury; real names as Portsmouth') shows the track of country which Hardy wrote about almost exclusively. If it is checked against the real map it will be found to comprise the whole of Dorset, with parts of Hampshire, Wiltshire, Berkshire, Devon and Somerset (and Cornwall on a sketch-map in the corner). More detailed notes on places which were important in Hardy's life and writings follow.

Berkshire

GREAT FAWLEY. This is a small village, nestling among the Berkshire downs, where Hardy's grandmother, Mary Head, grew up. He depicted it as 'Marygreen', the childhood home of Jude Fawley. The ugly Gothic church which he describes in the novel can still be seen.

READING. Known in *Jude* as 'Aldbrickham'. This was the kind of bustling industrial town which held little interest for Hardy.

WANTAGE. Appears in *Jude* as 'Alfredston', the place where Jude was apprenticed. There is a statue of King Alfred in the market place. (Hardy's last novel is the only one which has a setting some way to the north of Dorset.)

Cornwall

BEENY CLIFF, also known as 'the Cliff without a Name'. Hardy visited it in his youth with Emma, and wrote one of his most famous love poems about it. In *A Pair of Blue Eyes*, his only novel with a Cornish setting, it is almost a major actor; there is a most dramatic scene where the hero is trapped and nearly killed on this cliff.

ST JULIOT. The old church which Hardy restored is still standing. There is a memorial to Emma, written by her husband.

Devon

BARNSTAPLE (Downstaple) and EXETER (Exonbury) are both mentioned in Hardy's fiction.

PLYMOUTH was the childhood home of Emma Gifford. Tryphena Sparks was headmistress of the Plymouth Public Free School.

Dorset

The majority of the Wessex Novels are set here.

BEAMINSTER. The home of Angel Clare's parents.

BERE REGIS. This was one of the traditional seats of the aristocratic Turberville family, as described in *Tess*. There is a fine church with a Turberville window, showing the family crests.

BULBARROW. Mentioned in 'Wessex Heights', this is a hill south of Sturminster Newton which gives some magnificent views over the Vale of Blackmore. Hardy thought that these views were among the finest in the country.

CERNE ABBAS. Stands at one end of the road which runs through the *Woodlanders* country to Sherborne. It is particularly famous for the chalk giant on the nearby hill, which is of uncertain age. There is also a beautiful gatehouse, all that is left of the medieval abbey.

CRANBORNE. 'Chaseborough', the town where Alec d'Urberville's employees went on Saturday nights to get drunk.

DORCHESTER. The county capital is particularly rich in associations for the Hardy enthusiast. His house, Max Gate, stands on the edge of the town; it is privately owned, but can be seen on certain days of the week. The County Museum (which has a statue of William Barnes outside the door) contains a reconstruction of Hardy's study, the manuscript of *The Mayor of Casterbridge*, and several other documents concerning Hardy, mainly of interest to students. Readers of *The Mayor* will find several parts of the town familiar. There are 'walks', or avenues of trees, which have hardly changed since he wrote. The amphitheatre on the Weymouth Road, Maumbury Rings, is unchanged too. Following the London Road out of town one crosses Hardy's two bridges, the first covers a small stream flowing along the Mill Lane area; the second is Grey's Bridge, where Henchard often stood. It is a fine stone construction and carries a small plaque (the original can be seen in the County Museum) threatening that anyone who damages the bridge will be transported! Ten Hatches Weir is only a little way from this bridge, and across the meadows is the old hangman's cottage. From this end of the town, which merges rapidly into the countryside, there is a good view of the tower of Fordington church. The Reverend Henry Moule preached here for many years, and was active in the cholera epidemic which broke out in the slum quarter of Mill Lane when Hardy was a boy. This church is full of interest, and so is St Peter's (near the museum), which has some interesting monuments and two architectural drawings by Hardy. The monument to the writer stands on the Bridport Road at Top o' Town.

Two prehistoric camps, Poundbury and Mai-Dun, stand at a short distance from Dorchester.

EGDON HEATH. When Hardy wrote *The Return of the Native* there were 'at least a dozen' scattered stretches of heathland in Dorset, although for the purposes of his novel he united them under one name. Today the heath is not easy to find, as some of it has been planted with rhododendrons and other parts are used by the army. There are still several miles of heath around Puddletown, Wareham and Bere.

HIGH-STOY. Another of the 'Wessex heights' which Hardy loved. It stands near the Sherborne-Cerne Abbas road, giving a fire view over the countryside.

KINGSTON MAURWARD. The local 'great house' when Hardy was a boy. It stands near the road from Dorchester to Stinsford. The lady of the manor, Mrs Martin, made a great favourite of the child Hardy and gave him lessons. It is now an agricultural college.

HIGHER BOCKHAMPTON. The cottage where Hardy was born and grew up now belongs to the National Trust. It has not changed a great deal, and it is a picturesque place. It is open to visitors.

MARNHULL. Tess Durbeyfield's village. There is an interesting church.

PUDDLETOWN. Hardy knew this small village very well, and described it as 'Weatherbury' in *Far from the Madding Crowd*. Tryphena Sparks grew up there.

SHAFTESBURY. 'One of the queerest and quaintest spots in England', Hardy said when he described this little Dorset town under its old name of Shaston in *Jude the Obscure*. He found it strange that this interesting place was so little known. Standing on a hill, it gives some extensive views which Hardy mentioned as being among the finest he knew. There is one lovely street, Gold Hill, which is full of old-fashioned houses and must be one of the steepest climbs in any English town.

SHERBORNE. 'Sherton Abbas' in *The Woodlanders*. There is a magnificent Norman abbey which Hardy knew well.

STINSFORD. The village between Dorchester and Bockhampton whose church contains graves of the Hardy family, to which has now been added that of Cecil Day Lewis. The church boasts several unusual 'gurgoyles'.

STURMINSTER NEWTON. Hardy and his wife lived at Riverside Villa here while he was writing *The Return of the Native*.

TOLPUDDLE. One of a number of small villages near the Trent or Puddle River whose names are based upon it. It is famous for its contribution to trade union history. The Martyrs' Oak where the six labourers met is still standing, and there is an excellent museum in one of the six cottages which have been built in their honour.

WEYMOUTH. Appears in several of Hardy's writings as Budmouth. It was a fashionable watering-place in the time of George III, of whom there is a great chalk figure on a hill outside the town. Hardy worked as an architect here from 1869 to 1870.

WIMBORNE MINSTER. Hardy lived here while he was writing *Two on a Tower*. It is an ancient town with an interesting church.

WINTERBOURNE ABBAS. Interesting because the church has an old minstrels' gallery which is one of the few that have not been pulled down. The choir survived longer here than in most villages, and there is a memorial to the last surviving member of it, a shepherd, who did not die until the Second World War.

WOOL. Described in *Tess* under the name of 'Wellbridge'. There is an old manor house here which belonged to the Turberville family, and contains the pictures of the two sinister Turberville women which so alarmed Tess. Nearby are the ruins of Bindon Abbey, and a flour-mill, which are both described in the novel.

Hampshire

BASINGSTOKE. Described in *Jude* as Stoke-Barehills, the site of the big agricultural show.

WEYHILL. 'Weydon-Priors', where Henchard sold his wife to the sailor. A great sheep-selling fair was traditionally held here every year.

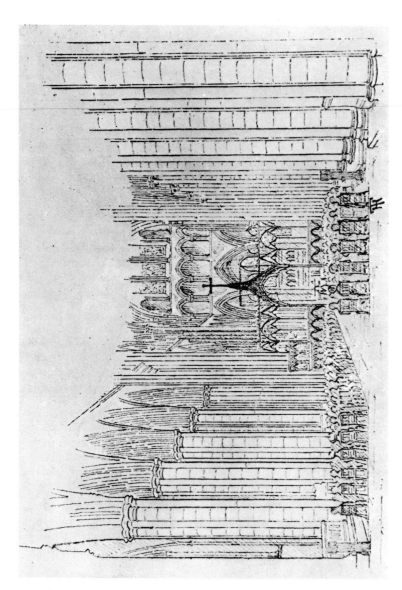

Melchester, 'the most homogeneous pile of medieval architecture in England' from Hardy's own sketch.

WINCHESTER. Hardy knew this ancient cathedral town well. He gives a long description of it in the last chapter of *Tess*, where he indirectly relates how she is hanged at the County Gaol for Alec's murder.

London

Greatly changed since Hardy knew it. His grave can be seen in the Poets' Corner at Westminster Abbey.

Oxford

As 'Christminster', the ancient university town is the emotional centre of *Jude the Obscure*. The landmarks of the novel are still there — the Cathedral, the High Street which he described as the loveliest in Europe, Christ Church Meadow, and the 'Church of Ceremonies' — St Barnabas, in the working-class part of the town which he called 'Beersheba'. Although he never lived in Oxford, Hardy seems to have known it very well. Real colleges are satirized under the names of 'Rubric' and 'Biblioll'. The University was not flattered by his last novel. It did not honour him until he was a very old man.

Somerset

BATH. Mentioned several times under its own name in the Wessex novels. Bathsheba went there to get married, as did Viviette in *Two on a Tower*.

WELLS. Hardy probably knew this small cathedral town closely, but he did not write about it much. It appears on his map as 'Fountall'.

Wiltshire

SALISBURY. Hardy wrote enthusiastically about the cathedral which dominates the city—'the most graceful architectural pile in England'. An important section of *Jude the Obscure* is set here ('At Melchester'). His sisters went to the training college here, which he described as the temporary home of Sue Bridehead.

STONEHENGE. This is where Tess and Angel take refuge just before the police catch up with them — Tess lying on the stone altar in the centre.

Further Reading

Editions of Hardy's writings

The Greenwood Edition of the Wessex novels (Macmillan) comprises all Hardy's novels and almost all his short stories; there are Papermac editions of all the major novels. They are well produced and have Hardy's original prefaces as well as the later prefaces he wrote for the new edition in 1912. In 1974 Macmillan's began to publish the New Wessex Edition with introductions, notes and indications of textual alterations as well.

Collected Poems, Macmillan, 1962, is the best edition of his poetry. It contains all his surviving poetry except *The Dynasts* which is available in a Papermac edition. There are many selected editions of the poems; one of the best and fullest is *Thomas Hardy*, ed. W.E. Williams, Penguin Poets, 1960.

Thomas Hardy's Personal Writings, ed. Harold Orel, Macmillan, 1967, presents various essays and minor works. There is no complete collection of his letters.

Dearest Emmie, Macmillan, 1963, contains letters to his first wife.

One Rare Fair Woman, ed. Evelyn Hardy and F.B. Pinion, Macmillan, 1972, consists of his surviving letters to Mrs Henniker, with an explanation of the part she played in his life.

Thomas Hardy's Notebook, ed, Evelyn Hardy, 1955.

The Architectural Notebook of Thomas Hardy, ed. C.J.P. Beatty, Dorset Natural History and Archaeological Society, 1966.

For Hardy's autobiographical contribution, see Biographies.

Bibliography

PURDY, R.L., *Thomas Hardy: a bibliographical study*, Oxford University Press, 1954, is the standard work.

Short Biographies

HARDY, F.E., *The Early Life of Thomas Hardy* and *The Later Years of Thomas Hardy*, Macmillan, 1928, 1930; reprinted in one volume, *The Life of Thomas Hardy* 1962. Though presented as written by his second wife this is known to have been largely written by Hardy himself, and was his attempt to give the world a standard autobiography.

Two good general biographies are:
WEBER, CARL J., *Hardy of Wessex*, Routledge, 1940; rev, edn 1965.

HALLIDAY, F.E., *Thomas Hardy: his life and work*, Adams & Dart 1972. Recently there has been a good deal of interest in Hardy's private life. The secret affair with Tryphena is discussed in:
DEACON, LOIS and COLEMAN, TERRY, *Providence and Mr Hardy*, Hutchinson, 1966, and:
SOUTHERINGTON, F.R., *Hardy's Vision of Man*, Chatto & Windus, 1971. The latter book is more scholarly and includes also a useful chapter on the novels. A new definitive study is:
GITTINGS, ROBERT, *Young Thomas Hardy*, Heinemann, 1975.

General background

LEA, HERMANN, *Thomas Hardy's Wessex* (1913) reprinted Toucan Press, 1969. An excellent guide to the Hardy country, written in consultation with Hardy himself.

BURNETT, DAVID, *A Dorset Camera 1855–1914*, Dovecote Press, 1974, for a series of contemporary photographs.

KAY-ROBINSON, D. *Hardy's Wessex Reappraised*, David & Charles, 1972, is more up to date.

PINION, F.B., *A Hardy Companion*, Macmillan, 1968, provides a mass of useful information on all aspects of Hardy's work and thought.

BAILEY,J.O., *The Poetry of Thomas Hardy*, University of North Carolina Press, 1971, gives detailed information about the personal, literary and historical background of every one of the poems and is invaluable to the student.

CHASE, MARY ELLEN, *Thomas Hardy from Serial to Novel*, University of Minnesota Press, 1927, is useful for anyone who takes an interest in the conditions under which Hardy wrote and the way he tried to cope with magazine readers' prejudices; this compares the serial versions of *The Mayor of Casterbridge*, *Tess* and *Jude the Obscure* with versions published later, in which Hardy had a much freer hand. hand.

The Thomas Hardy Year Book, published annually by the Toucan Press, often has interesting poems and articles. The Toucan Press has also published a series of monographs, edited by J. Stevens Cox; these are uneven, but well worth reading.

Criticism

LERNER, LAURENCE and HOLMSTROM, JOHN, *Thomas Hardy and his Readers: a selection of contemporary reviews*, Bodley Head, 1968, is perhaps the best book to begin with; it is both amusing and depressing for it shows how Hardy was consistently undervalued by his contemporaries and even abused for writing books which did not fit in with their ideas.

The main stumbling block for the Victorians was his 'pessimism', or rejection of the idea of Providence, and this has remained an obstacle for modern critics and readers because it is generally assumed that Hardy is a writer who invariably looks on the black side of things. The only book that deals adequately with this whole question is:

MORRELL, ROY, *Thomas Hardy: the Will and the Way*, Oxford University Press, 1965, an excellent corrective to conventional works on Hardy.

In spite of prejudice, Hardy has been recognized in this century as a truly great writer. Some critical studies are:

BROWN, DOUGLAS, *Thomas Hardy*, Longman, 1954.

GREGOR, IAN, *The Great Web*, Faber 1974

HAWKINS, DESMOND, *Thomas Hardy*, Arthur Barker, 1950.

JOHNSON, TREVOR, *Thomas Hardy*, Evans, 1968.

WING, GEORGE, *Hardy*, Oliver & Boyd, 1963.

WEBSTER, HARVEY C., *On a Darkling Plain*, University of Chicago Press, 1947, places Hardy skilfully in the intellectual context of his time.

WILLIAMS, MERRYN, *Thomas Hardy and Rural England*, Macmillan, 1972, is an attempt to place him in his social context.

Works on individual novels include:

BROWN, DOUGLAS, *Thomas Hardy: 'The Mayor of Casterbridge'*, Arnold, 1962.

PATERSON, JOHN, *The Making of 'The Return of the Native'* University of California Press, 1960.

TANNER, TONY, 'Hardy's *Tess of the d'Urbervilles*', *Critical Quarterly*, Autumn 1968.

WILLIAMS, MERRYN, '*Jude the Obscure*', Open University publication (A302 18–19.)

For those specially interested in the poetry:

DAVIE, DONALD, *Thomas Hardy and British Poetry*, Routledge, 1973.

HYNES, SAMUEL, *The Pattern of Hardy's Poetry*, University of North Carolina Press, 1961.

DAY LEWIS, CECIL, *The Lyrical Poetry of Thomas Hardy* (Warton Lecture), Oxford University Press, 1953.

Finally, the most brilliant and also the most perverse work:

LAWRENCE, D.H., 'Study of Thomas Hardy', written during the First World War and reprinted in *D.H. Lawrence: Selected Literary Criticism*, ed. A. Beal, Heinemann Educational, 1967.

Other references in this text

CECIL, LORD DAVID, *Hardy the Novelist*, Constable, 1943.

HAIGHT, G.S., *George Eliot*, Oxford University Press, 1968.

NICOLSON, HAROLD, *Swinburne* (1926), reprinted Archon Press, 1969.

ARCH, JOSEPH, *The Life of Joseph Arch* (1898) reprinted 1971.

Appendix:
Serialization and Hardy's Texts

Hardy's novels have reached us in their familiar form after surviving a process of censorship, dismemberment and reconstitution that is at times painful to contemplate but so essential as evidence of Victorian literary taste that no serious student can afford to ignore it. It was serial publication that caused so much irritation to writers and left indelible marks upon their books even when restored to the safety of the hardback version. To different degrees a forgotten hack writer and a serious artist alike had to accommodate original ideas to the demands of the serial editor if they were to reach the widest public instead of a more discerning body alone.

Leslie Stephen, Hardy's most distinguished periodical editor, stated as a general principle in one of his letters to the novelist: 'Though I do not want a murder in every number it is necessary to catch the attention of the reader by some distinct and well-arranged plot.' Some kind of strategy was then required to meet these demands. Ways of involving the minds of regular readers and retaining them as subscribers were various. A writer might simply favour the more melodramatic cliff-hanging incident for the end of the instalment, or embark upon a series of complex legal and financial problems hinging upon the favourite laws of inheritance and property, or create mysterious characters whose identities are slow to be revealed. In the end, when the novel emerged in the customary two or three volume form, no matter how much detail of dialogue, incident or description might be revised, these characteristics would remain. What follows here is by way of tracing the composition, erasures and revisions required by a magazine editor on two occasions.

To simplify a situation in which there were many variations let us consider three stages:

1. A manuscript as it was written and intended for the press.

2. A revised version prepared for a magazine with passages removed for reasons of length and cuts insisted upon in the interests of morality.

3. A return to a version of (1) usually abandoning all the cuts and revisions of the serial text and intended for the publisher of the hardback edition. While this often provides the modern text, it may be noticed that Hardy revised his texts voluntarily in various ways for collected editions of his novels in 1895 and 1912. This final establishment of a text is the sum total of years of alterations but is in itself rarely of great moment.

The Mayor of Casterbridge, first published in *The Graphic* from January to June 1886, documents most of the problems of serial authorship and is drawn upon for a number of revealing incidents. There

173

seems to have been no objection to the initial act of wife-selling since it created a sensational impact: it was the later marital tangles of Michael Henchard that called for reserves of patience in the novelist.

Lucetta, crossing the paths of the two principal male characters as she does, has been criticized even in the completed version. Her arrival at Casterbridge from earlier days in Jersey created many of the textual confusions. It is in chapter XII that the problems of her past present themselves in flashback. As it was originally defined, the incident was inconsistent with Victorian family reading, though it is, one would think, hardly substantial enough to raise objections. The original version is the one we know today:

> ...one autumn when stopping there I fell quite ill, and in my illness I sank into one of those gloomy fits I sometimes suffer from, on account o' the loneliness of my domestic life.... While in this state I was taken pity on by a woman—a young lady I should call her, for she was of good family, well bred, and well educated—the daughter of some harum-scarum military officer who had got into difficulties, and had his pay sequestrated.... This young creature was staying at the boarding-house where I happened to have my lodgings; and when I was pulled down she took upon herself to nurse me. From that she got to have a foolish liking for me. Heaven knows why, for I wasn't worth it. But being together in the same house, and her feelings warm, we got naturally intimate. I won't go into particulars of what our relations were. It is enough to say that we honestly meant to marry. There arose a scandal, which did me no harm, but was of course ruin to her.... At last I was well and came away. When I was gone, she suffered much on my account, and didn't forget to tell me so in letters one after another; till, latterly, I felt I owed her something, and thought that, as I had not heard of Susan for so long, I would make this other one the only return I could make, and ask her if she would run the risk of Susan being alive (very slight as I believed) and marry me, such as I was. She jumped for joy, and we should no doubt soon have been married—but, behold, Susan appears!

Here it is as Hardy altered it. It will be seen that a highly sensational boating accident is added and that, from here onwards, the book is overburdened with marriages and remarriages; in themselves the entanglements which readers of popular serials were known to appreciate.

> 'Well, this summer I was there, and met with an accident. I fell out of a boat in the harbour, and struck my head in falling. If somebody had not helped me instantly, I should have been drowned. An account of it was in our local newspapers at the time.'
> 'Indeed. And it's all haphazard in this life!'

'But the account was not complete. The person who saved me was a woman—a merchant's daughter—a woman who—God knows why, for I never gave her encouragement!—who has had a foolish liking for me more than five years; ever since I first knew her from going over there to deal with her father. So when I found I owed my life to her, in a moment of gratitude and excitement I offered to marry her. I did marry her—I married her at St. Heliers a fortnight ago. Three days after I came home here to get the house ready for her, and await her coming. But from the moment I landed, I felt I had acted rashly. It was not that I dreamed of Susan living; but I felt I did not care for this young woman, much as she might like me. Odd as it may seem to you, I've always liked Susan in my heart, and like her best now. Well, now Susan has returned to life, and you begin to see the color o't; for the other is coming by the packet tomorrow night.' Henchard's voice grew brokenly indicative of passionate revolt against eighteen years of caution. 'I've compromised myself by acting a fortnight too soon!'

Explanations are unnecessary but the return of Lucetta to the forefront of the action, alternately claimed by Henchard and Farfrae, occasioned an amount of accommodating minor revision. For example, take an incident in chapter XXVII as it stands today:

'But you ought to hear it,' said he [Henchard].

'It came to nothing; and through you. Then why not leave me the freedom that I gained with such sorrow! Had I found that you proposed to marry me for pure love I might have felt bound now. But I soon learnt that you had planned it out of mere charity —almost as an unpleasant duty—because I had nursed you, and compromised myself, and you thought you must repay me. After that I did not care for you so deeply as before.'

'Why did you come here to find me, then?'

'I thought I ought to marry you for conscience' sake, since you were free, even though I—did not like you so well.'. . .

This unluckily aroused Henchard. 'You cannot in honour refuse me,' he said. 'And unless you give me your promise this very night to be my wife, before a witness, I'll reveal our intimacy—in common fairness to other men!'

With this passage compare the following, the result of an editor's blue pencil and an obedient rewriting. (Only the important phrases are given):

'Had I found that you married me for pure love I might have felt the vow binding, though it was not legal. But I soon learned that you had done it out of mere charity—almost as an unpleasant duty—because I had helped save your life and you thought you must repay me in some way. . . .'

'I thought I ought to remarry you for conscience' sake.'...

'You belong to me and you cannot in honour refuse me.....And unless you give me your promise this very night to be my legal wife, before a witness, I'll disclose all—in common fairness to other men.'

Comparative study of different versions reveals Hardy's problems with the return of Richard Newson, the true father of Elizabeth-Jane. On his first visit to Casterbridge he is told that his daughter is dead and he departs; but there is a picturesque incident (XLIII) in which Henchard spots him through his telescope and which is his cue to depart. The serial version made for difficulties in consistency and motivation of character by making Elizabeth-Jane already aware of her father's identity and known to him. Having met him many times during her walks along the Budmouth road she is still obliged to return to her stepfather's home without any revelations or recriminations. The original (and final) text is overwhelmingly superior in this respect since her continued silence is completely improbable, threatening to pull the book's credibility apart, even though Hardy consented to produce this inartistic effect.

There were minor revisions to the text made between 1886 and 1912, some of them explained in an author's Preface. They concern passages in chapters 12, 18, 34, 43 and 44, and the ones with which many people are familiar concern the author's later thoughts on the Scots dialect attributed to Donald Farfrae. Without any external pressure Hardy, who it will be remembered was a devotee of William Barnes, would attempt to rectify linguistic matters. At the same time his conception of Wessex as an entity was growing more specific, rechristening places with new names and rendering the speech more correct on the principle that a spoken language is an index to the society that produced it. Thus he wrote 'zilver zaxpence' and ''oman' where standard spellings had originally prevailed. In the end Wessex had grown into an autonomous world of his own imagination that he was at times loath to identify with the map of Dorset and its neighbouring counties.

Chapter IV of *The Mayor of Casterbridge* follows two women into the town and the eye travels to collect a bird's eye view of the whole scene. In the shop windows is arrayed a great profusion of scythes, reap-hooks, or in the words of Gerard Manley Hopkins, 'all trades, their gear and tackle and trim'. Even so, in the serial edition of the opening chapter Henchard is shown with what is called merely an 'implement'. In the novel it was to be identified; although all Hardy's novels have their quota of literary references, biblical allusions and the like, the implement is given as a 'hoe': when he wished Hardy could call a spade a spade.

The second part of this Appendix is devoted to *Tess of the D'Urber-*

villes or *Too Late Beloved* as it was originally known. In this case Hardy had begun writing in 1888, designing the text for a rather different means of dissemination: a newspaper fiction syndicate which would buy a novel and lease it to a chain of local newspapers up and down the country for simultaneous publication. The manuscript was under contract and was in the printer's hands in 1889 without any alterations, the seduction scene and the illegitimate child notwithstanding. However, as the narrative came fully to the attention of the editor he cancelled the contract and returned portions already standing in print. To the author's mortification it was the prelude to a period of frustration and evasion: not until 1891, when he prepared a revised text for *The Graphic* once more, was he able to place the novel with an editor and one of the greatest of his works was cynically submitted to a process he called 'dismemberment'.

We shall document the late-night seduction scene: chapters X and XI. Hardy's original conception is one that would seem to the modern reader to have come under a mild censorship already, for there is a restraint and ambiguity in the presentation of Alec's approach to the sleeping girl:

> D'Urberville stooped; and heard a gentle regular breathing. He knelt and bent lower, till her breath warmed his face, and in a moment his cheek was in contact with hers. She was sleeping soundly, and upon her eyelashes there lingered tears.

At this point the author's viewpoint changes and he turns to a historical meditation. The bowdlerized text jettisons the whole of the village dance that leads to the seduction and treats the incident in flashback (as if it were no more urgent than Henchard's behaviour in Jersey) when Tess returns to her mother. The differences are startling:

> 'Well!—my dear Tess!' exclaimed her surprised mother, jumping up and kissing the girl. 'How be ye? I didn't see you till you was in upon me! Have you come home to be married?'
>
> 'No, I have not come for that, mother.'
>
> 'Then for a holiday?'
>
> 'Yes—for a holiday; for a long holiday,' said Tess.
>
> Her mother eyed her narrowly. 'Come, you have not told me all,' she said.
>
> Then Tess told.
>
> 'He made love to me, as you said he would do, and he asked me to marry him, also just as you declared he would. I never have liked him, but at last I agreed, knowing you'd be angry if I didn't. He said it must be private, even from you, on account of his mother; and by special licence, and foolish I agreed to that likewise, to get rid of his pestering. I drove with him to Melchester, and there in

a private room I went through the form of marriage with him as before a registrar. A few weeks after, I found out that it was not the registrar's house we had gone to, as I had supposed, but the house of a friend of his, who had played the part of the registrar. I then came away from Trantridge instantly though he wished me to stay; and here I am.'

'But he can be prosecuted for this,' said Joan.

Even without the disclosure of the fraudulence of the ceremony, a marriage by special licence strikes against the credibility of characterization. There is no illegitimate child in the serial so that neither its baptism nor burial need to be recorded, but less probable still is the behaviour of Angel Clare. Because Tess is perfectly justified in living with Alec, to whom she believes herself married, Angel is made monstrously unfeeling to reject her on that score. These are the dismantlings of a work of art caused by the susceptibilities of an editor but tolerated by its creator in a way that shocks us today.

Hardy, aware that this novel represented his art extended to the full ('I have put in it the best of me') was reluctant to see it sink in periodical form without a fight. In May 1891 before the serial began to appear there was published in the *Fortnightly Review* a piece entitled 'Midnight Baptism, a Study in Christianity'. This is the incident that was not to be allowed to stand in its due place in the serial. Then, in November of that year while the serial was in progress, he published the night seduction scene separately in the *National Observer* under the title 'Saturday Night in Arcady'. Even with all the instalments and the two fugitive pieces together the reader was still puzzled, because the fragments bore none of the names that identified them with the new novel: in the end, with all the cancelled passages visible in the three-volume copy, the novelist's method of self-defence should have been obvious, and not, in the long run, unheeded.

Still consistent with Victorian magazine ethics words like God, Hell and Damnation disappeared from the serial copy of *Tess* and when Angel Clare finds Tess with Alec in the hotel at Sandbourne he is made to imagine perfect discretion and separate rooms occupied by Mr D'Urberville and Miss D'Urberville for reasons simple to understand. Finally, however, an instance that amused Hardy in later years. Angel Clare carries the milkmaids one by one across a flooded road but not in the pages of *The Graphic*. It is a happy incident, but at a late date in the preparation of copy for the paper Hardy was made to give Angel a wheelbarrow to transport the girls. Agricultural implements are always in evidence in the Wessex novels.

Mary Ellen Chase's study, *Thomas Hardy, from Serial to Novel*, has a wealth of further documentation and also takes *Jude the Obscure* into detailed account. It has been pointed out that without recourse to the manuscripts where the changes are evident Miss Chase is not entirely correct in some of her judgements, but she shows us without the slightest doubt the extent of the tyranny of editorial taste over the creative writer. Indeed, it exposes a piece of cultural history and provides texts for the history of censorship and a discussion that is still in progress.

Regarding the process we have been tracing, the American Hardy scholar, Joseph Warren Beach, writing in 1927, remarked that English fiction in the latter half of the nineteenth century was lacking in profundity, seriousness and depth. It is a verdict that may well spring from the same casual and patronising habit as Henry James's. His verdict on 'the good little Thomas Hardy' was that *Tess*, though much impaired was a surprising success. Hardy with a more peasant-like isolated and rocky quality about himself and his work accorded very little with a man of James's refinement and those mannered novels which at times appear to be endlessly undulating and circling in their moral refinements, turning in upon themselves and sometimes disappearing altogether. Possibly as a result of technical expectations that Hardy did not acknowledge in the first place and his consequent failure to observe them in his novels Hardy's standing has been depressed for too much of the present century.

Finally, it is tempting to compare him with another figure that now emerges so clearly out of the Victorian and Edwardian eras, Sir Edward Elgar. This most distinguished composer had to establish himself in spite of the tyranny of Victorian oratorio which had almost contrived to set the entire Bible to music. What Elgar recognized (like Hardy with *Tess*) in *Dream of Gerontius*, his setting of Cardinal Newman's poem, as 'the best of me' was first performed much against the grain of the nonconformist conscience of the English provinces. But both Hardy and Elgar displayed the courage to work and to grow, overcoming contemporary prejudices and now stand firm as masters of their arts.

MAURICE HUSSEY

General Index

Index to Hardy's Poetry and Prose

Acknowledgements

We are grateful to the following for permission to reproduce copyright material:

Author's Agents for an extract from *Hardy The Novelist* by Lord David Cecil. Published by Constable Ltd; The Bodley Head Ltd. for extracts from *Thomas Hardy And His Readers* edited by L. Lerner and J. Holmstrom; Author's Agents and The Viking Press Inc. for an extract from *The Rainbow* by D. H. Lawrence in 'The Complete Short Stories Vol. III'. Reprinted by permission of Laurence Pollinger Ltd. and the estate of the late Mrs. Frieda Lawrence; Macmillan London and Basingstoke, The Macmillan Company of Canada Ltd. and Macmillan Publishing Company Inc. for extracts from *Life, Jude The Obscure, Hardy's Personal Writings, Woodlanders, The Mayor of Casterbridge, Tess, Far From The Madding Crowd, Return Of The Native, Two On A Tower, Under The Greenwood Tree* and *Collected Poems* all by Thomas Hardy also *Selected Stories* by John Wain. Copyright for *Collected Poems* of Thomas Hardy 1925 by Macmillan Publishing Company Inc. and the Trustees of the Hardy Estate, Macmillan London and Basingstoke and Macmillan Company of Canada Ltd. The Novel extracts reprinted by permission of The Trustees of the Hardy Estate and Macmillan London and Basingstoke and The Macmillan Company of Canada Ltd.

The author and publisher are grateful to the following for permission to use photographs:

Crown Copyright, The Science Museum, London, page 57; Fitzwilliam Museum, Cambridge, page 42; Gernsheim Collection, University of Texas at Austin, page 55; Martin F. Gostelow, pages 27 and 140; National Gallery, London, page 95; Radio Times Hulton Picture Library, page 109; Mark Sealey, pages 31, 47 and 103; Tate Gallery, page 74; Trustees of the Thomas Hardy Memorial Collection, Dorset County Museum, pages 11, 21, 38, 105, 112 and frontispiece; Victoria and Albert Museum, page 45. The cover picture is by courtesy of the City of Manchester Art Galleries.

Brooklyn
Beckham

The Secret Diary

A.C.Parfitt

JOHN BLAKE

Published by John Blake Publishing Ltd,
3 Bramber Court, 2 Bramber Road,
London W14 9PB, England

First published in paperback 2000

ISBN 1 903 402 04 2

British Library Cataloguing-in-Publication Data:

A catalogue record for this book is
available from the British Library.

Typeset by t2

Printed in Great Britain by
Creative Print and Design (Wales),
Ebbw Vale, Gwent.

1 3 5 7 9 10 8 6 4 2

Papers used by John Blake Publishing Limited are natural,
recyclable products made from wood grown in sustainable
forests. The manufacturing processes conform to the
environmental regulations of the country of origin.

Brooklyn
Beckham

The Secret Diary

Contents

MARCH
1999

Thursday March 4th

Hello world!

Born today. I must say it was quite a relief to get out into the open. Nine months of bobbing around not doing much isn't really my idea of a good time. Still, everything seems to be in good working order – two hands, two feet, nose, eyes, etc. I'm a bit worried that I don't seem to have any teeth yet, but I'm not sure I'm really going to need those – I found out which part of Mum was serving the drinks pretty quickly, and that seems to keep me nice and full.

Mum and Dad seem OK, but it's a bit early to start having any real opinions, as they're still acting a bit daft and gooey: everyone keeps bursting into tears every time they look at me (including Dad which is pretty uncool behaviour for such a big lad). If I didn't know any better I'd get a complex, but I suppose they're all just pleased to see me – at least I *hope* they are …

I don't know what they're going to call me yet. I hope it's something good.

Friday March 5th

Mum and Dad must think I was born yesterday. OK, so I *was* born yesterday, but that's not the point! They keep telling me that they're really famous, and that I'm going to be the most well-known baby in the country. Now, I don't want to speak disrespectfully about my parents – they *are* very sweet and everything – but between you and me *I'm not sure that they're all that bright.* Quite what they could possibly do to make them so famous is anyone's guess.

Having said that, I must admit that the hospital is very posh. Mum's bed seems nice and comfy, and they do have a superior line in cuddly toys. Dad's been playing with them all day long, though, and I've hardly had a look-in. The point is that all this must be costing them a fair whack, which is a very good sign – it looks like they are able to keep me in the style to which I intend to become accustomed.

No mention of my name yet, but no news is good news, I suppose. They must be thinking up something really cool.

Saturday March 6th

OH MY GOD, I DON'T BELIEVE IT!!!!
This is terrible. This is more than terrible,

this is a catastrophe. I'll never be able to show my face in public. I'll be a laughing stock. They've called me *Brooklyn!* What the hell kind of a name is that? I'll tell you – a rubbish one. Of course, Mum and Dad think it's a great idea – they look pleased as punch, and talk about overkill. They say the word Brooklyn at every available opportunity: 'Who's a beautiful little Brooklyn?' 'How's my little Brooklyn today?' I'll tell you how I am today – *NARKED OFF!!!*

Sunday March 7th

I've calmed down a bit – probably helped by the fact that I had a good old scream in the middle of the night to punish Mum and Dad for the error of their ways.

I suppose I should be grateful for small mercies. I overheard Mum telling someone that I was named after the place where I was

conceived. It could have been worse –
Brooklyn is a far better name than Kitchen
Floor …

Overheard a couple of the nurses talking
today, and gleaned a bit of information
about Ma and Pa. It seems Mum is a famous
singer called Posh (daft names run in the
family, obviously). I find this a bit difficult
to believe because:

a) I've heard her sing (she tried to croon
me to sleep last night – hence the
screams …)
b) I've heard her speak, and you wouldn't
call it posh in a month of Sundays.

According to the nurses, she sings with a
bunch of other girls called Scary, Sporty and
Baby. I'm not sure how I feel about this –
there's only one 'Baby' in Mum's life, and
he ain't no singer. I'll have to put this other
Baby in her place when I meet her.

So Mum's a singer, which sounds unbelievable enough. But get this – Dad's a football player. Now I'd hate to perpetuate stereotypes, but aren't sportsmen meant to be rugged, athletic and manly? Dad seems to spend more time doing his hair than Mum, and that's just in a hospital room where no one is going to see him. Don't get me wrong – looking good is fine (I'm a bit of a stunner myself, actually), but I can't quite see him on a football pitch.

The nurses seemed pretty sure though, and on the whole I'm quite pleased. Pop star and footballer – looks like I've got pretty good genes!

Monday March 8th

I'm getting a bit bored of hospital. I mean it's all very swanky and everything, and the nurses are quite pretty, but there's not a whole lot to do apart from watch Mum eat grapes and catch Dad trying to work out what the bidet in Mum's bathroom is for. It's about time I hit the outside world – I've got things to do, people to see.

To top it all, all this cootchie cootchie coo nonsense is beginning to get on my nerves. They *are* grown adults, after all – you'd think they could talk to each other properly.

We leave tomorrow.

Tuesday March 9th

Now that's what I call an exit! Dad spent most of the day packing up all my toys (he's a good lad, really). Then, at about five o'clock, the three of us went to the hospital doors and there was this sleek, silver limo waiting to take us away. We got bundled into the back like we were some kind of royalty, and off we sped with six coppers following us on bikes as an escort. It's good to see that I've made an impact.

Home is a modest four-bedroom penthouse flat – hey, it's not much, but it keeps the rain out. It looks like Mum and Dad weren't joking when they said how rich and famous they were. I take it all back!

Wednesday March 10th

Mum's band is called the Spice Girls. Don't ask me why. There's a picture of them up in my bedroom, and they're a right funny-looking bunch. I can recognise Mum in the picture (I wish she wouldn't pout like that – it's *so* undignified) but the funny thing is there's *four* others. Now I know about Scary, Sporty and Baby (although I can't work out which is which – none of them look scary or sporty, and like I already said, this town's only big enough for one Spice Baby). I've no idea who the fifth person is, but one of the girls in the picture has a target drawn over her face with something written above it. It looks like 'TAKE THAT GERI YOU OLD COW'.

I wonder if Mum wrote that. I think it's quite likely, as she has got a bit of a temper on her sometimes. She gave Dad a right telling off for playing football in the hallway this morning.

Thursday March 11th

8. p.m. Overheard Mum saying to Dad that she fancied an early night, and then giggling. I don't know what she's laughing at – early nights are boring. I think I'll have a bit of a scream to liven things up.

10. p.m. Oh dear, they didn't like that very much. Mum lost her rag a bit after about an hour and a half of me yelling, and told me that if I wasn't quiet, the Big Bad Evil Ginger One would come and get me. Dad was in the room at the time and he looked completely shocked, and no sooner had Mum said it than she made the sign of the cross. Dad told her not to talk about his friend Chris Evans like that, but Mum told him off and said, 'Be quiet, David.

You know I'm not talking about him.'

Who is this Big Bad Evil Ginger One? It sounds awful. I hope it doesn't come and get me. I'm terrified.

Friday March 12th

Had my first visitors today. Mum told me that Scary Spice was coming to say hello, and that she was bringing her daughter. I was a bit nervous, to tell you the truth, a) because I wasn't sure how scary Scary Spice was going to be and b) because this was going to be my first encounter with a girl my own age. I spent ages getting ready – Mum decked me out in a funky little denim number (Versace, only £199 – perfect) – and I took a good couple of hours deciding how to do my hair. In the end I decided that both of them should be brushed back. Though I say so myself, I looked pretty damn hot.

So then Scary arrived. *Scary?* The only thing that's scary about you, sweetheart, is your haircut.

I shouldn't be bitchy – she was actually quite nice, and she did give me a good old laugh when she introduced me to her daughter. 'Brooklyn, meet Phoenix Chi.' *Phoenix Chi?* Ha Ha Ha!!! What a stupid name! And I should know about stupid names, I'm an expert. Fortunately, I'm still too little to start smiling, so they didn't know I found it so funny.

Phoenix Chi is pretty cute in the looks department, I suppose, but she's not quite my type, if you know what I mean. We hit it off quite well, though, and I had an interesting conversation with her whilst Mum and 'Scary' (ha!) were gossiping:

Brooklyn: Yo, Phoenix, how's it hanging?
Phoenix: It's Phoenix *Chi* to you, dude. Have some respect for your elders.

Brooklyn:	Hey, take it easy Phoenix *Chi*. So why's your Mum called Scary? She doesn't look that scary to me.
Phoenix:	You wouldn't say that if you wet your nappy three times in one morning, dude. And anyway, you're hardly one to talk. What's all this 'Posh' stuff about?
Brooklyn:	Yeah, good point. Tell me, have you heard of the Big Bad Evil Ginger One?
Phoenix:	Hey, dude, keep your voice down. Don't you know that our Mums start shaking and sweating every time you mention that *thing*?
Brooklyn:	How am I supposed to know? I'm only a week old. What is it?
Phoenix:	You're too young to handle it, man. And anyway, you'll find out soon enough. Until then,

it's enough that you know that the Big Bad Evil Ginger One is the one thing that *everyone* should fear.

I couldn't question her any more because Mum and Scary picked us both up and started fussing. I think we hit it off quite well though – Phoenix Chi seems to know quite a lot of stuff. I'd better make friends with her.

Saturday March 13th

Spent day playing with Dad. Well, I say playing *with* Dad; what I really mean is watching Dad playing with my toys. He made two football teams: one out of toy cars, and one out of furry animals. Manchester United won. In fact, not only did they win, they drove all over Boca Juniors, who then had Dad jump up and down all over them shouting, 'Take that, Diego!' To be honest, he'd been wound up enough already, when the referee, Mr Potato Head, adjudged one of his Ford Escorts offside. Then Mum came in and told him off for ruining my toys. Quite right, too!

Sunday March 14th

Heard Mum saying that she wants to be an actress. Doesn't sound too unreasonable to me. I've seen how much dosh she's made out of singing, and she hasn't got much talent in that department. Obviously you don't need to be much cop at these things to be successful at them. I wonder if Dad's really any good at football. I haven't seen him play yet (apart from by himself in the back garden, where he seems to score a goal every thirty seconds!)

Monday March 15th

Mum was out shopping today. She does that a lot, I've noticed – I hope she's not an addict.

So I had Dad looking after me. It was all very well, right up until the point when he tried to change my nappy. It took him absolutely ages, and by the time he'd finished I was – ahem, how can I put this delicately, ready for another one. So we had to start all over again.

Then we had a good old time together – Dad tickled me a bit, and I cooed like, well, like a baby (works every time). Dad put a nappy on his head to make me laugh. At least, I *think* it was to make me laugh. He did keep looking at himself in the mirror to see what he looked like. I hope he's not thinking about using my nappies as a new fashion accessory – he *does* wear the strangest things sometimes.

So anyway, there's Dad crawling around for my entertainment, wearing a nappy on his head, and in walks Mum. 'David,' she says, 'how many times have I told you about wearing underwear on your head? Now you're doing it with Brooklyn's.' And she sends him off to do the washing up.

Poor old Dad, he was only having a laugh. Mum can be terribly bossy sometimes.

Tuesday March 16th

Had terrible nightmares last night that the Big Bad Evil Ginger One was coming to get me. It must be a terrifying creature, from the way everybody talks about it. Screamed and screamed until Dad got up and took me into their bed.

Entre nous, their bedroom isn't quite to my taste – all very lavish but, how can I put this, *not what you'd call posh!* They've got this huge picture on the wall of them kissing. It's funny, Mum seems very keen on kissing Dad, but I've done it myself a few times and it's really not that great. (Well, I suppose it's more of a gumming than a proper kiss, but it's the best I can do at the moment.) He's got this funny little beard on his chin that makes it all scratchy. What she sees in it, I'll never know.

Fortunately for me, this beard thing doesn't seem to be hereditary. At least, *I* don't seem to have one!

Wednesday March 17th

I'm getting a bit bored of the all-milk diet. It's very kind of Mum to lay it all on and everything, but her and Dad get to eat all sorts of interesting-looking stuff. Maybe a nice set of teeth would be quite useful after all. I wonder how I go about getting some. I'll see if Phoenix Chi can shed any light on the matter next time I see her.

Thursday March 18th

Welcome to Brooklyn's Restaurant. On the menu today:

Breakfast: Milk
Lunch: Milk

Dinner: And tonight's special is, er –
                 Milk

Friday March 19th

I'm going to turn into a bottle of bleedin' milk
if I'm not careful. I'm thinking of going on
hunger strike, but what's a kid to do? After
all, I gotta eat.

Saturday March 20th

You know, Dad may not be the sharpest pencil
in the box, but he is awfully sweet. He's had
'Brooklyn' stamped in each of his football
boots. Isn't that nice?

I'm a tad worried, though. The last pair had
'LEFT' and 'RIGHT' embroidered into them,
and for a very good reason. It takes him long
enough to work out how to tie his laces up, let
alone work out which foot to put the shoes on.

Must stop now – it's dinner time. Milk again.
Yum yum, I can hardly wait (*not!*).

Sunday March 21st

Mum's taking me shopping tomorrow. Better
be on my best behaviour today and hopefully
she'll splash the cash!

Monday March 22nd

Boy oh boy, we just shopped till we dropped.
Far too pooped to write anything. Will fill
you in tomorrow.

Tuesday March 23rd

Wow! I can see why Mum likes shopping.
That was one of the best days of my life – OK,
so I'm only 19 days old, but it was still pretty
good. The day went like this:

8.00 a.m.	Get up
8.30 a.m.	Brekky (no prizes for guessing what was on the menu)
9.00 a.m.	Leave house in chauffeur-driven limo. Dad was in a bit of a panic as we left, as he was late for football practice. He was still trying to work out which foot to put his boots on – I knew that was going to be a problem.
9.30 a.m.	Arrive shops. This is where the fun starts. Mum carried me around in a groovy little leather and sheepskin papoose (£210 – sounds a lot, I know, but hey, I *am* a Spice Baby. I gotta look the part.)
10.00 a.m.	SHOP SHOP SHOP!!! Mum's an expert. She bought: three pairs of trousers (£250 each); two dresses (£800); five (*five!*) pairs of shoes (£150 *each!!!*). We spent ages in a

shop that sold kids' clothes, looking at some rather nifty togs that I've definitely got my beady little eyes on. Unfortunately – this was the only downer of the day – Mum told the shop assistant that I had too many clothes already. *Too many clothes?* Look who's talking, dollface! I'll have to take an inventory of my wardrobe at some point, see what she's talking about.

1.00 p.m.   Lunch at PizzaExpress. Mum had a rather tasty looking salad; I had – yep, you guessed it!

2.00 p.m.   This was the high point, the tour de force, the real deal. Mum went to a jewellery shop and bought a bracelet for Dad. The price tag? *Fifteen grand!* Lumme, guv'nor – *that* is what I call flash.

When we got home, Dad was in a right mood. I think he'd got in trouble for being late for football practice. He kept muttering something about 'that miserable grey-haired old git Fergie'. Still, he perked up a bit when Mum gave him the bracelet.

I've got to say, Dad's habit of wearing jewellery and stuff is a bit disconcerting. It's getting to the point where I can only tell which parent is which by remembering that Mum's the one wearing the skirt – I *think*. I hope he doesn't take it to extremes.

Wednesday March 24th

Thinking about it, the best thing about going shopping is that you don't seem to need any money to do it. Mum just kept flashing this little bit of plastic around, and hey presto, Bob's your uncle. I don't know why more people don't do it.

Thursday March 25th

My wardrobe:

1 pink Versace dress – I think Mum got a bit carried away when she first found out about me. I'm dreading the day they decide to try it out.

5 woollen objects – I can't for the life of me work out what they are, but they've got enough bobbles, ribbons and tassles to sink a battleship.

1 Manchester United football kit – and it's not even the most recent version! Come on, Dad, you must have *some* influence at work …

14 romper suits – Nice and comfy, but not the sort of thing you'd really want to be seen around town in.

3 pairs dungarees – Definite no-nos. Fortunately Mum has the good sense not to dress me up in them. I've got a feeling they must have been presents from Granny.

5 pairs trousers – Two Gucci, two D&G, and

one, to my eternal shame, without a label. I don't know whose idea that was.

26 T-Shirts – All Calvin Klein. I definitely need a bit of variety there.

3 pairs booties – Too embarrassed even to describe them.

So what Mum was talking about when she said I had enough clothes is anybody's guess. A kid like me needs an ensemble for every occasion – that little lot wouldn't last me a week ... Time she changed her ideas, I think.

Friday March 26th

Here's the plan. Every time Mum decks me out in something duff, I'll scream my lungs out. She'll soon get the idea.

Saturday March 27th

Woke up, Mum dressed me in trousers, T-

shirt and pink booties (yeeeuuuchh!!!).
Screamed my head off. Mum looked a bit
confused, but don't worry, she'll soon get the
message.

Watched Dad playing football on the telly this
afternoon. I gotta hand it to him, he knows
what he's doing with that ball. He's obviously
picked up a few tips from me – I'm a bit of a
mean dribbler myself.

We're off to some posh restaurant called The
Ivy tonight. I'm hoping that this will see the
end of the all-milk diet.

Sunday March 28th

Well, that was a waste of time. The evening
started out quite hopefully with Mum and
Dad getting kitted out in some pretty groovy
gear. I figured that they'd want me to match,
but, can you believe it, they put me in a
bleedin' romper suit!

To make it even worse, we arrived at the restaurant and there was a whole bunch of photographers there, trying to get a picture. I was so embarrassed. Don't get me wrong – I'm as happy to pose for the cameras as the next baby, but only if I'm looking funky. As it was, I felt like a right dork.

Anyway we got into the restaurant, and Dad ordered a bottle of champagne. The waiter brings it and pours a glass for Mum, a glass for Dad ... but a glass for Brooklyn? Oh no. What's the point of taking me out to a swanky restaurant if I don't even get to glug a drop of shampoo? Mum made the kind offer of a drink of milk, but somehow I couldn't quite stomach it. I decided to have a bit of a cry instead, but Mum trotted out the old Big Bad Evil Ginger One routine. I wish she would shut up about that – she knows it terrifies me.

Then the menu comes. Well, you've never seen anything like it – truffle this, foie gras that. It all sounded pretty 'orrible to me. Dad seemed to agree. He asked the waiter if he could have sausage and egg, but Mum told him off so he had to make do with confit of larks' tongues or some such nonsense.

Et moi? What did I get to eat at this temple of gastronomic elegance? I don't think I need to tell you.

Monday March 29th

Spent all day making them suffer for Saturday night. Actually, it's quite hard work, what with all the screaming and being grumpy. Mum and Dad are looking pretty knackered so I think my mission's accomplished. I'll be on my best behaviour tomorrow. In fact, we've got visitors. Sporty Spice is coming round for an audience with yours truly!

Tuesday March 30th

Well, Sporty seems nice enough. Why is it though, that everyone seems determined to state the obvious? Every time I meet someone the conversation is pretty much the same:

Sporty Spice: Who's a gorgeous little thing, then?

Brooklyn: Gurgle gurgle [*Me, obviously. Tell me something I don't know, sweetheart!*]

Everyone had a good old natter about what football team I was going to play for. Dad seemed pretty much fixed on me playing for Manchester United, but Sporty reckoned I was more of a Liverpool kind of kid. I'm not quite sure what they think they're on about – who says I'm going to be a footballer? They're all jumping the gun a bit, anyway – I can't even crawl yet, let alone kick a ball. And I might just surprise them all and run off to be a ballerina.

Wednesday March 31st

You are not going to believe this. Dad's old boots have just been auctioned off for charity, and they fetched five thousand quid. *Five grand* for those old things! I mean, I'm sure he's a great footballer and everything, but have you *smelt* them? It'd be like walking around with a couple of old stiltons on your feet. Oh well, each to his own.

APRIL
1999

Thursday April 1st

Well, the screaming tactic is half working. The good new is that Mum's bought me a new top. The bad news is that it's pink. *Pink!* Doesn't she know I've got an image to maintain? I thought it was some kind of April Fool to start with, but it seems not.

Look Mum, here's the deal. I'm a boy. Boys don't wear pink. She's a fashion icon, you'd think she'd understand this sort of thing. Sometimes I think she's got no idea at all. She's been going around telling everybody that I've got her nose and Dad's thighs. Well, the nose bit is OK – Mum's nose is quite cute – but Dad's thighs? I should hope not. His are all big and hairy; mine are much smaller, and, well, sort of pink – altogether more sophisticated.

Tomorrow I meet Baby Spice. I'm gonna have to lay down the law – I don't want her muscling in on my act.

Friday April 2nd

Joy! Rapture! I'm in love! I've just met the most beautiful creature on the planet. Baby Spice – the very words are like music to my ears. When she waltzed in this morning, my world was turned upside down. She picked me up, gave me a little tickle, and I went all funny in my tummy. Her eyes are like azure, her hair is the colour of sunlight. When she smiles, it's as if an angel is smiling.

I am putty in her hands. Before she arrived, I

was all ready to act the hard man – now, all she has to do is say the word and I'll do anything she asks of me. The hour she spent with me was the happiest of my short life. She seems to be quite good friends with Mum, so hopefully I'll be seeing quite a lot of her from now on!

Saturday April 3rd

I can't stop thinking about my sweetheart. Is it me, or did I detect a look of complete and utter devotion when she sneaked a look in my pram? I'm sure the seeds of love are planted in her heart. I shall water them with adoration until they blossom and bear fruit.

Sunday April 4th

One month old today. Too besotted to write anything.

Monday April 5th

She will be mine. Oh yes, she will be mine!

Tuesday April 6th

Mum and Dad are getting married! It's obviously something in the air. To be honest, I thought they were married anyway. I'm terribly glad that they're doing the decent thing. I know they're a bit weird, but they do make a lovely couple.

Wednesday April 7th

The oldies have been designing their wedding invitation, and they've made themselves this coat of arms. Now, I don't want to sound mean or anything, but I think it's a bit naff. It consists of a swan on a gold crown – Dad wanted a football going into a goal, but Mum put the kibosh on that one pretty swiftly.

I'm not sure about this crown stuff. I know they're rich and famous and all that, but they're really *not* royalty. And a good thing too, as far as I'm concerned. If they were King and Queen, I'd be a prince. And if I were a prince, I wouldn't be allowed to marry Baby Spice (which I fully intend to do as soon as I'm old enough). Being a member of the Royal Family is all very well, but you don't get to do what you want. A cat like me needs his independence.

Thursday April 8th

Mum had lunch with Scary today, so it gave me a good opportunity to catch up with Phoenix Chi. She gave me some good advice:

Brooklyn: Phoenix Chi, my friend, what's happenin'?

Phoenix:	The usual, man. How's it hangin' in the Posh household?
Brooklyn:	Pretty good, pretty good. Can you keep a secret?
Phoenix:	Whaddya take me for, dude, some kinda big-mouth, cheatin' schmuck? Course I can keep a secret.
Brooklyn:	I'm in love!
Phoenix:	Gees, you guys are all the same. If you ain't fallin' for one chick, you're fallin' for another. Who's the lucky lady?
Brooklyn:	Baby Spice.
Phoenix:	Hey, man, you got *gooooood* taste. If I was that way inclined I'd have the hots for her myself. How you gonna play it?
Brooklyn:	I dunno, Phoenix Chi, I thought you could give me some advice.
Phoenix:	Lemme see. Well, obviously

	your main problem is the age gap. You gotta do something that makes her think you're mature beyond your years. Why don't you write her a poem? We chicks go for that kinda thing big time!
Brooklyn:	Nice idea, Phoenix Chi, nice idea. I'll give it a go.

She's pretty canny, that Phoenix Chi. I'd have asked her to write the poem for me, but unfortunately I wet my nappy with the excitement of it all and had to be changed.

Friday April 9th

I've got writer's block. This poem-writing stuff isn't as easy as you'd think. I'd like to ask Dad for some help – he's wise in the ways of the world. Problem is, he can only remember his own name half the time, bless him. The rumour going around is that my vocabulary is bigger than his, and all I can do is burp!

Saturday April 10th

Earth has nothing to show more fair,
Than Baby Spice, and her golden hair.

Nah, too flowery! I need something with a bit more pzazz – something to show her I'm red-blooded, virile – and *all* man!

Sunday April 11th

Gimme a peck and I'll be happy,
Spurn my love and you'll make me sad.
I'd rather have you than a nice dry nappy,
Just keep it quiet from Mum and Dad.

Hmmm ... not really mature enough, and I'm not sure she'd relate to the nappy imagery.

Monday April 12th

Overheard Mum and Dad planning the wedding. I do hope they're not going to go over the top. Presumably they'll buy me some new gear for the day – at least I hope so: I've got to look my best because I've decided that I'm going to make my move on Baby Spice at the reception. It should be perfect; she'll have had a few glasses of champagne, love will be in the air – what more can I say?

I've given up on the poetry – I don't think I've really got it in me. I'll just have to rely on my good looks and reckless charm.

Tuesday April 13th

It's Mum's birthday on Saturday, so I'll be seeing all the Spice Girls – including you-know-who. I've got butterflies in my tummy!

Wednesday April 14th

Blimey! I went shopping with Dad today – that boy could spend for England. The purpose of the trip was to buy Mum a birthday present, but he managed to slip a few little goodies in for himself – and a few for me, I'm pleased to report:

Dad's Shopping List

Sunglasses (Moschino – £200)
Leather Coat (Nicole Farhi – £850)
Present for Mum (Tiffany – £30,000)
Packet of J-Cloths (KwikSave – £2.99)

Brooklyn's Shopping List

Natty pair of corduroys (Gap - £50)
Hooded Fleece – nice and warm, lovely jubbly (Gucci – £199)
Bumper pack elasticated nappies (Mothercare – £12)

OK, so the nappies aren't the coolest, and perhaps the J-Cloths present a bit of an image problem, but that's Mum's fault. She made Dad buy them after he spilt his drink all over the kitchen floor whilst looking at his watch.

All in all, Dad's got good taste – he certainly bought me some groovy gear. I hope Mum lets me wear my new clothes when Baby Spice comes round on Saturday. They make me look like a bit of a hunk, though I say so myself. However, I'm not so sure about the earrings he bought Mum for her birthday. I've got to say thirty grand seems a bit steep for what he got. They're a bit, well, *small*, and they're all black, like little lumps of coal. I don't think he got a very good deal – after all, thirty grand could buy you 2,500 boxes of nappies (that's a lotta nappies), or 150 pairs of Gucci baby trousers! I hope Mum likes them.

Thursday April 15th

Only two days to go till I see my love again.
My little heart's all a-flutter.

Friday April 16th

A terrible thought has struck me. What if
Baby already has a man? Surely she couldn't
do that to me. If she has, I think the only
option open to me would be to take a vow of
celibacy and become a monk. I think I could
enjoy the contemplative life, and more
importantly I reckon I'd look pretty dapper
in a cowl.

One day to go!

Saturday April 17th

Happy Birthday, Mum! Funny kind of day.

All the Spices came round, and I was the complete centre of attention. The only thing that made me slightly peeved was the constant talk about which football team I'm going to play for: 'Who's going to make a lovely little Man United midfielder, then?' 'Who's going to play for Liverpool and score more goals than his Daddy, hey?'

What *are* they talking about? For all they know, I might grow up to be a rocket scientist. Come to think of it, I sort of doubt it looking at Mum and Dad.

Had a pretty encouraging chat with Baby, but I'm not sure she quite understood my gurgles:

Baby Spice: Who's a beautiful little boy, then?

Spice Baby: Gurgle Gurgle *[Hey babe, less of the little!]*

Baby Spice: Yes, you are, aren't you? Come and give your Aunty

	Emma a big hug!
Spice Baby:	Gurgle Gurgle *[You betcha boots, Honey-Bun!]*
Baby Spice:	What tiny little hands you've got!
Spice Baby:	Gurgle Gurgle *Gurgle! [You know what they say about men with small hands! Whaddya say we dump these bozos and go paint the town red, just you and me?]*

I think she seemed quite keen, but Mum dumped me back in my cot at that point. I've laid some important groundwork though. Phoenix Chi was quite encouraging, but she wasn't too impressed that I'd given up on the poetry idea: 'You guys ain't got no sense of style!' What's she talking about, no sense of style? I didn't notice *her* wearing any Gucci!

Most importantly, Mum seemed to like her present. It's been worrying me ever since Dad bought it, actually, but there's no accounting for taste.

So everything was going absolutely swimmingly until Sporty mentioned the Big Bad Evil Ginger One. She looked quite shocked that she'd said it, and everyone fell completely silent. Then Phoenix Chi started to cry, and the girls all made their excuses and left.

I can't understand it. What is this Ginger One that strikes fear into everybody's hearts, including mine? My feeling is that it must be some terrible ghoul that terrorises Spice Girls and Spice Babies. The mention of it even makes the blood run out of Dad's face, and to be honest he's a bit too daft to be scared of much.

Sunday April 18th

I think I may have got to the bottom of my inability to write poetry – it's genetic. Mum played a Spice Girls record today, with some very peculiar lyrics about really, really wanting to do something called a zig a zig.

Hmmm! Not quite sure what that's all about. I may only be a few weeks old, but I can tell gibberish when I hear it. If that's what my mum comes out with, I've obviously got no chance as a bard.

Funny thing is, Dad seemed to quite like it. He sat there nodding his head and grinning like a loon – but then, he does that quite a lot. He's easily pleased, poor lad.

Monday April 19th

Heard another Spice Girls track – yet another masterpiece of lyricism, imparting some wonderful nugget of advice about never weeing with your knickers on!

Oooh! Great information, girls. Thanks – I

must remember that: never wee with my knickers on.

Tuesday April 20th

Damn! Wet my knickers twice in the night. Mum was really cross. I think I'd better keep my big mouth shut in the future.

Wednesday April 21st

Had some funny man sneaking round outside the house with a camera today taking pictures whilst Mum was serving dinner (yep, milk again). Dad was furious, but not half as furious as me. Why is it that whenever I get snapped I'm looking my absolute worst? Like today, this bloke got pictures of me in mid-dribble, and a particularly ignominious one of me burping. It's just not fair. I'm actually a well-dressed, groovy-lookin' kinda guy. All the pictures the world sees are of me being a slob!

Thursday April 22nd

Oh dear, I think Dad's lost it. I suppose I should be flattered, but I can't help thinking he's ... how can I put it ... one player short of a football team. So what's he done this time? He's only gone and had BROOKLYN tattooed on his back. Apparently he likes the idea of touching the tattoo during football matches – dunno why. Mum's as bad as he is – she thinks it's great. I do wish she wouldn't encourage him. I know he means well, but I don't think I'd want DAD tattooed just above *my* bum, thank you very much.

They're going round telling everybody that it's not a fashion accessory. *Not a fashion accessory?* Of *course* it's a bleedin' fashion accessory – what's wrong with that? If, like me, you're born to shop, then fashion accessories are the most important things in life. Come to think of it, I'm beginning to think that *I'm* a bit of a fashion accessory myself (and a pretty damn exclusive one at that ...)

Friday April 23rd

He's obsessed. The boy is obsessed. Do you know what he's doing now? He's carrying my dummy with him everywhere he goes. And as if that weren't bad enough, he's *telling* everyone about it.

When's he gonna learn about this stuff? *Dummies ain't cool, daddio.* Even I'm embarrassed to be seen with one and I'm only a few weeks old.

Saturday April 24th

Feeling a bit peaky today – something funny in the tummy region. Maybe it's just the effects of unrequited love.

Sunday April 25th

Really not feeling good. Had a good old cry to get Mum's attention. She looks quite worried – but not half as worried as me. This can't be anything to do with Baby Spice. My love would never inflict such a thing. My own suspicion is that the Big Bad Evil Ginger One is coming to get me. Help! I hope Mum and Dad let me sleep with them tonight.

Monday April 26th

I'm going to hospital! I've got something called a hernia – no idea what it is but it sounds pretty scary for someone of my tender years. I won't be taking my diary in case it falls into the wrong hands. If I don't pull through, I hope whoever finds it will do the honourable thing and destroy it immediately to keep it safe from prying eyes. I thought it might be sensible to write a will – I don't want to be melodramatic or anything, but you never know. Anything could happen out there:

The Last Will and Testament of Brooklyn Beckham

I, Brooklyn Beckham, being of sound mind, do divide my estate as follows:

My collection of dummies I leave to Dad. May they give him as much pleasure as they've given me (only not in public, please Dad!)

My cuddly toys I leave to, well, Dad can have those too, I suppose – he seems to get more use out of them than I do, to be honest.

My crayons I leave to Mum. May she put them to good use in teaching Dad how to spell his name.

My togs I leave to Phoenix Chi. I know she's a chick and everything, but a lot of these baby clothes aren't very gender-specific (I've been meaning to have a word with Mum about that). Oh, and

I won't be at all offended if you ditch the romper suits. I would too in your position.

Signed this 26th day of April, nineteen hundred and ninety-nine

Brooklyn Beckham

I think that covers everything. We leave in ten minutes. Goodbye, cruel world ...

Tuesday April 27th

Wednesday April 28th

Thursday April 29th

Friday April 30th

MAY
1999

Saturday May lst

I'm back! That wasn't nearly as bad as I'd expected. Mum took me to this really posh hospital where I got mollycoddled by all these cute nurses – they seemed to dote on me completely, but hey, they're only human, I suppose.

I wasn't allowed to eat anything for a while, which was a bit of a downer: there's only one thing worse than too much milk, and that's no milk at all (I never thought I'd find myself saying that). I was absolutely starving when the doctor turned up. He gave me something to make me sleep – quite why I'm not sure, as falling asleep is something I'll quite happily do at the drop of a hat.

By the time I woke up I felt much better – at least I did after I'd had a good old nosh. I had absolutely everybody cooing over me non-stop:

Nurse: Who's a brave little thing, then?

Brooklyn: *Moi, actually.*

Nurse: Did you have a nasty little hernia?

Brooklyn: *Hey, baby! A man of my experience takes these things in his stride.*

Nurse: Did you have a little operation?

Brooklyn: *Aw, shucks, it was nothin'...*

She seemed quite impressed.

And that was about all there was to it. I had to hang around for a few days, but Dad came to see me every day, which was awfully sweet of him. I've got to say I was ready to come back home and get my hands on my diary. The moment I arrived at the hospital, I started worrying about having left my clothes to Phoenix Chi – the thought of her wearing my designer labels made me very uncomfortable, for some reason.

Dad's birthday tomorrow. Can't wait – I love birthdays.

Sunday May 2nd

May I say that I have the most fantastic taste? Mum bought Dad a whole pile of birthday presents on my behalf:

Dad's Birthday Presents from Brooklyn

1 Suit (Versace – £2,000)
1 Leather Jacket (Gucci – £850)
1 Mug with 'Daddy' written on it (Woolworths – £4.99)

Can you believe Dad's 24? Talk about over the hill. I wonder what I'll be doing when I'm 24. I'd better give it some consideration. After all, I need to be able to keep Baby Spice in the style to which she's become accustomed.

Monday May 3rd

Hey! Managed my first ever smile today. What a relief – I've been laughing inwardly for weeks just looking at Mum and Dad. Now I've got an outlet.

Tuesday May 4th

Woke up. Had a smile. Breakfast (milk). Had a smile. Cried a bit. Had another smile. Lunch (milk). Smile, smile, smile – you get the picture.

Wednesday May 5th

It's amazing the effect this smiling has on people. Flash 'em a cheesy little grin and they melt like butter. I'll have to try it out on Baby Spice – she's coming round tomorrow.

Thursday May 6th

Now that's what I call a result!!! As soon as Baby arrived, she made a bee-line for me (*naturellement!*) and took me in her arms. I squeezed out the biggest grin I could muster, and the result was electric:

Baby Spice: Come and give your Aunty Emma a big hug!

Spice Baby: *Hold on to your hat, darlin'.* [Smiles]

Baby Spice: [Squeals] Oh, aren't you just the most adorable little thing?

Spice Baby: *What can I say, babyface?*

	Looks – you're either born with 'em or you're not.
Baby Spice:	[To Mum] He's so beautiful.
Spice Baby:	*That's right … give in to your desires. You know you can't resist them …*

Then Mum did her old trick of dumping me back in the cot – she's got a terrible habit of interfering at the worst moment. Still, I don't want to rush things and Baby's practically pledged herself to me anyway …

Friday May 7th

Me and Mum are going to go and watch Dad playing footy on Sunday. Should be interesting to see what the fuss is all about.

Saturday May 8th

Took delivery of a pretty nifty piece of

machinery today. Four-wheel drive, specially imported European chassis, swivel suspension, high-rise mudguards and particularly impressive steering grip. Top speed? Well, that rather depends on who's pushing it.

Yep, my new pram is a groovy mover. Dad took me out for a spin this afternoon, and I have to say, heads were turning. We didn't really test it to the limit of its capabilities, but you know, power is nothing without control …

Sunday May 9th

Went to my first football match today. It was OK, I suppose (Dad's team were playing Middlesbrough, and I'm proud to report that he won), but I'm not sure I feel particularly inclined to fulfil everyone's expectations and start playing the beautiful game myself. To be honest, I couldn't quite see the point of it all. Having said that, I've got to admit that Dad was impressive, even though he unfortunately didn't score. I think he might have done better if he hadn't kept touching that stupid tattoo – everyone thought he was scratching his bum for the whole game ...

Monday May 10th

A very strange thing happened today. Mum and Dad were watching telly, and something came on about a person called Ginger Spice. Apparently she is an ambassador to the United Nations in America. As soon as they started talking about her, Mum and Dad went very quiet, and a sinister gloom fell upon the whole room. They turned the telly off, and hardly said anything for the rest of the day.

Tuesday May 11th

A terrible suspicion is beginning to dawn on me. Could it be that this Ginger Spice and the

Big Bad Evil Ginger One are the same? It would all fit together: Mum and Dad's reaction, the deathly chill when its name is mentioned, everything ...

If my theory is correct, somebody has to be told. The Ginger One has infiltrated the highest echelons of society. It is clearly planning world domination. We're all doomed!

Wednesday May 12th

Terrible nightmares last night. Kept dreaming that the Ginger One had grabbed me and was going to make a great big Baby Pie. Had a good old cry and then Dad came to look after me. If anyone can protect me from the Ginger One, he can.

Thursday May 13th

Dad came home last night after his football match in a terrible mood. He said some unrepeatable things about the referee – I'm far too shocked to write any of them down here. He kept muttering something about a 'yellow card'. I'm not quite sure what that is, but I can see why it must have upset him – yellow really isn't his colour.

Friday May 14th

Can't get the Ginger One out of my head. Maybe I'm paranoid, but hey, just because you're paranoid it doesn't mean they're not out to get you. Phoenix Chi is coming round tomorrow. That girl knows more than she's letting on about this whole thing. I'm gonna have to get her to squeal …

Saturday May 15th

It's far, far worse than I suspected. Scary and Phoenix Chi came round and I pumped her for information:

Brooklyn: Yo, Phoenix Chi, you gotta give me the low-down on the Ginger One.

Phoenix: Dude, I already told you: you can't handle the answers, so don't ask the questions.

Brooklyn: Hey babe, I'm sick and tired of being kept in the dark about this stuff, so here's what I know. My theory is that the Big Bad Evil Ginger One goes under another name ... Ginger Spice!

Phoenix: You catch on pretty quick, kid. OK, since you've got that far, here's how it is. In the beginning there were five

	Spice Girls: Ginger, Posh, Scary, Sporty and Baby …
Brooklyn:	[Sighs …]
Phoenix:	Hey kid, concentrate – keep your libido outta this. So like I said, in the beginning there were five Spice Girls – everyone loved them and they made a lot of dough. But then, one of the girls erred from the Path of Spiciness. She quit the group, and was cast out into the darkness.
Brooklyn:	[Gasp!]
Phoenix:	Pretty dramatic, huh? Many a long month did Ginger Spice wander in the void, howling tunelessly and threatening world domination so that she could wreak terrible revenge on the Spice Girls who deserted her.
Brooklyn:	My God, this is terrible. And now she's infiltrated the

	United Nations in a cynical manoeuvre to achieve her evil ends.
Phoenix:	What you talkin' about, dude? I ain't heard nothin' about no United Nations.
Brooklyn:	I heard it on telly a few days ago. She's become a United Nations ambassador.
Phoenix:	Hmmm … Things have become much worse than I expected. We must be vigilant.

This is terrifying news. It seems me and Phoenix Chi are the only people in the world that can see through Ginger Spice's plan. We're going to have to do something, otherwise the world is doomed …

Sunday May 16th

I'm pleased to report that my Dad scored a goal against Tottenham Hotspur today. This is good news, because it snapped Dad out of the foul mood he's been in since the ref made him wear yellow.

Actually, it's about time he scored. He's only scored five goals since I was born. He's paid twenty-four grand a week – that's about forty-eight grand a goal! Nice work if you can get it.

I wish he wouldn't run around kissing his team mates like that, though. I'd hate people to get the wrong idea …

Monday May 17th

Made a list of all the weapons I can draw upon should I ever find myself fighting against the evil Ginger Spice:

Brooklyn's List of Weapons

1.   My scream – I've got a great set of

lungs on me, and every military campaign needs a good warning system

2.   A state-of-the-art getaway pram
3.   I'm a pretty mean burper. OK, so I can't really see how that will come in useful, but it's as well to cover all your options.

Tuesday May 18th

Mum and Dad don't seem to be too concerned about the threat to national security posed by Ginger Spice. They're far too busy worrying about the wedding. After they get married, it seems we're moving house. I haven't seen the new pad yet, but it's costing them a cool two-and-a-half million. Wow! To put it in some kind of context, that's twelve thousand five hundred pairs of Gucci baby trousers.

Talking of baby trousers, it's about time I

went shopping again. I seem to be growing out of my clothes week by week.

Wednesday May 19th

The wedding is going to be at a big castle in Ireland. I'm quite excited actually – I've never been to a castle. Apparently the place had been booked by another couple, but Mum and Dad offered them 20,000 big ones to shove off and they accepted. It looks like they're really going to push the boat out.

I really hope they don't go over the top. They've got this nasty habit of decking me out in the most ridiculous-looking gear when they think it's an important occasion. They don't seem to give a stuff about my reputation.

Thursday May 20th

Dad seems a bit on edge at the moment. Him and Mum were talking about something called the FA Cup. I don't see why it's so important – one of his birthday presents was a cup, but he seemed far more interested in the leather jacket I gave him.

Anyway, apparently it's quite a big thing, and from what I can tell they've only got to win one more game before they can get this 'cup'. I guess I'll have to sit tight for a week or so and wait to see what happens.

Friday May 21st

Cripes! Went with Mum to a Spice Girls rehearsal today. They're a lovely bunch, but to be honest I'm more in tune than they are when I'm screaming. It pains me to report that even Baby Spice lacks a certain something in the old voice department. Not that it makes any difference to me – when you're in love, such things dwindle into insignificance.

Phoenix Chi was there, too, and she seemed to concur with my critical appreciation of our mothers' pop combo. Having said that, Phoenix has her heart set on a career as a rap star – she's really not into the pop scene. I think she could do well.

I asked her what the plan of campaign was re the Ginger Spice situation. She looked a bit shifty and said, 'Lay low, dude, I got my people on it.'

Saturday May 22nd

Manchester United 2, Newcastle 0. Thank God for that. I watched it all on telly, and I have to say I'm in two minds about whether this FA Cup thing is better than the mug I bought Dad for his birthday. On the plus side it is quite big and sparkly, and everyone seemed quite impressed that they'd won it; but on the minus side, he couldn't exactly use it to have his warm milk before he goes to bed at night, and it doesn't say 'Daddy' on the side …

Still, he seems quite pleased, despite the fact that he cut his lip during the game. It didn't stop Mum from kissing him, though. Yuk!

Sunday May 23rd

Dad stayed in bed all morning with a headache. I overheard Mum telling him that he had too much beer to drink last night. Took a mental note: don't drink beer (Ha – a chance would be a fine thing). It's obviously pretty 'orrible stuff if it makes you feel like that. Dad kept saying, 'Don't tell Alex, he'll do his nut. We're playing the Krauts on Wednesday.'

Monday May 24th

Good news about the wedding. Mum and Dad are asking everybody to wear black and white. This is fantastic – I look great in black and white. Even they can't go wrong with that.

I've grown a few more hairs on my head lately. I'll have to give some serious thought to how I'm going to style them. Dad uses this funny white stuff in his hair to make it stay in place, but I don't think I'll bother with that, a) because I'm not quite hairy enough to make it worthwhile, and b) because it doesn't half stink – it'd make the chicks run a mile.

Tuesday May 25th

Dad's gone to Germany ready for the match tomorrow. Apparently if they win this game, they'll have done something called 'The Treble'. Don't ask me what that is. Football's full of this funny lingo that I don't understand. I suppose I'll have to pick it up if I'm going to support Dad properly. Between you and me, though, I think I understand more than Mum. She still thinks Old Trafford is an aftershave.

Wednesday May 26th

Well, we did the treble. Haven't got a clue what it means, but we did it anyway. Phoenix Chi came round our place to watch it on telly, and I think she's beginning to suspect that I don't know much about football:

Brooklyn: Come on you reds!
Phoenix: Dude, what you talkin' about? You ain't got no idea about this football thang.
Brooklyn: Course I have, er, It's a game ... um ... We was robbed ...
Phoenix: Dude, you ain't foolin' nobody!

She's right. I think I'd better mug up.

Thursday May 27th

Dad came back home today. He seems to be very popular. He and the team were paraded through Manchester on a big bus. Everyone was cheering them. I don't mind saying I felt a lump of pride in my little throat. I gave him a nice cheesy smile when he came back, and he gave me a big slobbery kiss. I wish he wouldn't do that – I'll have stubble burn for days.

Friday May 28th

Having seen the reception Dad got, I wonder if perhaps I would like to be a footballer after all. I've been giving it some pretty serious thought, narrowing down my options one by one:

Brooklyn's List of Possible Careers

Racing driver – quite fancy that, but I do

sometimes feel a bit travel sick in my pram, especially just after breakfast, so I guess I'm not cut out for it.

Pop star – might be fun, but it's a bit early yet to decide whether I've got a good enough singing voice, and I've already established that I've no talent for writing lyrics. Still, neither of those things has stopped Mum …

Chef – no way, José! They say cooking's the new rock 'n' roll, but in my humble opinion it's too girly, and anyway, I've really no expertise in that field (unless you're talking milk – if anyone's looking for a milk expert, look no further …)

No, footballer definitely comes top of my list at the moment. It seems to me like the perfect job; you get paid a fortune, you only have to go to work a couple of times a week, and all the chicks fancy you. I'll have a bit of that, please!

I'm seeing Baby Spice tomorrow, so I'll sound her out about it.

Saturday May 29th

She seems keen:

Baby Spice:	Hello, Gorgeous!
Spice Baby:	*Hey, babe. Ever fancied hangin' with a footballer? Picture it – the glamour, the money. If that's what you fancy, I'm your man. Admit it, Honey-Bun, you're tempted!*
Baby Spice:	Ooh, you're so beautiful I could eat you up.

HOW ABOUT THAT??? Practically a proposal of marriage in my books. That's sorted, then. A footballer it is.

Sunday May 30th

I was far too excited about my conversation with Baby Spice last night to have any kip. Mum got completely the wrong end of the stick, so I had to endure her trying to sing me to sleep all night. Sing me to sleep? Squawk me to sleep, more like!

I'll tell you what I want, what I really, really want, Mum – a bit of peace and quiet!

Monday May 31st

Well, quite an eventful month, all in all. Discovered the evil truth about Ginger Spice, decided to become a football player, practically got engaged to Baby Spice. If life up till now is anything to go by, I've got a pretty busy future in store ...

JUNE
1999

Tuesday June 1st

Aw, bleedin' 'eck, it's happened again. There I am, enjoying lunch courtesy of Mum, and some photographer starts taking pictures through the window. Dad went spare and started chasing him, but the bloke got away.

Mum was really upset. She started crying. I know how she feels – I hadn't even had a chance to do my hair.

Wednesday June 2nd

I am so embarrassed. No, embarrassed isn't the word – humiliated, distraught. Those pictures got published all over Germany. Mum and Dad are absolutely furious. Mum said that it was 'an invasion of our fundamental right to privacy as a family unit'. Dad looked a bit confused when she said that – I don't think he quite understood what she was on about.

But she's right. I can't be expected to look fantastic all the time. I need my privacy in order to maintain my image as a Spice Baby – that's what the public loves me for. Now a whole nation has seen pictures of me in large expanses of white nappy. What's a kid supposed to do?

Baby Spice will go right off me if she sees them.

Thursday June 3rd

Calmed down a bit today. I suppose if I'm going to be an international celebrity baby, I'm gonna have to take the rough with the smooth.

Friday June 4th

Wicked! Three months old today, and Mum's bought me a football game called Subbuteo. Actually I'm a bit too young to play with it, but Dad's not. In fact he got quite excited when Mum brought it home. It's good for me, though, because I can watch Dad's ball skills while the two of them play together, and pick up a few tricks of the trade.

Saturday June 5th

Hmmm … I think Dad's a bit better at real

football than toy football. He keeps forgetting that it's not a proper game, kicking the football for all it's worth, and then spending about three hours trying to find it again. Come on, Dad! You're supposed to be a soccer role-model here. I'm really not learning much.

Sunday June 6th

Mum's had to confiscate the football game from Dad. He got a bit upset and kicked one of the members of her team. Mum said it was that kind of behaviour that got him into trouble before, and that he needs to learn to channel his aggression into a more positive mode of expression. Personally I think he had a point – the guy was clearly off-side.

Monday June 7th

Mum and Dad spent the day deciding what

wedding presents they would ask for. It's quite a pertinent question, actually, because to be honest they've got everything they need – four cars, nice house, more clothes than you can shake a stick at, etc., etc.

In the end, they decided to ask for money, a decision I heartily approve of. Green readies, chaps; stick a cheque in the post. American Express? That'll do nicely. After all, they'll need to keep the wonga coming in if they're going to keep me in the lap of luxury, aren't they?

Mum said that in Greece it's the custom to stick money all over the bride and groom at the wedding ceremony. How vulgar! All those grubby old tenners spoiling your natty wedding garb.

Tuesday June 8th

Only about three weeks to the wedding. Mum

seems to be getting quite excited. She got a bit upset that somebody called Fergie wasn't going to be able to make it, but Dad said he was sure he must have a good excuse. Mum said she just hoped he'd give him time off for a decent honeymoon.

I don't know who this Fergie bloke is, but he seems to be a pretty powerful dude. He'd better not overstep the mark. Nobody tells Brooklyn Beckham's Dad what to do.

Wednesday June 9th

Mum's been telling people that she wants to have another baby. Dad's been wandering around with a slightly wild look in his eyes.

I'm not sure how I feel about Mum's plans. On the one hand, it'd be quite nice having another kid in the house – at least I'd be able to get a bit of intelligent conversation. On the other hand, being an only child does have its advantages – I've got their undivided attention so that they can attend to my every need. I'll have to give the matter some more thought.

Thursday June 10th

Sometimes I just don't understand Mum and Dad. A couple of days ago they were cursing photographers, now they're persuading them to come and snap the wedding. I thought that it was the tradition for the bride and groom to pay the photographer. In Mum and Dad's case, it seems to be the other way round.

Ah well, the extra lolly will come in handy, I suppose. I wonder how much they'll get.

Friday June 11th

YABBADABBADOO!!! Mum and Dad have just signed a deal with the wedding photographers. Guess how much – a million quid! One million notes – can you believe it? And they get to call the shots on the day. For that kind of dough, I'd stand on my head and paint my bottom blue and they could still take pictures …

There'll be no need for that, though – at last the world will see pix of Brooklyn Beckham looking like the dude he is!

Saturday June 12th

Shopping with Mum. Too angry to write.

Sunday June 13th

Life isn't fair. Life just isn't fair. I'm given the opportunity of a lifetime, and Mum goes and blows it. Here's how I thought it was going to be:

1. Everyone has to wear black and white to the wedding.
2. Brooklyn looks terrific in black and white.
3. We're going to get some decent photos.

Well, that's how I *thought* it was going to be, but Mum, it appears, has different ideas.

We went shopping for my wedding clothes yesterday. Was there a hint of black? Was there even a hint of white? Nope. Not a jot. Not a smidgen. Instead, Mum's hit upon a great idea. Brooklyn is to wear … purple. PURPLE!

I felt like screaming. In fact, I did scream – quite a lot, actually.

Monday June 14th

She's meant to be one of the most fashionable people in the world. How can she do this to me?

Tuesday June 15th

Purple, I ask you!

Wednesday June 16th

The worst thing is, it's not so much a purple suit as a purple dress. It's so humiliating. I hope people don't think I'm a poof …

Thursday June 17th

The horror, the horror …

Friday June 18th

Not even a million quid is worth this sort of ignominy.

Saturday June 19th

Please don't make me wear purple, Mum. Please ...

Sunday June 20th

Saw Phoenix Chi today. She tried to persuade me that purple is the new black. It's very kind of her, but she ain't foolin' nobody.

Monday June 21st

I think I'll run away. I'll miss Mum and Dad, it's true, but they'll have brought it upon themselves. It'll be tough without the money, too; but what's the point of having money if you only ever get to wear purple bleedin' dresses?

The only problem is that I can't run. I can't even walk, come to think of it. Or crawl, for that matter. I think I'd better review the masterplan ...

Tuesday June 22nd

Only two weeks to go. Mum's really upset because this Fergie person is going to another wedding. 'You're his star player, David. You'd think he could make an effort.'

Personally, I'm not too worried. The fewer people who see me in the ridiculous wedding garb the better, as far as I'm concerned.

Wednesday June 23rd

Everything's being packed up ready for the move to the new house after the wedding. I shall have to hide my diary in case it gets lost in the confusion. I don't know quite how I'm going to cope without having an outlet to express my inner turmoil.

Farewell diary! So many things could happen before I see you next: Baby Spice might think I'm a poofter; Dad might forget his name when they're saying the wedding vows. Oh, and we're going to a tropical island for the honeymoon. World, here I come …

Thursday June 24th

Friday June 25th

Saturday June 26th

Sunday June 27th

Monday June 28th

Tuesday June 29th

Wednesday June 30th

JULY
1999

Thursday July 1st

Friday July 2nd

Saturday July 3rd

Sunday July 4th

Monday July 5th

Tuesday July 6th

Wednesday July 7th

Thursday July 8th

Friday July 9th

Saturday July 10th

Sunday July 11th

I am absolutely cream-crackered. I haven't stopped for two weeks. I've got so much to say I don't know where to start – the wedding seems as good a place as any.

I have, quite honestly, never been so embarrassed

in my life. Despite all my screaming and shouting, they wouldn't relent about my garb, so I got decked out in this poncy purple dress. I looked like something out of *Queer as Folk*. I tell you, my manhood has taken a severe knocking here.

To make it worse, everywhere I looked there was a pesky photographer. I couldn't do anything without being snapped. Lunch – snap snap. Have a good old burp – snap snap. Drool (deliberately) all over my gear – snap snap. Hey guys! I know you're paying a million spondoolies and everything, but come on! Certain things are for my eyes only (especially when I look like I've just fallen out of a box of Quality Streets).

As for the ceremony itself, well, you've never seen anything like it. I mean, I know it was never going to be what you'd call understated, but there *are* limits. Mum looked like a bleedin' meringue for a start, and as for Dad – if you think *I* looked a little too in touch with my female side, you should have seen him. They both started crying as they said their vows, and I don't blame them – I would too if I looked like that.

As they walked out of the church, a hundred white doves were set free. The problem with Mum and Dad is that they don't think these things through properly. It looked great and everything, but then a couple of guests got, ahem, a little message in the eye. They looked as embarrassed as I felt.

And so to the reception.

Mum and Dad's Wedding Menu

Red Pepper Soup
***

Turkey Breast
Grilled Mediterranean Vegetables
***

Sticky Toffee Pudding
Terrine of Summer Berries

Brooklyn's Wedding Menu

Milk

But worst of all, and I can hardly bring myself to write it, *Baby Spice was with another man!* Oh, the treachery! Oh, the fickleness! Frailty, thy name is woman! I don't know his name, and to be honest I don't want to know it. Baby Spice seemed oblivious to the pain she was causing me – she even had the gall to pretend that nothing was happening:

Baby Spice: Hello, Gorgeous. How are we today?

Spice Baby: *Well, Judas, I don't know about you, but to be honest I've had better days.*

Baby Spice: [Concerned] You've got a bit of a grumpy little face today, haven't you?

Spice Baby: *You ain't seen nothin' yet, Honey-Bun. I ain't fallin' for your crocodile tears. Go on, go*

back to your lover boy. I hope
you'll both be very happy ...

I think she got the message, because I started bawling and she put me back in my cot.

As far as I'm concerned, I'm through with relationships. From now on women will just be my playthings. I shall use them and discard them just as I have been used and discarded by Baby Spice. I tried to explain this to Phoenix Chi after dinner, but she was completely unsympathetic:

Phoenix:	Hey, pal, why the long face?
Brooklyn:	Woman trouble.
Phoenix:	Gees, you guys, you're always blaming your problems on us chicks. Lemme guess, it's Baby Spice, huh? What've you done to upset her?
Brooklyn:	Nothing, unless you count showering her with adoration, hanging on her every word,

Phoenix: and pledging my life to her … Hey man, you're living in the dark ages. The modern girl needs more than that. She needs a bit of excitement in her life, a bit of get up and go. I mean look at ya – you can't even get up by yourself, let alone go! She needs something extra, and if you can't supply it, she's going to go to someone who can … And between you and me, what's with the purple dress, anyway? Kind of a fashion faux pas, huh?

Thanks a bunch, Phoenix Chi – that's done my self-esteem a load of good.

So all in all, what with that and looking like something out of Madame JoJo's Piano Bar, I was too upset to enjoy the party. Everyone else seemed to have fun though – especially the guys from Dad's football team who got rather merry and started singing a very rude song about Arsenal supporters. You've never heard such a racket in your life – gimme the Spice Girls any day ...

The next morning we toddle off on the honeymoon, which I was really looking forward to – a couple of weeks by the pool, catching some rays, watching the girls go by. First stop South of France – but funnily enough we bumped into Fergie on the plane out. Now, I've heard a lot about this Fergie bloke, but he wasn't a bit like I expected him to be. He was much podgier for a start, and had long ginger hair – between you and me he looked a bit girly. And Dad didn't speak to him once about football, he seemed far more interested in playing with his daughters, Beatrice and Eugenie. I don't know why Mum moans about him so much – he seemed perfectly nice to me ...

We stayed at the villa of a friend of Mum and Dad's called Elton. He wasn't there himself, which was a shame because I reckon we'd have got on well. We've got a lot in common – well, we've got a daft name in common, which would have been enough to break the ice.

Still, it was a good chance to get away from it all, and for me to start the long process of recovery after the Baby Spice débâcle. I think I could grow quite fond of French women – they have a certain style that I find so lacking in their English counterparts.

Of course, nothing ever goes quite according to plan. We were supposed to go on to a tropical island in the Indian Ocean. Now that sounds like my kinda scene: blue sea, golden sands, steel drums playing a little light calypso in the background for me to shake my butt to – I can boogie with the best of them if the mood is right. Alas, it was not to be. Fergie, curse him, told Dad that he had to cut his honeymoon short so that he could be back for stupid old football practice.

So, back we came. It's been a very eventful couple of weeks – I feel I've grown up a lot ... well, by precisely two weeks, actually. The Baby Spice stuff was distressing when it happened, but I'm beginning to get my life back on track. After all, there are plenty of fish in the sea ...

Monday July 12th

This new house is taking quite a bit of getting used to. It's very swanky – several squillion bedrooms, and acres of land. I don't quite know why they need such a huge place, but I'm not complaining. It's great for my image.

Suffering from a rather sore mouth today. I hope it's nothing serious.

Tuesday July 13th

Mouth too sore to think. Mum v. grumpy

because I kept her up all night. And she's the one that wants more babies – you gotta learn that it goes with the territory, doll.

Wednesday July 14th

I think I'm growing teeth! This is so exciting. Finally I can see an end to the all-milk diet. I'm going food shopping with Mum tomorrow. I wonder what my first solid grub will be. Oysters? Caviar? I can hardly wait.

Thursday July 15th

Went to Marks & Spencer with Mum. Here's what we bought:

'Gourmet Selection' Chicken in White Wine Sauce – quite like the sound of that, especially the gourmet bit, being, as I am, a connoisseur of fine things.
3 packs Jammie Dodgers (Dad's favourite)

2 jars mushy peas

Yum yum, looking forward to my first proper meal. I pity the poor sod who's got to eat the mushy peas, though – they look 'orrible.

Friday July 16th

Well, I hope Mum and Dad enjoyed their 'Chicken in White Wine Sauce'. I do hope they found their 'Gourmet Selection' to their satisfaction. They certainly seemed terribly pleased with themselves, but not as pleased as when they started feeding me my first proper tuck. Of all the things I could have had. They've got more money than they know what to do with – I could have been eating anything, but no! Not an oyster in sight. Not even half an oyster. Not even a bleedin' winkle!

Yes, dear diary, the mushy peas were for yours truly. Have you ever eaten a mushy pea? My advice is to steer clear – they are vile. Come back milk, all is forgiven.

The strange thing is, Mum seems to quite like them. After I spurned my tempting supper, Mum scoffed the lot.

Saturday July 17th

Dad's been showing off his BROOKLYN tattoo. He doesn't seem to have too many qualms about exposing himself in public, that boy. He takes his top off at every available opportunity. I suppose he has got quite a good physique, but even so – you don't see Mum doing it.

Sunday July 18th

Oh no! Mum's been in the papers saying how much she likes mushy peas, and now some mushy pea company have given her a lorryload as a publicity stunt. No prizes for guessing who's going to have to eat their way through that.

Phoenix Chi's coming round for tea. She looks like a girl with a healthy appetite – maybe I'll be able to off-load some of the green sludge on to her.

Monday July 19th

Well don't say I didn't try:

Brooklyn: Phoenix, sweetheart, have I got a treat in store for you …

Phoenix: What you talkin' about, dude?

Brooklyn: Mmmm … lovely mushy peas, my favourite. You can have some if you like.

Phoenix: No way, dude. I got my own diet – none of that poor-boy trash.

Brooklyn: So what do you eat, then?

Phoenix: Soul food, brother.

Mmmm … soul food. Dunno what it is, but you can bet your bottom dollar it's tastier than mushy peas. I wish Mum could take a leaf out of Scary's book sometimes.

Tuesday July 20th

That's it, I give up. I disown him. Dad went out today wearing a skirt. He calls it a sarong, but he's not fooling anyone. A skirt's a skirt, that's the bottom line. Mum's just as bad – she's actively encouraging him, telling him he looks great.
Dad! Take it from me! You look a right 'nana. If you dress up in girls' clothes, you look like a girl. Simple as that!

Wednesday July 21st

This is no good. I can't tell which is which any more.

Thursday July 22nd

Now, let me get this right. Mum's the one with the fringe and the skirt. Or is that Dad? No, no, that's definitely Mum. This is very confusing. I'll just have to remember that Mum's the one with all the jewellery.

Friday July 23rd

No, that won't work either. Dad's got more jewellery than Mum. I wish he'd just start wearing trousers again – it made life a whole lot easier.

Saturday July 24th

I know – Dad's the one with the beard. Easy-peasy.

Sunday July 25th

Doh! Dad's shaved his beard off. Sometimes I think he actively *wants* to look like a girl.

Monday July 26th

That's much better. Dad's started wearing trousers again. Apparently some bloke pinched his bum in the street, so it made him think twice about all this cross-dressing stuff.

Talking of cross-dressing, I'm pretty cross with the way they're dressing me at the moment. I haven't been shopping for ages. We're going on a bit of a spree tomorrow, though, so hopefully I'll be able to put things right.

Tuesday July 27th

That's the first time I've been shopping with

Mum and Dad. Talk about spurring each other on. They bought presents for their best man and bridesmaids, presents for each other, and most importantly presents for me – a few rather natty little outfits, with, I'm pleased to report, not even a hint of purple.

That Jezebel Baby Spice will see me and weep.

Wednesday July 28th

Dad's dead pleased. He's been walking round like that cat that got the cream. From what I can tell, there's been a piece in the papers about how scientists have decided that he's as clever as some bloke called Albert Einstein. Dad didn't know who Albert Einstein was, so he got Mum to look it up in an encyclopaedia: 'World's greatest thinker, formulated theory of relativity, successfully described the nature of the universe.' He seemed rather pleased at that. Apparently Dad is the perfect example of somebody with a high level of 'bodily-kinesthetic' intelligence.

I hope it doesn't go to his head. I can think of loads of reasons why Dad isn't the intellectual equal of the world's greatest ever thinker. It takes him three hours to drink a glass of orange squash, for Chrissakes. (The label says 'concentrate'.)

Thursday July 29th

The footy season starts again soon. To be honest, I'll be glad when Dad has something to put his mind to – he keeps coming out with some very funny ideas. He told a magazine today that he's looking forward to the day when I'll want to have DAD tattooed in the same place he's got his BROOKLYN one.

Sorry to disappoint, Dad, but I wouldn't hold your breath. You may be into that kind of thing, but the top of my butt remains tattoo-free, d'ya hear?

Friday July 30th

Mum and the girls are going to go and start recording a new album soon, and I'll get to go with her. I'm a bit worried about how to act in front of Baby Spice. I was kind of uncompromising last time – not that she wasn't asking for it. I guess I'll just have to play it cool. It would really help if I was seeing some other chick when I meet her, but you know it's difficult. I don't really get much chance to meet other women. Sometimes I feel like a bird in a gilded cage.

I'll ask Phoenix Chi for some tips next time I see her.

Saturday July 31st

Another month older, another month wiser. I've had a funny few weeks – been jilted by Baby Spice, suffered severe confusion regarding my parents' sexual identity. It's a miracle I'm so level-headed. Let's hope August calms down a bit …

AUGUST
1999

Sunday August 1st

Aaaaaaaaaaaaaaarrrrrrrrrrrggggggggggggghhhhh
hhhhh!!!!!!!!!!!!!!!!!!!!!!!! Mum and Dad have
bought two Rottweilers. They're absolutely
massive – big slobbery lips and nasty sharp
teeth. What do they think they're doing? One
of those could eat me up in one bite, and still
have room for a bowl of Winalot.

They haven't let them in the same room as me
yet, but it's only a matter of time.

Monday August 2nd

I can hear the dogs snarling around outside. Too scared to write anything.

Tuesday August 3rd

A terrible realisation has dawned upon me. The Rottweilers are in the employ of the Ginger One. They are her harpies, her familiars. What am I going to do?

Wednesday August 4th

Tried to explain my fears to Dad, but unfortunately he didn't understand a word I was saying:

Dad:	Who's got a wet little nappy then?
Brooklyn:	Gurgle Gurgle *[Don't patronise*

	me, daddio. If you knew what I knew, you'd have a wet nappy as well.]
Dad:	Shall we change you?
Brooklyn:	Gurgle, gurgle, gurgle *[You do what you like, pal. As soon as I'm old enough to walk, I'm outta here. Can't you see that the spawn of evil is among us?]*
Dad:	If you're a good boy, I'll take you out to stroke the doggies.
Brooklyn:	Waaaaaaaaaaaahhhhhhh!!!!

It's very frustrating not being able to speak. I'll have to make an extra special effort to learn. Fortunately I cried so much I wasn't deemed good enough to go anywhere near the so-called 'doggies'. I have a feeling I'll be doing quite a lot of crying in the near future …

Thursday August 5th

Cried all day.

Friday August 6th

Ditto.

Saturday August 7th

Cry, cry, cry, cry, cry.

Sunday August 8th

So far it's working – I haven't been anywhere near the dogs yet. Mum and Dad are a bit narked off with me, but it's for their own good. They'd be devastated if I was delivered into the hands of the Ginger One.

Monday August 9th

Went to a Spice Girls recording session today. The situation *vis à vis* Baby was the last thing on my mind, actually. When your life and soul are in danger, such trivialities as unrequited love cease to matter. She seemed quite unembarrassed about the whole affair:

Baby Spice: Hello beautiful!
Spice Baby: *Hey, babe. I got things on my mind at the moment more important than you could ever imagine. Don't go messin' with my head, OK?*

I think she got the message, as she hardly spoke to me for the rest of the day.

Phoenix Chi managed to put my mind at rest a bit:

Phoenix: Hey, dude, you look like you seen a ghost.
Brooklyn: Maybe I have, Phoenix Chi. Maybe I have …

I explained all about the Rottweilers, but she

didn't think that sending spies in the guise of evil beasts was quite Ginger Spice's style: 'She's more subtle than that. She's far more likely to try an' destroy the Spice Girls by knocking them off the number one spot in the charts. Rumour is she's working on an album as we speak …'

We then had a listen to the girls practising. Don't tell Mum, but my money's on Ginger Spice any day of the week.

Tuesday August 10th

I'm going to be a TV Star! Some guys want to film an 'At Home with the Beckhams' documentary. I'm not quite sure why. The Beckhams don't do much when they're at home these days. Dad spends a few hours a day doing his hair, and Mum practises her singing. It drives the dogs up the wall, I'm pleased to say. Unfortunately it drives me up the wall too. I'm sure Dad's not wild about it, either, but he knows better than to say anything. Last time Mum got cross with him, he had to do the washing up every day for a week.

Wednesday August 11th

I overheard Mum saying that the guys who want to film this documentary are the same ones that did a documentary about Fergie, who apparently lives in a big palace. How come he gets to live in a palace, and Dad doesn't?

Anyway, Mum and Dad are insisting on being treated like royalty. They're charging fifty thousand big ones (that's one hundred thousand jars of mushy peas to you and me – yeuch!) and are insisting on being able to hire and fire all the staff. This seems to me to be completely reasonable. I remember what it was like with those pesky photographers at the wedding. I couldn't wet my nappy without having someone take a photograph of me.

Charging people a whole pile of dosh to take some pictures is one thing, but expecting them to intrude on your private life is quite another. I don't know why everyone's so interested in them, anyway. Mum and Dad scrub up quite nicely, I suppose, but you should see them when they've just got up. Not a pretty sight!

Manchester United beat Sheffield Wednesday 5–0 today. Talk about a trouncing!

Thursday August 12th

Dad's playing Leeds on Saturday. I hope Mum lets me go.

Friday the thirteenth tomorrow. Hope the Rottweilers don't get too excited …

Friday August 13th

Nothing sinister to report. What a relief.

Saturday August 14th

Well, Mum took me to the game, but I wish she hadn't. I've never been so scared in my life.

Dad's team won 2–0 (Ha! Take that, Leeds!), but then things turned a bit nasty. I know there's supposed to be a load of chanting at football matches, but at one point they all started singing, 'We're going to kill Baby Becks.' That's me they're talking about!

Mum started crying, and Dad made a very rude sign at the supporters. Can you blame him? I'd have done far worse if I wasn't safely cocooned in my designer baby carrier. Lemme at 'em.

Sunday August 15th

I fear for my life. I know I live on the edge sometimes, what with the Ginger Spice conspiracy and then the Rottweilers, but this is the first time I've had my life threatened so openly.

Mum's been cuddling me all day, which has made us both feel a bit better. She's very sweet sometimes.

Monday August 16th

Mum and Dad are getting me my own bodyguard! How about that? I reckon I must be a pretty important kinda dude. We start interviewing tomorrow.

Tuesday August 17th

Blimey, some of these bodyguards make Dad look like a brain surgeon. Mum's very choosy – we've interviewed loads of 'em. None of today's batch were suitable. Of the ten we interviewed:

3 were too stupid
2 were scared of the dogs
4 supported Manchester City
1 said he fancied that bird out of All Saints (Dad started agreeing with him, until Mum shot him one of her looks)

We've got more to see tomorrow.

Wednesday August 18th

I'm sick of the sight of bodyguards. None of them are right for Mum – too big, too small, too thick, too thin, too this, too that. Make up your bleedin' mind, Mum! My safety is at stake here!

Thursday August 19th

Look, Mum, it's perfectly simple. I've constructed a very straightforward little questionnaire to determine which bodyguard has the attributes I expect:

1. Mum sends you out to buy Brooklyn's tea. Do you buy:

a) Steak tartare, pommes soufflés and Haagen Dazs

b) Mushy peas

c) Milk

2. You are accompanying Brooklyn on a shopping trip, and need to look the part. Do you wear clothes bought from:

a) Nicole Farhi

b) Marks and Spencer

c) Mr By-Rite

3. You are around and about with Brooklyn, and you sense the presence of the Ginger One. Do you:

a) Make the sign of the cross, draw a chalk pentangle and mutter obscure prayers of protection.

b) Put your head down, walk a bit faster, and hope she

doesn't catch you.

c)   Cast Brooklyn aside and run off into the horizon, shouting 'Aaaarrrggghhh ... the Beast is among us.'

4.   You're looking after Brooklyn on a shopping trip, and his nappy needs changing. Do you:

a)   Roll your sleeves up, find a suitable place, and do what needs to be done.

b)   Pretend nothing has happened and ignore the people who wrinkle their nose as you pass by.

c)   Say at the top of your voice, 'Uuuurrgghh ... look what you've done now, you horrible little sprog!'

Anyone who answers (a) to all of the above is the one for me. Easy-peasy.

Friday August 20th

Well finally, they've made their minds up. I'm now the proud owner of not one, but two brand spanking new bodyguards. I think they'll come up to scratch. I have a bit of trouble telling them apart, to be honest, as they look almost identical – big, beefy, oozing testosterone. Not unlike me I suppose. Anyway, you know the type.

I am quite impressed with them both – and they *do* have a good line in shades. We're talking Samuel L. Jackson and John Travolta here. Very cool. Too cool, in fact, to talk very much, so I haven't worked out their names. But hey, they're not being paid to talk, they're being paid to act – and to take the bullet if necessary. I'm the brains, they're the muscle …

I'll refer to them as Number 1 and Number 2. Number 1 used to be a copper, and Number 2 was in the SAS. Pretty good credentials. Most importantly, they are quite presentable, so I'm not embarrassed to be seen with them.

I hope they shape up OK …

Saturday August 21st

8.00 a.m.	Woken up by Number 1 staking out my bedroom, checking for bugs, hidden explosives, etc.
9.00 a.m.	Mum gets the all clear to serve brekky. Number 2 has to taste my mushy peas to check they haven't been tampered with. Looked sick as a dog – Ha ha ha!
1.30 p.m.	Number 2 refuses to touch my mushy peas for lunch. Number 1 has to do the honours.
1.31 p.m.	Number 1 calls Number 2 some very rude things. Hope Dad didn't hear.

| 3.45 p.m. | Number 1 tries to frisk Mum in the corridor. |
| 3.46 p.m. | Mum slaps Number 1 and tells him to 'stop being such a bloody idiot'. Way to go, Mum! |

Sunday August 22nd

Having a bodyguard isn't as exciting as I thought it would be. They just get in the way half the time. Still, we're going into town tomorrow – they'll probably come into their own then.

Monday August 23rd

That's more like it. Mum took me to the shops in the Merc. Number 1 accompanied us in the car, whilst Number 2 provided an escort in the Ferrari. Some bloke made a bit of a spectacle of himself in the jeweller's shop. Mum bought

Dad a watch, but when this bloke heard it ticking he thought it was bomb. Still, better safe than sorry, I suppose.

Tuesday August 24th

I think I'm going off having these bodyguards. It was much more fun when it was just me, Mum and Dad. Still, that's the price of celebrity, I suppose.

Wednesday August 25th

The stupid documentary producers have pulled out of doing the film, so bang go my chances of being a TV star – thanks a bunch, guys! They said Mum and Dad were charging too much money, but these people have no conception of the expenses involved in being a Beckham. Even in the last two weeks we have spent the best part of a hundred grand on basic necessities:

List of Basic Outgoings

2 Bodyguards @ £35,000
His 'n' hers matching Cartier watches @
£10,000
10 x M&S Microwave Dinners @ £3.49

I mean, we've got to subsist …

Thursday August 26th

Dad's in a very grumpy mood – something to do with getting another of these yellow card things. Mum was very cross: 'Oh, David, that's the second in two games. When will you learn?'

Dad stomped off in a huff and went to play with his toy cars.

Friday August 27th

Mum's bought Dad a Manchester United

colouring book. He seemed quite pleased with it, but I'm a bit worried that he's got his beady eyes on my crayons.

Saturday August 28th

Sunday August 29th

Monday August 30th

Tuesday August 31st

SEPTEMBER
1999

Wednesday September 1st

Thursday September 2nd

Friday September 3rd

Saturday September 4th

Sunday September 5th

Monday September 6th

Tuesday September 7th

Wednesday September 8th

Thursday September 9th

Friday September 10th

Saturday September 11th

Sunday September 12th

Monday September 13th

Tuesday September 14th

Wednesday September 15th

Thursday September 16th

Friday September 17th

Saturday September 18th

Sunday September 19th

Monday September 20th

Tuesday September 21st

Wednesday September 22nd

Thursday September 23rd

Friday September 24th

Saturday September 25th

Sunday September 26th

Monday September 27th

Tuesday September 28th

Wednesday September 29th

Thursday September 30th

OCTOBER
1999

Friday October 1st

Found crayons! Dad nicked them weeks ago to do his colouring in, and then left them under his bed. He only found them because Mum told him to go and tidy his room. Honestly, sometimes I feel like *he's* the kid around here.

Hence my silence for all of September – not that I'd have had much to write about even if I could. Dad got two more yellow cards (I've found out what they are – apparently Dad gets them for kicking people in a football match, just like he did when he was playing

Subbuteo with Mum. It seems he does it quite a lot.)

Oh, and Mum and Dad were voted Coolest Couple by a magazine called *Elle*. Coolest couple? I don't think so. As if to prove my point, Dad turned up at the awards ceremony with a silk hanky on his head. Q.E.D., daddio …

Dad seems to have a thing about wearing stupid things on his head. Since I've been around he's been wearing silk hankies, woolly hats, bandannas – everything bar a bleedin' tea cosy. You name it, he's made a hat out of it. Anyone would think he's ashamed of his hairstyle; but then, why would he spend two hours a day with the old Brylcreem pot if that was the case?

Maybe he should just shave it all off. Nah, on second thoughts I don't think I fancy that very much. I'm a bit of a slap-head myself, but I don't really want to make it worse by having a skinhead Dad.

Saturday October 2nd

Oh dear, Dad's in trouble with Fergie again. He went out partying the night before a game, and got fined two weeks' wages. *Two weeks!* That's £50,000!!! Talk about unreasonable.

Now if they'd charged him £50,000 for wearing that stupid silk hanky on his bonce then I'd understand. When are you going to learn, Dad? If you want to put something on your head, get a hat!

Sunday October 3rd

Hey, way to go! I had my first ever crawl today. A whole new world has opened up in front of me. I'm mobile!

Gave Number 1 and Number 2 a bit of a runaround. This could be fun ...

Monday October 4th

Seven months old today. Crawled all day to celebrate – boy, can I move …

Tuesday October 5th

The great thing about being able to move around is that I can have a good old rummage about. Found Dad's Manchester United colouring book, today, which made interesting reading. I don't know why he needed to nick all my crayons for it. All he's done is go through and draw a false beard and moustache on the pictures of Fergie.

You know, I'm beginning to think that there might be two different Fergies. Even without the false beard and moustache, the one in Dad's colouring book doesn't look a bit like the one we met on the plane that time. Ah well, you live you learn.

Wednesday October 6th

I'm growing up real quick. Caught a glimpse of myself in the mirror today, and I don't mind telling you that I was rather impressed with what I saw. My hair has grown fuller, more in keeping with a man of my experience; my cheeks are less chubby – the whole effect is, well, pretty zingy!

It's about time I sorted my love life out. I'm completely over Baby Spice now. To be honest I've moved on. I need a woman with a bit more dignity. I wonder if Phoenix Chi knows anyone. She's coming round tomorrow. I'll have to ask her.

Thursday October 7th

Showed Phoenix Chi my crawling antics, but she wasn't impressed. She's been crawling for a few months now. So we settled down and had a good old gossip:

Brooklyn: Hey Phoenix, I'm not getting much action in the old romance department. You got any friends that are looking for luurrve?

Phoenix: A few, dude, but hey, don't take this the wrong way – you ain't quite their type.

Brooklyn: Whaddya mean, not their type? I'm the most eligible bachelor in town – young, rich, single, handsome. What more could a girl need.

Phoenix: Experience, man. These chicks are nine, even ten months old. What've you got to offer them? They need a man that can show them a few tricks.

What a blow to the ego. I'm going off Phoenix Chi a bit – she's so superior all the time. I don't know what she thinks she's got to be superior about. I haven't noticed her being protected by two crack babyguards lately.

Friday October 8th

I've been overhearing some very odd conversations from Mum and Dad's bedroom. She put me to bed, went into her bedroom, and then I heard her whispering, 'David, take my dress off, darling …'

Why can't she take her own dress off? She's a grown woman, after all.

Saturday October 9th

Same thing last night. 'David, take my stockings off, my darling …'

What is going on? I've never heard her ask him to take her stockings off before.

Sunday October 10th

So they go to bed last night and I hear Mum say under her breath, 'David, darling, take my bra off.' By this time I'm blushing bright red, but then I hear, 'Now David, that's the third night in a row I've caught you wearing my bloody clothes. It really has got to stop.'

Oh, the shame of it. Wearing skirts is one thing, but that! I hope nobody finds out. I'll be a laughing stock.

Monday October 11th

Aw, Mum! She's been going round telling people that football matches are too scary for me because of the noise. I don't think so! Given some of the stuff I've had to contend with – baby-eating Rottweilers, the constant threat of Ginger Spice, Dad in a skirt – I think I can manage a few noisy football supporters, even if they are making unkind comments about my parentage.

I hope she doesn't stop me going to matches. If I'm going to impress the birds by being a top footballer, I need all the help I can get …

Tuesday October 12th

Mum's really upset. Everyone's been making all sorts of mean comments about her looking too thin. Well, if it's any consolation, Mum, I think you look gorgeous.

And anyway, there's no question of her not eating enough. I took an inventory of everything she ate today:

> 6 bags crisps (cheese and onion – did nothing for her breath)
> 1 jar mushy peas (perfectly happy with that – it's one jar less for me to eat …)

2 chocolate bars
1 Indian takeaway
2 tins Ambrosia real dairy custard

Posh Spice? Nosh Spice more like …

Wednesday October 13th

Dad's taking me to football training tomorrow. Can hardly wait.

Thursday October 14th

Well, I finally met the real Fergie. He seemed quite nice, even if he was a bit grumpy. I flashed him one of my winning smiles, though, and that melted even his stony old heart. Works every time – maybe I should become a male model. Everyone in the team did exactly what he said, especially Dad. He was a bit like Mum in that way – really bossy. If only Fergie could see what Dad had made him look like in the Manchester United colouring book.

Fergie made them do all sorts of funny things – to be honest, there wasn't much football involved. It was more a case of making everybody wiggle their hips and all sorts of other undignified things. I was with Number 2, and he said they looked like 'a bunch of bleedin' ballerinas'. I'm inclined to agree with him.

I've slightly gone off the idea of becoming a footballer.

Friday October 15th

Uh-oh! Dad's in trouble yet again. He's being hauled in front of the FA because of his behaviour – something to do with all those yellow cards, I suppose.
They don't know the half of it – if they think his conduct is ungentlemanly on the pitch,

what would they think if they knew about the conversations he's been having with Mum about him wearing her clothes?

If only I could talk, what secrets I could tell (don't worry, Dad, they're safe with me.) But you know, it can't be long before I start talking. I'm going to have to give some serious thought as to what my first words will be. I really must avoid tired old clichés like 'Ma' or 'Da'. I need something with a little more pzazz – I don't know what Phoenix Chi is considering, but I'll definitely have to upstage her. That girl is getting a bit too big for her booties.

Saturday October 16th

Sunday October 17th

Monday October 18th

Tuesday October 19th

Wednesday October 20th

Thursday October 21st

Dad nicked my bleedin' crayons again. I *wish* he wouldn't do that – he's got enough money, can't he buy his own? Without them, I have no artistic outlet, no mode of expression. All Dad uses them for is to practise writing DAVID – which I suppose means that they're at least being put to good use …

Friday October 22nd

Dad's sister got married today. I've got to say, Dad can look pretty funky when he's not dressing up in girly clothes. Me and Mum didn't go to the wedding – she said she was too tired after I kept her up all night screaming. That'll put the cat among the pigeons.

Given some more thought to my first words. I reckon 'Brooklyn in da house!' would probably go down well. I hope I can manage it.

Spice Girls rehearsal tomorrow. I'll see if I can work out what Phoenix Chi's got in mind.

Saturday October 23rd

Ha ha ha! Phoenix Chi has said her first word, and all she could come up with was 'Mama'! Gave her a good old ribbing:

Brooklyn: So, Phoenix Chi, first words, hey? 'Mama'. Pretty inventive, huh?

Phoenix: Hey dude, don't give me none of yo' lip. This speakin' thang ain't so easy as it seems. So how's the love life, or lack of it?

Brooklyn:	No need to rub it in, Phoenix Chi. Since you ask, it's pretty quiet.
Phoenix:	Why not have another crack at Baby Spice, dude? She's a single woman again, you know.

Well, that got my little mind working overtime. I thought I was over her, but maybe I've been kidding myself all along:

Brooklyn:	What about all that stuff about experience? I thought I was too young to go for the older woman option.
Phoenix:	Maybe, maybe not. You know, I can see you and Baby as an item. You look kinda cute together.

Sunday October 24th

My mind is in turmoil. Do I really want to go down the path of loving Baby Spice with all my being once more? Maybe I have no choice. Maybe it is destined to be.

She tried to give me a kiss yesterday, but I wriggled around and cried and got out of it. I don't want her thinking she can muscle in again so quickly – this cat's gonna play hard to get.

Monday October 25th

I had to listen to those 'orrible dogs snuffling around outside the house all night. It's not long now till Hallowe'en – I'm sure I've noticed a difference in the dogs. They are more intense, more purposeful somehow. It's the calm before the storm ...

Tuesday October 26th

Cripes! All hell's broken loose. Mum's in real trouble for not going to that wedding the other day. Dad's family believes Mum thinks she's too posh for them. Mum thinks Dad's family's over-reacting.

Personally I think it's a load of old baloney. Talk about a storm in a teacup. Should I ever get it together with Baby, she'll have to be content to live in sin with me. All this marriage stuff seems like more hassle than it's worth.

I wonder how much Dad's sister got for her wedding photos.

Wednesday October 27th

Only a few days until Hallowe'en. Something sinister is afoot. Ginger Spice has a new record out. They were playing it on the radio and out of the window I saw the dogs stop what they were doing and prick up their ears. She is calling to them.

Thursday October 28th

I hope Number 1 and Number 2 are aware of what is happening. I feel I shall need protection before the week is out. They seem to spend their whole time arguing about whose turn it is to test the mushy peas.

More important things are happening, guys! The dogs are planning to gobble me up on Hallowe'en. I know it. I can feel it in my water. I've got to think of some kind of way to get out of the house on Hallowe'en, otherwise something terrible will happen.

Friday October 29th

Dad! My hero! I've overheard him saying to Mum that he's going to take me out tonight to do something called Trick or Treating. I don't know what it is, and I don't care. As long as the evil Ginger Spice doesn't know where I am, I'll be happy … I gleaned a bit of information about it from Mum:

Mum: Who's going to be a scary little monster on Hallowe'en, then?

Brooklyn: *Hey, what are you trying to say? Is there something wrong with my hair? Aren't I smiling enough?*

Mum: That's right! We're going to dress you up as something horrible, aren't we?

Brooklyn: *Look, Mum, after the purple dress fiasco, nothing would surprise me. However, on this one occasion, a disguise would*

*be handy. Just don't go over
the top, there's a good girl.*

OK, guys, so I'm sacrificing my principles. So I'm not going to look like the cat I should on Sunday night. But hey! I got my reasons!

Later on in the day, I overheard Mum and Dad saying that they are going to dress me up as the evil Ginger Spice for trick or treating. This is great. In fact it's better than great – it's perfect! If the real Ginger One comes to get me, the last thing she'll be looking for is someone who looks like herself.

I've out-manoeuvred them all. You gotta get up pretty early in the morning to catch Brooklyn Beckham!

Saturday October 30th

Overslept.

Sunday October 31st

Tonight's the night.

The dogs are getting excited. There's something in the air (but that could just be a result of the mushy peas). Tonight we must act with all the skill and precision of a military operation. If all goes well, dear diary, I will fill you in tomorrow …

NOVEMBER
1999

Monday November 1st

I live to tell the tale! We started dressing up about an hour before dark. Mum put a ginger wig on my head – it felt a bit funny having so much hair. She said that to make me look authentic I'd have to look a bit fatter, but Dad told her not to be a bitch and stopped her from putting cushions up my jumper. Dad dressed up as a vampire (Black Cape –Versace £399). To be honest, he looked much scarier when he was wearing his silk hanky. Mum put a kind of slinky catsuit on that made Dad want to pinch her bum. Honestly, grown ups! I'll never understand them.

As we left the house, I caught a glimpse of the Rottweilers. They looked sick as ... well ... dogs. Number 1 and Number 2 followed us at a respectful distance. I got the impression that they were a bit embarrassed and didn't really want to be there. To be frank, I was unimpressed. It's a dangerous world out there; they need to be constantly vigilant.

Trick or treating involves going round to everyone's house and giving them a choice – either they give me a treat or Mum and Dad give them a trick. Fortunately everyone came up with the goods, which was lucky because Dad forgot to bring the eggs and flour. Mum got a bit upset when the grumpy bloke down the road said, 'Anything to stop you singing, sweetheart,' before handing over a fiver, but fortunately she didn't let it spoil the evening.

Came away with quite a good haul:

£32.86
1 pack Jammy Dodgers

Loads of sweets

Dad scoffed the Jammy Dodgers on the way home. Typical.

But best of all – no sign of Ginger Spice all evening. I have escaped her grasp!

Tuesday November 2nd

I think Mum and Dad have finally twigged that I'm not too keen on the dogs. They're talking about sending them to another home.

Wednesday November 3rd

Yippee!!! The dogs are going tomorrow! Farewell, mutts, it's been nice knowin' ya!

Thursday November 4th

I'm master of my own domain again. Thank God I don't have to put up with those snivelling hounds watching my every move. What a weight off my mind.

Bonfire night tomorrow. It's just one excitement after another round here …

Friday November 5th

Wow! That was great. We've just been to a wicked firework display. Dad wanted to have one in the back garden, but Mum reminded him that last year he put all the fireworks in the ground upside down, and that maybe it would be better if we let someone else do it this year. He sulked a bit, but he soon came round.

I only wish Baby Spice had been there. It was so romantic, she'd have been putty in my hands…

Saturday November 6th

Dinner tonight at a posh restaurant with Mum and a lady called Mrs Madonna. Why do all Mum's friends have funny names: Madonna, Elton, Scary, Sporty … It would be so refreshing to find out that she had a chum called Fred.

Ah well, I'll fill you in tomorrow.

Sunday November 7th

What an eventful evening. Mrs Madonna was very nice – and quite sexy too, between you and me. But it wasn't her I had eyes for. Oh no! Her daughter is the one for me!

Lourdes! If I could speak I would sing your name to the heavens. The thought of your golden locks sets my heart a-thumpin' (I definitely prefer blondes). OK, so she's a bit older than me, but that only adds to her charm.

She toddles with such grace, and when she opens her mouth to speak it is like poetry: 'Mummy sack servant!'; 'Mummy take clothes off again!' She is *so* sophisticated.

We got on like a house on fire. Despite the difference in our ages she understood me perfectly well, although she is very posh:

Brooklyn:	Lourdes, baby, what's happening?
Lourdes:	I say, must you speak in such an uncouth manner?
Brooklyn:	Ooops! Sorry! How do you do?
Lourdes:	Very well, thank you for asking.
Brooklyn:	So, Lourdes, were you named after where you were conceived, too?
Lourdes:	I should hope not, my dear fellow. Otherwise my name would be 'Chandelier'.
Brooklyn:	Oh I see. Well, maybe you and me could hook up sometime,

	have dinner. Mum does a great line in mushy peas.
Lourdes:	One is used to something a little more elegant.
Brooklyn:	Well, I'm sure we could rustle something up – a little puréed carrot, perhaps?
Lourdes:	In that case, I would be delighted to accept.

We couldn't fix a time and place as we both agreed that we were slightly at the mercy of our mums. It's probably no bad thing, as she's a pretty classy kinda chick. I need some time to brush up on my manners.

Monday November 8th

No good looking to Dad for inspiration about manners. He burps more than I do.

Tuesday November 9th

Lourdes, my love! When will I see you again?

Baby Spice came round today:

Baby Spice: Hello, Gorgeous. Have you got a kiss for your Aunty Emma?

Spice Baby: *'Fraid not, sweetheart. You're yesterday's news.*

Baby Spice: Come on, don't be grumpy!

Spice Baby: *Nice try, but no dice. You had your chance, you blew it …*

She looked a bit upset, but what can I say? That's the way the cookie crumbles.

Wednesday November 10th

Mum's turning on the Christmas lights in Oxford Street tonight. I don't know why they need her to do it. It's not like she's a qualified electrician or anything.

Thursday November 11th

Between you and me, I found the Christmas lights a little vulgar. I'm glad the beautiful Lourdes wasn't there – they wouldn't have been her scene at all.

Friday November 12th

Mum's been telling everyone that she wants to be a comedian. I think she's got it the wrong way round. Dad's the funny one – he went out today wearing a banana-coloured bandanna. Laugh? I almost wet myself. In fact, I did wet myself. Good thing Lourdes wasn't around to see ...

Saturday November 13th

Lourdes, my love. My life is empty without you. My heart aches. When will I see you again?

Sunday November 14th

Not long now 'til Christmas. I'll have to start thinking about my present list.

Monday November 15th

Brooklyn's Pressie List

- Lots of posh clobber to impress Lourdes.
- Football – I'll be needing it soon; can't be long before I take my first step.
- My two front teeth – the rest seem

to be coming through quite nicely, but I haven't heard a peep out of these two   yet. I wouldn't mind, but it just makes me look a bit odd. What kinda chick's gonna go for a toothless baby?

• My own set of wheels – this crawling is all very well, but a kid like me needs more independence. I saw a rather nifty little Ferrari in the toy shop the other day. It's just so *me* – and if Lourdes saw me in it, her eyes would pop out of her head.

Tuesday November 16th

Been worrying about my present list all day. I wonder if I'm going over the top. Maybe I should cut out the non-essential items.

Wednesday November 17th

Brooklyn's Pressie List – Second Draft

> • Clobber – Absolutely essential. I've
> got to look the part.
> • Ferrari – See above.

I've cut out the football – it's jumping the gun a
bit, and I can always nick one of Dad's – and the
two front teeth. It would be nice to have them,
but when you're on a diet of mashed vegetables,
there are more essential items.

Thursday November 18th

Dear Father Christmas

How's it hangin'? Thought I should drop you a
line well in advance of Chrizzy to give you
plenty of opportunity to get to work on my
presents. I've given it some careful thought,

separated the wheat from the chaff, and come up with the following:

- 1 baby Ferrari – we're looking at about forty grand, which sounds a lot I know. But look, Santa – I'm not like other kids. I've got a reputation to maintain – your run-of-the-mill soft toys just won't cut the mustard.
- New baby gear – I've saw a pretty groovy D&G cardigan the other day: any colour except purple would do. Otherwise, you know that kind of thing: Calvin, Armani – just stay clear of anything without a label.

If you could just drop the gear at the end of my cot on the night, that'd be great. Oh, and please try and keep the noise down – I get pretty grizzly if I'm woken up in the night.

Yours, etc.

Brooklyn Beckham

Friday November 19th

Way to go! Mum's taking me to LA tomorrow. Have decided not to take my diary. I can't be sure that it will be safe from prying eyes.

Saturday November 20th

Sunday November 21st

Monday November 22nd

Tuesday November 23rd

Wednesday November 24th

Boy oh boy, what an eye-opener. LA – now that's what I call a town. If I thought Mum knew how to shop in England, well, you should have seen her on the other side of the pond!

We had a pretty eventful trip over there. Mum was in a filthy mood when we left, because she'd just been voted Britain's Most Miserable Female Star. I don't know where anybody got that idea from. She normally seems pretty chirpy to me when she's out and about. It's when she's at home that she gets miserable. She got really cross with Dad the other day because he spent so long doing a jigsaw puzzle. The box said '1 to 2 Years' so Dad thought he was doing really well.

So anyway, Mum got in an argument with a traffic warden at the airport and called her some *very* rude things. I didn't know she had it in her. People wouldn't call her posh if they'd witnessed that little scene. She got told off for parking in the drop-off area, and Mum screamed at her that she didn't have any dark glasses and would be mobbed if she had to park further away. She needn't have worried though

– nobody even recognised her. Come to think of it, that made her even crosser.

We were going over to film a Spice Girls Special, so all the others were there, including Phoenix Chi. I had a quick chinwag with her on the plane, and told her about my new-found love:

Phoenix: So how's the love life, dude?

Brooklyn: I found myself an older woman. Maybe you know her – her name's Lourdes?

Phoenix: Hey, classy, dude.

Brooklyn: Well, you know, nothing's official yet, but we have an understanding. I like her, she likes me – we'll take it from there.

Otherwise the flight was pretty uneventful ...

LA is my kinda town. We shopped 'til we dropped, and then we shopped some more. Mum bought me a rather stylish Louis Vuitton bottle-carrier, and more clothes for her and Dad than they could ever possibly wear. More importantly, I've found a whole bunch of extra stuff to put on my Christmas list. I'd better send another letter to Santa updating him.

It was a whirlwind trip, but I must admit it was nice to get back and see Dad. I know he's a bit dim sometimes, but I do miss the lad.

Thursday November 25th

Jet-lag. Too tired even to write a coherent, erm …

Friday November 26th

Just about getting back into the swing of things. It's not easy being a jet-setting superstar baby, but I guess I'll just have to get used to it.

Saturday November 27th

You know, Number 2's one helluva good-lookin' dude. We hit town today, and anything in a skirt seemed to be trying to chat him up. The girl in Next looked a bit flustered, but between you and me I think that was more to do with the presence of yours truly than anything else. Some people can handle the presence of celebrities, others just get star-struck.

Anyway, Number 2 had better watch out. Mum was giving him some filthy looks.

Sunday November 28th

Number 2 had better watch out. Dad told Mum that he'd seen the chicks eyeing him up as well. The clock is ticking, dude.

Monday November 29th

I woke up to find that Number 2 had gone. Unfortunately this means I'm down to one bodyguard. I hope Lourdes doesn't find out – she was a bit sniffy about me only having two.

Tuesday November 30th

Another end to another month. I hope December's everything I've been hoping for – which reminds me, I must write to Santa again …

DECEMBER
1999

Wednesday December 1st

Dear Father Christmas

Re: Brooklyn's Presents

I hope you got my last letter. I'm sorry to mess you around, but I have a few additions to make to my Xmas requirements:

1 kiddy's drumkit (available from all good LA department stores – perhaps you could despatch an elf to pick one up for me)
1 bespoke baby buggy (4-wheel drive,

power steering – you know the deal)

In addition, I think it would be a nice gesture if you could sort Dad out with his own set of crayons. He's beginning to get the hang of them, and it would stop him from nicking mine all the time.

Hope this is OK. Look forward to seeing the loot on Xmas a.m.

With best wishes

Brooklyn

Thursday December 2nd

Mum and Dad are taking me out to see their friend Elton tomorrow. He's a very rich pop star, so it should be quite interesting.

These pop stars seem to be very rich in general. If Santa comes up with the goods at Xmas, I should be the proud owner of a new set of drums. They should offer a suitable fall-back position if the footballing gig falls through.

Friday December 3rd

Hey! Elton's really nice, but between you and me I think Mum and Dad have got his name the wrong way round. Elton John? Erm … I don't think so. John Elton, I think you'll find.

The only problem with him is that he dresses in even funnier clothes than Dad. And he came along with his friend David whose hand he kept holding. Still, I'm sure they were just being friendly.

Saturday December 4th

Cripes! I think Dad's gawn mad!

He decided to take me to footy practice today,

and so after brekky we bundled into the Ferrari. We were just going out of the drive when all of a sudden we see these other cars with photographers hanging out the windows.

Dad absolutely floored it – it was a good job I was safely strapped into my baby carrier (Gaultier, £399 heh heh heh!). I saw my life flash before my eyes, which was an uncomfortable experience as it seemed to focus on the purple dress at Mum and Dad's wedding, and for a few terrifying minutes I thought I'd never see my beloved Lourdes again.

It was all very scary – but I *am* pleased to say that the bozos with the cameras couldn't see us for dust. Nice one, Dad!

So everything was going hunky dory until Dad got pulled over by the coppers. They didn't believe his story about trying to escape, so they've told him he's got to go to court.

Sunday December 5th

Poor old Dad. He's in trouble with Mum as well as with the law, and he seems to be far more scared of her. She's banned him from Jammy Dodgers for a week. I don't know how he's going to cope.

I don't know what everyone's getting so worked up about – OK, so it was a bit scary, but hey, a guy's gotta live a little …

Monday December 6th

Court tomorrow. I hope Dad wears something sensible, otherwise they'll send him down for crimes against fashion.

Tuesday December 7th

Well! Dad looked perfectly presentable,

which is more than you can say for the judge. He had the most ridiculous haircut you ever saw (and living in my household you get to see some pretty ridiculous haircuts) – I almost burst out laughing when I saw him! *And* he was wearing what looked like a big red dress. Lordy me – he'll be the first against the wall when the style police hit town.

Despite his ridiculous get-up, he had the gall to ban my Dad from driving. So it has come to this. I am now officially the son of a convicted criminal. This is the beginning of the end.

More worryingly, this means that Mum is going to have to drive us everywhere. This is terrifying. Mum isn't a very good driver …

Wednesday December 8th

Dad's going to appeal against his conviction. I hope he's successful – if not I don't know what he's going to do with all his cars. He's got enough of the things:

List of Vehicles in the Beckham Household

Ferrari Maranello – top speed 199 mph,
0–60 in 4.3 seconds
Porsche 911 – top speed 149 mph, 0–60
in 6 seconds
Mercedes 300 – top speed 149 mph,
0–60 in 6 seconds
Range Rover – top speed 150 mph, 0–60
in 10 seconds
Pierre Cardin pram – top speed
untested, 0–3 in 5 seconds

OK, so the pram's performance doesn't rank so highly, but you've got to make do with what you've got. I hope Dad gets his licence back, though – the pram's groovy and everything, but it's really not his style.

And there's another reason why it's imperative for Dad to get back behind his four steering wheels: it reduces the risk of him having to chat to the general public and, therefore, the risk of me suffering EXTREME EMBARRASSMENT.

Until the bloke with the white hair and the red dress makes his mind up, Dad, Mum and me have had to resort to having our own driver and sometimes … you're not going to believe this … taking a normal taxi!! Like ordinary people!! It could take years of therapy to get over this. But the worst thing is: the taxi drivers insist on chatting – probably because they recognise me, even with my Ray-Ban baby shades on. And if that happens, Mum and I have a tactic that usually works – I puke up, and she fusses over me until we get out. That means that Dad doesn't get drawn into a debate on Britain joining the Euro or the state of the rainforests. But yesterday …

After Dad's conviction, we all toddled off to a swanky restaurant nearby to raise our spirits. Well … Mum and Dad raised a couple of spirits and I got lumbered with the usual tipple – *jus de vache.* Then we all piled into a taxi to go home. The following conversation will be etched on my brain for years to come:

Taxi Driver: Yeah, where to? [He turns round.] Blimey!

Mum: Home – aim for Hertfordshire. It's north.

Taxi Driver: Right you are then. [He looks at Dad in the mirror – I get ready to puke.] Soooo … where you been then, David?

Dad: Err … hmmm … a restaurant.

Taxi Driver: Yeah, which one?

Dad: Hmmmm … It was … just near … errr … name me some London train stations.

Taxi Driver: Oh, OK. Paddington?

Dad: No.

Taxi Driver: Euston?

Dad: No.

Taxi Driver: Victoria?

Dad: Yeah, that's it! Victoria, which restaurant did we go to?

The taxi driver didn't ask any more questions after that. The sooner Dad gets his licence back, the better

Thursday December 9th

Phew! He got the licence back. The man with the funny hair agreed that he was 'speeding under duress'. Dad's dead pleased – Mum's said he can start eating Jammy Dodgers again.

The Spice Girls are playing some really big gigs on Saturday and Sunday. I hope I get to go.

Friday December 10th

Fifteen days till Chrizzy! I hope Santa's doing his thing with the presents – I'll be pretty disappointed if he turns up with a load of boring old cuddly toys.

Saturday December 11th

Mum's concert tonight – can't wait to see her in action.

Sunday December 12th

Blimey! I think I've gone deaf! And no, it's nothing to do with Mum's singing. That concert was the noisiest thing I've ever been to. Even Dad had to pull his bandanna over his ears at one point to block out the sound of all the screaming fans. I've got to admit, though, it was pretty damn impressive.

I hardly recognised Mum when she came out on stage – they were all wearing rather natty-looking black leather outfits. I've got to admit that the sight of Baby Spice in all her Spicey glory got my eyes popping – I'd better not let on to Lourdes. The songs sounded great – even that funny 'zigga zigga' one.

But the most amazing thing was the audience – they went *nuts*. I felt like shouting, 'Hey guys, calm down, it's only Mum!' Unfortunately all I could manage was 'Gurgle gurgle' (I must put my mind to this speaking malarkey). Even if I could have spoken, though, they wouldn't have heard me, as they were far too busy screaming their heads off. To be honest, it's a wonder they heard any of the songs.

We went backstage after the gig, and I decided that it would be churlish to be rude to Baby Spice after such a performance:

Baby Spice: Did little Brooklyn enjoy his first concerty-woncerty?

Spice Baby: *Hey doll, don't concerty-woncerty me. But since you ask, yeah, it was pretty cool.*

Baby Spice: How about a kiss for Aunty Emma, then?

Spice Baby: *OK, but don't think you're gonna make a habit of this.*

I'm saving these cherry-red lips for one person and one person only. Apart from Mum, of course. And Dad.

Sporty was acting kind of weird. She spent the whole concert doing the splits up in the air, and she could hardly walk straight afterwards. That girl will do herself an injury if she's not careful.

Monday December 13th

Oh my gawd! Dad's just blown a hundred grand on a snooker table. It hasn't been delivered yet because – wait for it – he's designing it himself!

Now don't get me wrong. My Dad has many skills. Well, he's got a few skills. OK, OK, so he can kick a ball. This is my point: of all the tasks that are within the sphere of his capabilities, snooker table design is not one.

Mum's just as bad, encouraging him. The reason it's so expensive is because she doesn't like the colour green, so they're having it made out of … gold! Would you Adam and Eve it? It's going to go wrong. I just know it's going to go wrong.

Tuesday December 14th

Dear Father Christmas

I'm really sorry to keep pestering you, but I thought I'd better lay my cards on the table. Here's the deal. Mum and Dad have just ordered a gold snooker table that Dad designed. It's costing a hundred grand, but between you and me, spending that kind of dough on something designed by Dad is the equivalent of throwing your money down the potty.

What I need to know is this: if the table arrives and it's only got three legs, or the holes are in the middle instead of round the edge, and Mum and Dad decide they've wasted the lolly, how does this affect my pressie situation? I'm embarrassed to ask really, but you see the drum kit, the Ferrari and the clobber are all instrumental to the ongoing Lourdes situation, so without them I'll kind of be up the stream without a paddle. You dig?

Perhaps you could let me know how I stand.

Yours, etc.

Brooklyn Beckham

Wednesday December 15th

Ten days to go. I'm getting kind of nervous.

Thursday December 16th

No word from Father Christmas. I guess I'm just going to have to sit tight and see what happens.

Friday December 17th

Dad bought a great big Christmas tree today and spent all day decorating it. It looked absolutely great, but then Mum came home and said she wanted a star on the top. So off she went and cut out a picture of herself and up it went.

I do wonder sometimes if fame has gone to that girl's head.

Saturday December 18th

Only a week 'til Christmas, and Santa still hasn't replied. Sort your priorities out, Santa dude …

Sunday December 19th

Overheard Dad talking to John Elton on the phone. He's plotting something for Mum for Christmas. I wonder what it is …

Monday December 20th

Went carol singing with Mum and Dad. Earned 38 pence. Mum was a bit upset when somebody shouted out, 'Oi sweetheart, Hallowe'en was weeks ago!' I must admit, it wasn't a very Christmassy thing to say.

Tuesday December 21st

I knew it! I *bleedin'* knew it! Dad's gold snooker table arrived, perfectly constructed apart from one thing – the legs were 3 inches high! If anyone's going to mix up their feet and inches, it's my Dad. It was so embarrassing – the delivery men thought he was a complete fool.

He's sent it back to be altered – I hope this doesn't affect my pressie situation.

Wednesday December 22nd

I'm going to go mad! Mum's been singing Christmas carols all day. It'd be enough to make little baby Jesus turn in his manger. It's certainly enough to make little baby Brooklyn turn in his Pierre Cardin cot.

Thursday December 23rd

Aw, Mum, please stop … for pity's sake!

Friday December 24th

Mum! If I weren't so little I'd take your holly

and your bleedin' ivy and stick it where the sun don't shine.

To top it all, Dad keeps kissing me under the mistletoe. My skin is a mess of stubble burn. As you may have guessed, dear diary, the Christmas spirit is yet to descend upon me. Santa had better come up with the goods ...

Saturday December 25th

Zowee! That's what I call a haul. I don't understand why we don't have Christmas every day.

8.00 a.m.   Woke up. Distressed to see that Santa hadn't left any presents at the bottom of the cot.
8.01 a.m.   Started crying.
8.05 a.m.   Dad takes me downstairs. Relieved to see big pile of pressies under the tree.

8.06 a.m.   Start unwrapping pressies.

Brooklyn's Christmas Presents

1 Baby Ferrari – bingo! Diesel engine, CD/DVD player, top speed 30 mph – and best of all it's a mini-version of Dad's!
1 Baby Drum Kit
Assortment of Prada, Gucci, etc.

Mum and Dad had decided to limit their spending on each other this year; they promised each other that they wouldn't blow more than ten grand each. I'd have been worried – I mean, what does ten grand buy you these days? Still, they managed to come up with rather nice little gifts – platinum and diamond cufflinks for Dad, and a white gold necklace for Mum.

But then Dad sprang his surprise on Mum – he'd got her John Elton's piano!!! Mum was over the moon. She proceeded to spend all morning trying to play it.

I hope Mum gets some piano lessons soon.

The best part of the day was lunch. Finally a bit of variety in my diet: mashed turkey, mashed parsnips; Dad particularly enjoyed the mashed carrots, but Mum had to tell him off for spilling it all down his chin.

Sunday December 26th

Mum's been at the piano all day. What a bleedin' racket.

Monday December 27th

Dad's walking around with his head in his hands looking like he's made a terrible mistake.

Tuesday December 28th

Gave Mum a taste of her own medicine today. Had a good old bash on the drums – I think I may have the inkling of a talent there.

Wednesday December 29th

Welcome to the Beckham household musical extravaganza:

Brooklyn:	Boom, crash, Boom-boom, crash
Mum:	Plink plonk plink
Brooklyn:	Boomty crash crash kerbang
Mum:	Plinkety plink plonk

Dad's spent most of the day in the garden. He looks slightly drawn.

Thursday December 30th

Went to the wedding of a bloke in Dad's football team called Phil. It was all much more understated than Mum and Dad's wedding – but perhaps it's just that I've matured a bit since then. Best of all I got to wear my first ever tuxedo – even the stupid bandanna that Dad made me wear couldn't detract from the zappiness of the ensemble.

Friday December 31st

And so the year draws to a close, and what a year it's been. You know, I've a feeling that I'm a twenty-first century kinda guy, but it was good to catch the end of the last Millennium. It's been eventful too – lots of stuff has happened that I'll be able to tell my grandchildren about (I hope Lourdes is thinking long-term).

What the New Year has in store is anybody's guess ...

JANUARY
2000

Saturday January 1st

Brooklyn's New Year Resolutions

1. I will not be mean about Dad. He can't help it.
2. I will be tolerant of Mum's singing. I can't promise to extend the same tolerance to her piano playing, but I will do my best.
3. I will not leave my baby Ferrari out in the rain.
4. I will win the heart of Lourdes.
5. I will learn to speak.
6. I will learn to walk.

Sunday January 2nd

Dad's found another jigsaw puzzle to do. I haven't seen it yet, but apparently it's of a tiger. It's taking him ages. He'd better finish it soon – he's off to Brazil in a few days for a match.

Monday January 3rd

Dad's really worried about the jigsaw puzzle. I heard him talk to Fergie on the phone today. 'Hi, boss. Yeah, I'm really worried. I've got this jigsaw puzzle of a tiger and it's really, really difficult. I've got this nasty feeling that I won't be able to finish it in time for the Brazil match, which would be terrible – I just won't be able to concentrate on the game.'

Fergie's coming round tomorrow to help Dad out with the puzzle.

Tuesday January 4th

Fergie came round today – he wasn't at all pleased. Dad emptied the tiger jigsaw out on to the table, and Fergie just said, 'David, put the Frosties back in the box,' and stormed out.

It's going to be very difficult to stick to New Year Resolution Number 1 if Dad carries on like this.

Wednesday January 5th

Mum went on telly today and said that Dad likes to wear her thongs. I hope she meant her *things* … Everyone knows Dad puts a skirt on now and then, but I'd really rather the underwear stuff got kept under wraps.

Thursday January 6th

That's it! That's the last straw – Mum, you've got to learn when to shut your big mouth. It's all over the papers – she *said* thongs, and she *meant* thongs. I can't believe she told everyone that Dad likes to wear her pants! Oh the shame! Oh the ignominy! Now the whole nation knows what goes on in their bedroom. It's *so* humiliating.

Poor old Dad – don't get me wrong, it's not that I approve of these sartorial faux pas, but he really doesn't deserve this. He got sent off in his game against Brazil, which is hardly surprising. I'm amazed he had the bottle to go on in the first place.

Friday January 7th

Too embarrassed to show my face in public. Mum seems pretty sheepish – but at least she's stopped playing the bleedin' piano.

Saturday January 8th

Help! Someone's plotting to kidnap me. The cops have been round and everything. My life is in the balance. I haven't even got Dad here to protect me. Mum and Number 1 are going to have to protect me from these nefarious criminals.

I've got to find out who's at the bottom of this. I've constructed a list of possible suspects:

1.   Ginger Spice. She must be a strong contender. She's got the motive; after I foiled her cynical Hallowe'en plot she must have me down as an obstacle to world dominion.

2.   Baby Spice. OK, so it's not quite her style, but she's been distinctly

cold with me since I spurned her love. Hell hath no fury like a woman scorned …

3. Fergie. Not as unlikely as it sounds. He must have his eye on future Manchester United stars, and I am from good footballing stock, after all.

4. Lourdes. Perhaps she wants to whisk me away to live in luxury with her on desert island. Then again, perhaps not.

I'm absolutely terrified – I never realised I had so many potential enemies. We're going to a safe house tonight. I shan't be able to take my diary. This may be my last ever entry – I hope the world remembers me fondly …

Sunday January 9th

Monday January 10th

Tuesday January 11th

Wednesday January 12th

Thursday January 13th

Civilisation at last! I have just spent five nights in a police safe house, and I was distinctly unimpressed. A lad like me is used to a little luxury, but this place didn't even have en suite facilities. Still, I took it in my stride (not that I have much of a stride) and weathered the storm.

Mum was a tower of strength. She did insist on singing me lullabies to calm me down, though, which to be honest in my endangered state I could have done without. (Oooops! Bang goes Resolution Number 2.)

Anyway, I think the heat is off. Mum and Dad

have upped the security at home, and they're talking about getting a replacement for Number 2. This is good news – I'll need at least two bodyguards if I'm going to impress Lourdes.

Friday January 14th

Hey! I'm going to appear as a comic strip in *The Beano*. Dad's dead impressed – Mum reads him *The Beano* every week.

Saturday January 15th

Some mean old woman has been saying nasty things about my mum. She's the mother of somebody called Naomi Campbell, and she said that Mum is thick and talentless. She doesn't know what she's talking about. Mum's not at all talentless …

Sunday January 16th

Mum's got her own TV show! It's going to be called *Victoria's Secrets* and she gets to interview lots of famous people including John Elton and – wait for it – Dad.

I've seen the tapes, and the questions she asked Dad are nothing like the ones she normally asks him. On telly she says, 'When did you sign your first autograph?' and 'Who has more clothes, you or your wife?' In real life she asks very different things: 'David, have you been using the sofas as goal posts again?' and 'David, why are you wearing that skirt? You know I wanted to wear it tonight.'

Still, I'm glad she kept off that kind of stuff – after the thong débâcle you never know what she's going to say.

Monday January 17th

Wahey! Stood up for the first time. OK, so it only lasted about five seconds before I landed back on my bum (thank God for the nappy cushioning) but it's a start. I'll be walking before you know it.

Tuesday January 18th

Had another little stand today. I'm growing up fast! I'd better start making an effort to speak. 'Brooklyn in da house' are definitely going to be my first words – I just hope I can manage them.

Wednesday January 19th

Phoenix Chi came round today. She thinks I'm being too ambitious with my speaking and suggested that I started out with something a bit less challenging, like 'Da!' She's only jealous, of course, but I must say her speaking is coming on in leaps and bounds. She can already say, 'Phoenix is bad' – I'd grudgingly have to admit that her rap career seems a dead cert.

I told her about the kidnapping scare, and she agreed with me that Ginger Spice seemed the most likely suspect. To be honest, though, the Ginger One has ceased to be a worry to me. I've already foiled her twice, I'm almost walking so I'll be able to run away if the situation does get too hairy, and I've got a nippy little baby Ferrari if I need a getaway car at any point.

Thursday January 20th

First step! You'll notice I say step, not steps – I only managed the one. But you know what they say – from tiny acorns, mighty oaks do grow.

Friday January 21st

The gardeners have just chopped down the mighty oaks at the bottom of the garden. I feel a bit discouraged.

Saturday January 22nd

Mum and Dad spent the day interviewing bodyguards again. I spent the day trying to speak. Brooklyn in da house, Brooklyn in da house …

Sunday January 23rd

Well, they've chosen a new bodyguard. Number 3 is an ex-copper, and he looks pretty beefy.

Monday January 24th

Brooklyn in da house, Brooklyn in …

Tuesday January 25th

… da house. I'm almost ready. I'll have a good sleep tonight and then hit them with it in the morning.

Wednesday January 26th

Doh! What a disaster!

I was all ready to go – Brooklyn in da house and all that – when Dad picked me up and gave me a tickle. All of a sudden out it popped, without so much as a by your leave – '*Da!*'

Dad couldn't believe it, and looked delighted and a little upset all at the same time. It's not surprising – I'm not even one yet and already I'm a quarter of the way to matching his complete vocabulary.

Phoenix will laugh her head off.

Thursday January 27th

All I can say is 'Da!' This is so embarrassing. Even Dad can still say more words than I can, and if he were any less articulate they'd have to keep him in the zoo.

Friday January 28th

Mum and Dad are obviously worried. They've put me down for some really posh school out in the sticks somewhere. I start when I'm four – I hope I manage to formulate a few sensible sentences by then, otherwise I'll be a laughing stock.

Actually, I'm quite pleased about the school. Lourdes is a classy kinda chick. She'll appreciate breeding; she'll go for the educated type. Excuse me whilst I go and practise my Latin verbs …

Saturday January 29th

It's amazing what you find when you have a bit of a toddle around this place. Today I was pottering about, minding my own business, when what should I find but a little diamond? Pretty neat, huh? I shoved it in my nappy and then hid it under the cot ready to give to Lourdes when I ask her to marry me.

Mum and Dad have got plenty of the things, so I can't imagine they'd really miss it.

Sunday January 30th

Oh dear, oh dear, oh dear. Mum's in a right

old state. She's lost the diamond from her engagement ring. I can't think where it can have got to. She played absolute havoc in the shops, making all the shop assistants scramble around on the carpet looking for it.

My face was a picture of innocence, of course. I don't think anyone latched on to the fact that I'd nicked it.

Monday January 31st

The police were round today to talk about the missing diamond. It's in all the papers that Mum's lost her rock. (Makes a change from all the stories about Dad being off his rocker.) I'm wracked with guilt. What am I going to do?

FEBRUARY
2000

Tuesday February 1st

Phew! Dad found the diamond under the cot and guess what? It's not Mum's diamond after all, but a half-sucked Fox's Glacier Mint. Mum's been telling Dad not to spit those things out on the carpet for ages. Still, this little episode has taught me one thing – I'm not cut out for a life of crime. I just can't stand the tension …

Dad's getting completely obsessed by these silly tattoos. He's had this daft guardian angel inked on his back, looking over the 'BROOKLYN' tattoo. Apparently it's meant to protect me.

Now look, Dad, here's the deal. It's all very sweet of you and everything, but I'm not even a year old, and look what I've had to contend with in the last few months, kidnap threats, Ginger Spice, the Hounds of Hell. I hardly think a little tattoo on Daddy's back is going to protect me from stuff of that kind of magnitude, do you?

And if you think I'm going to have one done myself, you've got another thing coming. What if Lourdes saw it? She'd go right off me. She might even go for another celebrity youngster. I've heard that that Prince William is a bit of a charmer – OK, so he's a wee bit old for her, but I've got to be on the look out for the competition.

Wednesday February 2nd

On second thoughts, I don't feel too threatened by Prince Wills. After all, he only gets to live in that dodgy gaff in Green Park, whereas I get the splendour and luxury of Beckingham Palace. And if I were a chick, I know which would impress *me* the most …

Thursday February 3rd

I don't believe it. Dad's been doing the crossword. It's taken him all day so far, but this is a definite sign of improvement. He must learn not to scratch his head so much when he's concentrating, though – he gets Brylcreem all over his fingers.

Friday February 4th

Only one month 'til my birthday. I hope Mum and Dad are planning something good. I'm a bit worried, actually. Dad doesn't seem capable of doing anything at the moment. He's still got his nose in that crossword.

Saturday February 5th

He's still at it. The tension in the house is unbearable.

Sunday February 6th

Dad finished his crossword just after lunchtime. He was extremely chuffed with himself, and so was Mum. She said, 'Oh, David, that's the first time you've managed to finish a whole crossword puzzle all by yourself. I'm so proud of you.'

And she has good reason to be proud of him. I sneaked a look at the puzzle myself, and I must say I was impressed. He'd coloured all of the squares in a different colour, and very neatly too. I could hardly have done better myself.

Monday February 7th

Only a week to go till Valentine's Day. I'd better start composing my missives of love to Lourdes. I thought of sending something to Baby Spice – after all, despite everything she has played a formative role in my emotional development – but on balance I reckon it would be too cruel. She's clearly pining for me, and when one is a super-stud like me it is important to act responsibly when it comes to affairs of the heart.

No, Lourdes will be the only one who receives a Valentine from Brooklyn Beckham this year. I think I'll stay away from the old poetry – I've already discovered that I've no particular talent for that. Something short, sweet and to the point is what's called for, I think. A guy like me doesn't beat about the bush.

Tuesday February 8th

Lourdes

I am in torment. My life is as nothing, until we are reunited.

???

Hmmm … I'm not sure if that's quite the tone I want to achieve. I don't want to sound too desperate, or she'll run a mile. I'll have to give it some thought.

Wednesday February 9th

My darling Lourdes [A bit more passion. OK, so it's slightly over the top, but the chicks go for that kind of thing.]

I think of you every waking moment.

When my nappy is being changed, I think of you. Whenever I say 'Da!' I say it for you. In the morning, when I put on my Prada romper suit, I think of you. In the evening, when Mum puts me to bed in my Moschino cot, you are foremost in my thoughts. [I'm name dropping, I know, but Lourdes is the kind of girl that would be impressed with a little style ...]

Be my baby, sweet Valentine.

I think that hits the spot just right.

Thursday February 10th

I hope Lourdes is putting as much thought into her Valentine's message to me as I am in mine to her. I know that no true declaration of love has been spoken between us, but now's her chance!

Friday February 11th

I overheard Mum and Dad talking about my birthday party:

Dad:	We'd better do something special for Brooklyn's birthday, Victoria. After all, he *is* going to be two.
Mum:	He's going to be *one*, David. You really must get the hang of counting to ten. Go on, try and do it like I told you.
Dad:	Erm… Two…
Mum:	One, David.
Dad:	Oh yeah, one … um … what was next again?

I despair sometimes, I really do. Anyway, once they'd got past that little obstacle they started getting down to the nitty gritty. It sounds like it's going to be quite an event, with clowns and everything (although quite why they want to do that, I don't know. One clown in the family is quite enough, thank you very much.)

Saturday February 12th

I hope they invite Lourdes to the birthday party. It'll be the perfect time to make my move. After all, I'll be the centre of attention, all the girls will want a piece of the action. I don't know what kind of food they'll be laying on, but I hope the jelly and ice cream is up to scratch. There'd be nothing more embarrassing than sub-standard jelly …

Sunday February 13th

Valentine's Day tomorrow. I wonder if she'll send me flowers …

Monday February 14th

Nothing! Not a sausage – not that I particularly wanted a sausage, but you know what I mean. All I got was one poxy card, and I can tell that was from Dad because he spelt my name wrong. I can't believe she's ignored me. Then again, maybe she's just playing hard to get.

Dad got 136 Valentine's cards. I wonder if he'd be such a sex symbol if everyone knew that he has trouble putting his pants on *before* his trousers. I saw some of the cards, and to be honest they rather made me blush. They didn't make Mum blush, though – she told Dad to wipe that stupid grin off his face and throw those revolting cards away. He did as he was told, of course, but he's been in a very good mood all day …

Tuesday February 15th

Mum and me went round to see Phoenix Chi today. She was less than impressed with my Valentine's card situation:

Phoenix: Brooklyn, dude, how many Valentines d'ya get?

Brooklyn: Just the one this year, actually.

Phoenix: Only one? You need to be playing the field a bit more, my friend.

Brooklyn: Why, how many did you get?

Phoenix: Six of the little beauties.

Brooklyn: Six? Who from?

Phoenix: Who knows, dude? Could have been from any number of admirers …

Between you and me, dear diary, I think she's making it up. I've suspected that she's been getting a bit jealous of yours truly lately – she went a bit quiet when I told her that I was going to have a birthday party *with clowns*.

I wish I'd fibbed about how many cards I got now.

Wednesday February 16th

I'm worried about Dad – he's really getting a bit big for his boots. First of all he gets all these Valentine's cards, now it turns out that some university is starting a course in David Beckham studies.

David Beckham studies? Gimme a break. The geezer running the course says that 'nobody embodies the spirit of our times as well as David Beckham'. That's my dad they're talking about! If studying him is an academic discipline, then I'm a world expert. What would the eggheads make of him dressing up in Mum's thongs? What would their critical analysis be of the fact that he keeps nicking my crayons to practise writing his name? I could tell them a thing or two ...

Thursday February 17th

Oh dear me – Dad's started walking about the house wearing a mortar board. I hope this academia stuff doesn't go to his head. He's really not cut out for the life of the intelligentsia – in fact if his IQ were any lower you'd have to start watering him ...

Friday February 18th

Mum and Dad are taking me shopping for my birthday party gear tomorrow. They're keeping the arrangements for the actual day under wraps pretty successfully – I know there are going to be clowns but that's about it.
I hope they don't go over the top like they did at the wedding. And I certainly hope they don't bung me in a purple dress again. Not on my birthday – it would just be too cruel ...

Saturday February 19th

Wow. Those two never cease to amaze me when they go shopping together. Spend, spend, spend and then spend some more. They just bought me a Louis Vuitton papoose with a sixteen grand price tag. *Sixteen thousand big ones!* Between you and me I think a new baby carrier is a bit superfluous, as I can walk with the best of them now – admittedly, I'll need to wait for my legs to grow as long as Dad's before I can quite keep up with him, but I'm getting there.

But the papoose was just the start. After we'd bought that, we went to a car showroom and Dad bought a fifty grand motor. To be honest it's not quite my scene – a TVR Cerbera (although I am quite interested in the 180 mph top speed…) – but it has two fantastic redeeming features. First, it has a rather nifty little built-in kiddy seat – just perfect for a little dude like me to nip around town in – but best of all it has 'BROOKLYN' embroidered on the seats!

Could anything be funkier? I'll bet even Lourdes doesn't have a personalised sports car. She'll be dead impressed when she sees me in it – I hope she's coming to the party. I haven't heard Mum and Dad mention her, but I'm sure they wouldn't make an oversight like that. I don't know if Mrs Madonna is going to be there, but to be frank it's not her I'm interested in …

Sunday February 20th

Dad's been dropped from the team! This is unbelievable. I was feeling a bit under the weather this morning, so he missed footy practice to look after me, and before you can say 'Yaboo-sucks to Fergie' he's been dropped.

The poor lad's in a terrible state – he's been

crying more than I have. I must say I think he's been a little hard done by. If I could see that scoundrel of a manager I'd give him a piece of my mind. Well, I'd scream a bit – I'm sure he'd get the point.

Monday February 21st

I'm sure there's something Mum and Dad aren't telling me. They've been looking so worried all day, and Number 1 and Number 3 have been extra vigilant. It can't just be to do with Dad not making the team. I know he was upset, but this is something far more serious.

I feel a bit scared.

Tuesday February 22nd

Mum and Dad keep coming in and giving me a big hug and saying things like, 'We won't let anyone harm you, will we?'

Who wants to harm me? I'm not even one yet – what can I have done to upset everyone so much?

Wednesday February 23rd

Mum and Dad have had death threats. Too shocked to write anything.

Thursday February 24th

Who on earth would want to hurt my mum and dad? They wouldn't harm a fly. Somebody's been sending them nasty letters with pictures of me. No wonder they seem so upset.

You know, being a Spice Baby has its advantages, it really does. But sometimes I wonder if it's really worth it. You get jeered by football crowds, you get kidnap threats and now this. Sometimes I wish Mum and Dad would just whisk me away and we could go and live like normal people, away from the photographers and the glitz and the glamour.

I'd miss the lifestyle, I'm sure – but as long as I had Mum and Dad everything would be all right …

Friday February 25th

Mum and Dad have perked up a bit. The letters seem to have stopped, and I think Number 1 and Number 3 have put their minds at rest a bit. All talk is about my birthday party – I think they're more excited about it than I am, bless 'em.

Saturday February 26th

One week to go. I can hardly wait …

Sunday February 27th

Overheard Mum and Dad talking to the chefs about my birthday menu. From what I can make out, us kids are having burgers and chips and jelly and ice cream (yum yum), whereas the grown-ups are having something called Lobster Thermidor. It sounds bleedin' 'orrible to me – these grown ups do eat some funny things sometimes.

Mum's ordered Dad a family pack of Jammy Dodgers for the occasion.

Monday February 28th

I'm not sure quite how I feel about reaching the ripe old age of one. I've gotta say I've seen some action in the last twelve months, but now I've gained a certain maturity I think I really need to start settling down. I'll have to discuss the matter with Lourdes.

Tuesday February 29th

I wonder what they're getting me for my birthday. I could do with a new pair of baby trainers – I've only got thirteen, which is terribly unlucky …

MARCH
2000

Wednesday March 1st

I'm getting a bit nervous. There's going to be a hundred people there, all to see me, and I'll hardly know any of them. I've gotta be on good form – I hope Dad doesn't make me wear a bandanna.

Thursday March 2nd

The world's gone mad. The Spice Girls are being given a lifetime achievement award! Lifetime achievement? I've achieved more in my lifetime than that lot put together.

Brooklyn's Lifetime Achievements

1. Scuppered the evil plans of the wicked Ginger Spice
2. Learned to walk
3. Learned to talk (a bit – room for improvement there)
4. Fallen in love (twice)
5. Foiled a kidnap attempt
6. Learned to play the drums
7. Learned to drive a baby Ferrari
8. The list goes on …

The Spice Girls' Lifetime Achievements

1. Wrote some mumbo jumbo about wanting to zigga zigga
2. That's it …

If anyone deserves a lifetime achievement award around here, it's *moi*.

Friday March 3rd

I wonder if Lourdes and Baby Spice will have a catfight. I hope not – it *would* be so uncivilised. Then again, it would kind of impress Phoenix Chi. Ah well, *que sera sera* …

Twenty-four hours and counting. Mum's already told Dad off for nicking the Jammy Dodgers for the party.

Saturday March 4th

Happy Birthday to me.
Happy Birthday to me.
Happy Birthday, dear Brooklyn.
Happy Birthday to me.

One today! And what a day it was, even if it did have its share of heartache. Can you believe that after all the build-up, after all my expectations, and more to the point after I'd spent absolutely hours getting ready – Lourdes wasn't even there! I can't believe Mum and Dad didn't invite her. What an oversight …

To be honest, though, it was quite nice to be young, free and single. And I can't be too hard on the folks, as they did lay on a pretty classy bash. Everyone was greeted by the people with the funny hair and the make-up (before you say it, I'm referring to the clowns, *not* Mum and Dad). And there was everything the modern celebrity party needs – balloons, magicians, jelly – the works. Even Phoenix Chi was quite impressed:

Phoenix Chi: Pretty good bash, dude.

Brooklyn: Hey, Phoenix Chi, what can I say? We Spice Babies have got to do these things in style.

Phoenix Chi: You ain't no Spice Baby any more, man. You're one year old now. You can walk and everything. You're a Spice Toddler.

She's right, of course. I'm a man of the world now. A man of vast experience. Even Baby Spice treated me with a little more respect, and I found I was even able to bury the hatchet with her:

Baby Spice: Happy Birthday, Gorgeous!

Spice Toddler: *Thanks, Baby. Say, I've been thinking. I know you and me have had our ups and downs, but no hard feelings, huh?*

Baby Spice: Are you going to give me a little kiss?

Spice Toddler: *I knew you'd see it my way. OK then, for old times sake ...*

I've got to say that, despite everything, Baby is still the best kisser I know. Sorry, Lourdes, but that's the way it is.

But best of all were Mum and Dad. They gave me loads of lovely presents, including a pile of books (with lots of pictures so that Dad doesn't have too much trouble reading them to me). You know, they've got their faults, those two, but at the end of the day they've got hearts of gold. They've carefully nurtured me from the helpless babe-in-arms to the mean toddling machine I am now. They've given me everything I want (and a few things I didn't really want – but don't worry, guys, the purple dress fiasco is water under the bridge), and to top it all they've blown ten grand on a party for me and all my little friends. It doesn't get any better than this.

I've decided that this will be my last ever entry. People seem to be so interested in the three of us that I can't risk my innermost thoughts being read by just anyone. I've grown up now, and my life is for living, not for recording. If anyone should pick this diary up and read it, don't take it to heart. I don't mean it when I say Dad's stupid, and I don't mean it when I imply that Mum's neurotic. I can't be the easiest dude in the world to live with – I reckon they've done a grand job, and I love 'em to bits …

And so, here ends the secret diary of Brooklyn Beckham.